1848

*Great Revolutions*

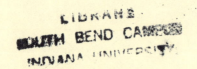

# 1848

## The Romantic and Democratic Revolutions in Europe

JEAN SIGMANN

**TRANSLATED FROM THE FRENCH BY LOVETT F. EDWARDS**

HARPER & ROW, PUBLISHERS
New York, Evanston, San Francisco, London

Translated from *1848: Les révolutions romantiques et démocratiques de l'Europe.* © Calmann-Lévy, Paris, 1970.

FIRST U. S. EDITION

ISBN: 0-06-013871-8

LIBRARY OF CONGRESS CATALOG CARD NUMBER: 79-181646

# Contents

## Part Two
### THE EUROPEAN REVOLUTIONS

## Some Problems


THE FRENCHMAN of today has, or thinks he has, some idea of some of the highlights of "the Great Revolution". From his old textbooks he retains a memory of stirring events like the oath of the Tennis Court, the storming of the Bastille, the night of 4 August (suppression of feudal rights by the Assembly and declaration of the Rights of Man), or of tragic individuals like Mirabeau, Danton, Robespierre, Saint-Just. Though imbued with the most genuine pacifism, he feels a secret attraction for the revolutionary armies poised for the conquest of Europe with the cry of "War to the châteaux! Peace to the cottages!" Everyday cares may well banish all memory of the epic; the champions of the soap-boxes bring them back to him at the hustings when, in default of policies adapted to the problems of our own time, they invoke the "immortal principles" and evoke "the greatness of our ancestors".

The men of 1848, abandoned to professional historians and the authors of scholarly works, knew neither "this excess of honour nor this humiliation". Nonetheless they were direct descendants of those who had either known or made the "Great Revolution", and they considered themselves, each according to his temperament, the heirs of the members of the Constituent Assembly, the Girondins or the men of the Mountain. The oblivion into which they have fallen is a result

[ 9

of the total discredit which enveloped them on the morrow of their failure. By a strange conjuncture, of which history provides few examples, the forty-eighters (the very expression implies a haughty disdain or a condescending sympathy) suffered both the insults of the supporters of established order and tradition and the criticism of the democrats. Born in the aura of Romanticism, they were condemned in the name of realism, of positivism and scientism. Denunciations fell equally upon their hollow rhetoric, their mystical idealism (how many hasty judgements have there been on Lamartine, the "minister-poet"!), and their generous illusions. The "year of folly" (*das tolle Jahr*) was to be for many years across the Rhine the inevitable epithet of that year 1848, whose commencement had received the poetic appellation of "the springtide of the peoples"!

From March to June 1848 hymns to liberty and fraternity had resounded from Paris to Poznan and Bucharest, from Holstein to Sicily. Two great States alone escaped the contagion: industrial England, capitalist and liberal, and agricultural Russia, feudal and autocratic. Continental Europe revealed its unity in the idea of revolution, but also its diversity in the development of that revolution. For the essential problems which the men of 1848 set out to resolve were posed in the States, or rather in the regions, because the existence of the States remodelled in 1815 was questioned almost everywhere, which reflected the original structures or combination of structures, political, ethnic, economic and social.

The political problem was to find its radical solution in France by the proclamation of a republic and the introduction of universal male suffrage. In most of the Italian States, and even more in the Slav lands, the middle class was too weak and the peasants too backward for the liberals to dream of demanding, at least at first, anything more than a constitution and an extension of the right to vote. Nevertheless, they had learnt from recent events, those of the eighteen-thirties, that the most solemn promises were forgotten as soon as the threat which had extorted them had disappeared. Only a strong new State able to weld together the dispersed fragments of the nation would be able to guarantee the individual his rights against princes summoned to submit or to abdicate. Poland restored, Italy and Germany united, were to form with France a brotherly community in a free and pacific Europe.

Adorned with magical virtues by the Messianic language of a Michelet, a Lamennais or a Mickiewicz, the principle of "nationalities", a word which had been common parlance since 1830, was to abandon the domain of dreams and speculations. In a few months the ambiguity of the expression was to appear under a harsh light. Did it mean the right of peoples to work out their own destinies according to the French revolutionary tradition? Or was it the right to unite, even were it by force, individuals supposedly of the same race because they spoke the same language, according to the conception of a Herder or an Arndt? It has been said a thousand times that impotence or complacence before the upsurge of aggressive nationalism was imputable to the lack of realism of an already distant past. After two World Wars, is contemporary Europe cured of the nationalist disease? Is not the contagion of racism being propagated even more in the new States of Asia and Africa, even when their leaders declare themselves to be socialist?

The forty-eighters, those impenitent idealists, could not incur the reproach of being disinterested in the fate of the lower classes. Most of them believed that social democracy would be the inevitable consequence of political democracy. The others, the socialists and communists (the words "socialism" and "communism" became common at roughly the same time as "nationality"), each in their own way appealed to the State to improve the lot of the "working classes". Believers in the force of the spirit, sometimes Christians for "social Catholicism" was one of the novelties of 1848, they rejected violence. In a climate of brotherhood, who would have dreamed of fighting against the transformations for which propaganda would have shown the moral necessity? The "organization of labour", the "right to work", these French catchwords were to be, in 1848, the two great keynotes of the progressive parties of Europe.

To free the workers from economic slavery, the individual

worker from political subjection, the peoples from foreign rule, such were some of the most exalted ambitions of 1848. There were also more commonplace ones! Their realization required that exceptional men should arise simultaneously in the four corners of Europe and powerful material forces spring up to smash the counter-offensives of the former authorities which withdrew without having joined battle. Could such a thing ever happen? The frightened reactionaries kept in their hands the apparatus of the State and the levers of the economy. What did it matter? The people, rendered conscious of its sacred rights, would be consulted. How could it not declare itself against its former oppressors? The spectacle, unique in the history of the world, of headlong revolutions, with apparently identical aims, kept this exhilarating dream alive.

The "complexity of 1848" (Pouthas) not only disappointed contemporaries, but also proved to thinking persons the uselessness of short-lived revolutions with little bloodshed which provoked no armed conflict between the great powers.

This book wishes to stress, if not the actual events, then at least the very modern character of the problems posed by 1848. A summary of the revolutions themselves will not be found here; many excellent ones already exist. Many of these, however, despite the talent of their authors, are scarcely comprehensible to the majority of their readers. Almost daily events, enigmatic heroes, contradictory slogans, ministers with conflicting views, more or less free elections, stillborn constitutions proclaimed eternal, succeed one another in an accelerated rhythm. The history of events inevitably acquires the appearance of a chronology embellished by the style of the narrator. The result is a choice, the reasons for which, even when good, escape the non-specialist. Certainly, these summaries are often preceded by chapters with reassuring headlines: "Causes and origins . . . !" Thus the reader is driven to admit the inevitability of revolutions which break out unexpectedly and to ignore the burden of foreseeable revolutions which miscarry.

The failure of the London manifestation of 10 April encouraged the supporters of law and order in Paris, in Austria and in Hungary to resist popular pressures, for the Chartist

agitation which we consider derisory had seemed able to shake
the foundations of English society. To contemporaries the
United Kingdom was not the model of the union of classes. In
what other country had strikes been more frequent or been
carried out with more determination? In what country had
the struggle for universal suffrage begun so soon or been so
bloody? Was not Engels right to believe that the English
workers would be able to overthrow the capitalist State which
was being sapped also by the irreconcilable Irish? In the
Europe of nationalities was it not in wretched Ireland that
religious, political and social hatreds, of the type needed
to provoke revolutionary explosions, intermingled, in that
Ireland which was to see the birth of the first popular Catholic
party?

The fate of the secondary States, those on the French
frontiers, has also been neglected. Has one not been taught for
a century that Switzerland and Belgium, endowed with
exemplary political wisdom, had necessarily to remain aloof
from the great movements? It remains to be determined why
these industrialized countries, one formed of three and the other
of two peoples, in close contact with France and Germany,
have known neither the class conflicts nor the linguistic quarrels
whence emerged, according to some, the revolutions of 1848!
Welcoming to the conspirators, was not Switzerland herself the
scene of a civil war which led to the revolutions of 1848? Was
the Belgian State, the product of the social movements of 1830,
with recent frontiers (1839) imposed by the great powers,
sufficiently strong to avert a fresh tempest? Did not the fine
façade of a prosperous country wisely governed by a French,
or Francophile, middle class conceal the sufferings of a proletariat deprived, as in France, of the right to strike, the sullen
fury of bourgeoisie excluded, as in France, from the right to
vote, and the resentment of the Flemish people, treated as
outcasts? Did not the Belgian democrats await from Paris the
signal to set up, with the consent of all the disinherited, a
Belgian republic? Did not the French democrats dream of
quite simply annexing the young monarchy, violating the
sacred creation of kings? In the Iberian peninsula, the chosen

land of revolutions and pronunciamentos, was not the French republic tempted to intervene with more or less discretion, if not to support the little republican groups then at least to facilitate the overthrow of the dictatorships in power?

Were the kingdoms of the north (Netherlands, Sweden, Denmark), States of the *ancien régime* protected, as we have been told, by their distance from the subversive ideas of the west? Did there not exist in 1848 régimes equally obsolescent in Northern Germany, notably in the Prussia of the "liberal" Frederick William IV? Did not Norway, subject to the political hegemony of Sweden and the linguistic hegemony of Denmark, provide the unique example of a peasant democracy whose independence seemed imminent? Could not liberalism, suffocated in the Netherlands, in Sweden and in Denmark, at last find its chance, because of the weakening of Russia and Austria, the vigilant guardians of absolutism? Did not the presence in Frankfurt of the delegates of the kings of the Netherlands and of Denmark justify the appetites of the Germans, freed from oppression by a Parisian revolution?

"Capital of the revolution in France", Paris was also, in foreign eyes, the "capital of the revolution in Europe". What other explanation was there as to how the action of a few thousand builders of barricades could overthrow a régime regarded as strong, and encourage everywhere even the most timorous opposition to present *en bloc* the boldest of claims and cause Governments to yield or to disappear? The pressure of the Parisian streets was aimed at the liberation of the workers and the peoples as was once again to be shown by the events of 15 May 1848, a transient conflagration of collective madness for those ignorant of 5 June 1832. For the first time in French history the Government had to take into account, by the introduction of universal suffrage, the opinions of the mass of Frenchmen, a crushing majority of whom were peasants. What did these illiterate peasants have against the monarchy? What did they know of the republic? Of socialism? Of war for the liberation of subject peoples? Would they reject the "notables" of the property-owning classes and vote for the candidates of the Parisian clubs? Interpretation of the results of the April elections could not overlook the structures and mentality of the French social system at the fall of the July Monarchy.

The revolutionary movements of the Austrian Empire and of Italy, as well as those of Germany, are incomprehensible without an exact knowledge of the Danubian monarchy. Despite the magisterial works of Droz and Minder, Austria is a victim of the myths which encumber German history and prevent one from comprehending, over and above the incidental, the deeper feeling of the "year of folly". The idea of a Prussia preparing, by the prosperity of twenty-five out of thirty-eight States, the political unity of Germany clashed with the opinion of the classes which represented the greatest numbers and that of the politicians who, above all, demanded political liberty and national unity. Between the advent of Frederick William IV (1840) and the undeniable progress of the liberal and national ideal during the eighteen-forties is there any correlation or coincidence? Why did the real revolution, which disavowed the existence of the Diet, start in the small States of the south? Why was the Frankfurt parliament, its emanation, dominated by middle class intellectuals? Why, finally, did the King of Prussia not profit in April 1849 by the serious difficulties of Vienna in Hungary by becoming emperor of a Germany from which Austria herself was excluded?

Of all the national movements which were to disturb Austria in 1848–9 the most powerful by far was the Magyar movement. Did satisfying the claims of the "Hungarian nation" mean any more than according an aristocracy the freedom to oppress serfs of every origin and to bully those who differed from them?

To what degree did the "Slav renaissance"—primarily a brilliant Czech renaissance—indubitable literary events, prepare the way for 1848? Was the "awakening" of the Slav nations, as Engels asserts, the work of a minority of romantic intellectuals, docile instruments of pan-Slavism nourished on German culture (the Poles, patriots by instinct and enemies of the Russians, naturally excepted)? How, finally, was the idea of uniting the Rumanians on one side and the Carpathians on other born in one of the most backward Hapsburg provinces?

Since the overwhelming majority of the peoples of the Empire were peasants crushed by feudal dues, was not the problem essentially a social one? Surely to imagine peoples resolved to claim the right to vote and to form independent nations is to give way to anachronism?

Was not the liberal and anti-Germanic revolution to break out first in Italy, where, up until 1848, the Hapsburg exercised a *de facto* power which they had never enjoyed in the Germanic confederation? Surely a few Austrian cavalry charges would have been enough to destroy movements inspired by hatred for absolutism and the Tedeschi? The brave but foolhardy attempts in 1849 to found republics at Rome, Florence and Venice are incomprehensible to anyone unfamiliar with their association with provincialism, the parochialism on the one hand, the exploits of the Carbonari (1820–1; 1831) and the incoherent insurrections of Young Italy (1833–45) on the other.

Did not the Risorgimento, a complex movement of committed writers formed in a romantic atmosphere, because of its lack of realism, prepare for the setbacks of 1848? Could "Albertism", behind an enlightened despot who in 1821 had betrayed successively reactionaries and liberals, resist the prestige of a Papal monarchy reconciled with liberty?

It is not only the Italian movements of January 1848 which prompt one to revise the traditional viewpoints which hold that the European revolutions should have commenced in February of that year. It was from 1846 that the Europe of subjected peoples united in suffering and in hope, the Europe of the princes in fear. A serious food crisis followed by an economic recession of exceptional intensity extended from the British Isles to Central Europe. Chartism seemed reborn. But why did the German workers, the Parisian proletariat, seem unaware of a combination of circumstances which could justify, if it took place, a great workers' movement? On the other hand political conflicts, whose study falls under the heading of international affairs, already opposed aggressive nationalism and the ideal of the brotherhood of peoples. Thousands of Germans, and the Left wing was not amongst the least ardent, were prepared to cross swords with little Denmark which, in

Schleswig-Holstein, had made a mockery of the "rights" of a great people. On the other hand, all the advanced elements considered the annexation of Cracovia (November 1846), a minor event, a new victory of reaction over the nations, and welcomed the defeat of the Swiss Catholics (November 1847) as the first success of the "Holy Alliance of the Peoples" over the "Holy Alliance of the Kings". Why, finally, at a time when French leaders were making fine speeches against a régime whose power made London feel uneasy, did manifestations of revolutionary type make the princes of southern Germany tremble? The unforeseeable Parisian revolution was to break out on a minefield.

To integrate the years 1846-7 into the movements of 1848-9, to try to answer the many questions posed, to try to justify affirmations apparently contradictory, is, in our opinion, to throw light upon a complex scene without taking unawares the good faith of the reader who is always a little suspicious of the certitudes which he demands.

*PART ONE*


EUROPE IN THE EIGHTEEN-FORTIES

# [ Chapter One ]

## The United Kingdom: Capitalism, Proletariat, Liberalism, Irish Nationalism

BETWEEN 1815 and the eighteen-forties the map of Europe suffered only two important modifications: Belgium and Greece snatched their independence from the Netherlands and the Ottoman Empire. This territorial stability was in contrast to a demographic increase hitherto unknown, the beginnings of industrialization, the appearance in certain countries of a factory proletariat and the rise of the middle classes. The middle class (let us adopt provisionally the singular which masks the social differences covered by this expression) claimed a place in the State commensurate with its economic importance. Eastern Europe, agricultural, aristocratic, apparently rooted in the absolutism of the past, was henceforth opposed to a new Europe, in the west, middle-class, constitutional, even parliamentary, the most characteristic facets of which were represented by England.

### Demographic Growth and Prodigious Urbanization

In the first half of the nineteenth century the demographic growth of the United Kingdom (71 per cent) attained a momentum unequalled in Europe (50 per cent). Between 1800 and 1850 the number of inhabitants rose from 16·2 to 27·7 million. Great Britain alone increased by 92 per cent (21·1 million as against 11 million) and Ireland by 27 per cent (6·6 million as against 5·2 million). This increase was, however, tempered by transatlantic emigration: almost 300,000 Irishmen left their country without hope of return between 1841 and 1845! The British increase was due to a considerable reduction in the death-rate and the maintenance of a high birthrate.

The average annual death-rate per thousand inhabitants of England and Wales fell from 27·7 (1781–1800) and 22·5 (1801–1830) to 21·4 between 1841 and 1845. This increase had begun before the year 1798, which saw the publication of the work in which Jenner revealed his discovery of the anti-smallpox vaccine, and the beginnings of the campaign of Malthus.

A conservative, Malthus recommended voluntary limitation of births among the families of the poor. But the propaganda of his supporters in no way modified British behaviour. The average annual birth-rate per thousand inhabitants in England and Wales was stabilized between 1841 and 1845 at 32·4. Then it continued its upward trend to go even beyond that to 35·5, the maximum of the century, between 1871 and 1875, which exceeded the figure for 1790. Its high level seemed linked to the urbanization and industrialization of England; promiscuity of the sexes in the factories and the slums of the smaller towns, now suddenly transformed into industrial centres, lowered the age of marriage and encouraged free unions.

The Europe of 1800 had only twenty-two towns with more than 100,000 inhabitants. Three of them were in France: Paris, Marseilles and Lyons. The British Isles had only one: London. The political and financial capital of the United Kingdom and of an immense empire it had, it is true, almost a million inhabitants (960,000). It was the largest city in the world. Also, the industrial revolution had modified, from the second half of the nineteenth century, the distribution of the population between the countryside and the towns. Forty-eight towns (London excepted) of more than 10,000 inhabitants accounted for 11·9 per cent of the English and Welsh population in 1801 and 15·2 per cent in 1831. In the France of 1836 all the

towns of more than 10,000 inhabitants (Paris excluded) only
accounted for 8·7 per cent of the total population. The lead of
England and Wales continued to grow. In 1851 there were in
the United Kingdom ten towns of more than 100,000 inhabitants—London had 2,363,000—and in France five; eighteen
British towns as against ten French had from 50,000 to 100,000
inhabitants; the agglomerations of more than 50,000
represented 20 per cent of the population in Great Britain and
6·5 per cent in France. By 1850 the United Kingdom was the
first State of the modern world to have an equal distribution
between town and country. A new urban England, daughter
of large-scale industry, stood face to face with the former
agricultural England. The struggle for power which in most of
the European States ranged the aristocracy of money against
the aristocracy of land here took the original form of a rivalry
between industrial capitalism and landed capitalism.

### The Economic Power of the Landed Aristocracy Menaced; Industrial and Commercial Capital against Protectionism

The England of the great estates did not resemble either the
western Europe of independent small landowners or the central
and eastern Europe of peasants still subjugated to feudal
restraints. The landlords had obtained from parliament, which
they dominated, the right to annex and enclose the common
lands (waste land, poor pasturage). The estates thus rounded
off were divided into huge farms handed over to farmers with
an adequate amount of capital for their exploitation. The
growth of the towns assured an easy market for meat. The areas
reserved directly or indirectly for stockbreeding made up
perhaps three-quarters of the lands exploited. On reduced
areas cultivation attained yields unknown on the continent.

This undeniable technical advance created profound changes
in society. The confiscation of the commons by landed capitalism deprived the small proprietor of the revenues of his meagre
stead, the rise of industrial capitalism deprived him of his
complementary wage as a home weaver. He risked becoming a
*metayer* or a farm labourer subject to endemic unemployment,

for the growth of stockbreeding tended to reduce the number of paid workers to a minimum.

Already by that time a part of the rural proletariat, the immense "reserve forces" of industrial capitalism, had begun to move. Between 1801 and 1831 the share of the agricultural sector of the active British population had fallen from 35·9 per cent to 24·6 per cent, and that of the industrial and mining sector had increased from 29·7 per cent to 40·8 per cent. The exodus from agricultural southern England to the industrial north must have been accelerated by the reform of social legislation. The law of 1834 "on the poor in England and Wales" imposed internment in the workhouse on the unemployed who were given assistance. A man was separated from his family. The "Bastille of the poor" was denounced in vain by Dickens in *Oliver Twist* (1838) and by the young Disraeli in *Sybil* (1845). Given a choice between the workhouse and penury, the majority of the proletariat chose penury, the first step towards the factory. The poor tax, levied on the proprietors, fell from eight million pounds in 1818 to four million pounds in 1837.

The representatives of industrial and commercial capitalism introduced into the Commons by the electoral reform of 1832 agreed to support a law demanded by the landed capitalists, but favourable to all forms of wealth. On the other hand, they looked with growing hostility on the agricultural protectionism which a minority had dictated to the nation. Masters of Parliament, the landed aristocracy had had the Corn Laws passed in 1815. Import was forbidden at a price less than eighty shillings a quarter. This rigorous protectionism was powerless to check a decline of international character which only penury, generative of social unrest, interrupted. The legislation of 1828 opened a breach in this system; the rise of 50 per cent in 1822–5 provoked too many riots, so that the Government had to take account of the interest of the consumers. The introduction of the sliding scale followed the first measures to reduce the entry dues on manufactured products (1822–5). For the first time since 1815 power eluded, timidly it is true, the influence of the dominant "pressure group".

For a dozen years the evolution of prices to some extent deflected public attention from legislation on cereals. In 1835 the price of wheat slumped but a bad harvest reversed this tendency and the rise continued up to September 1838. Under the leadership of Richard Cobden the Manchester industrialists took advantage of the occasion to start a great campaign for free trade; at the height of the crisis they founded the Anti-Corn Law League. Outside the political argument the League invoked economic arguments against the sliding scale, for example British industry would increase its outlets in the countries exporting cereals, as well as social arguments. All the consumers would benefit by the abolition of indirect taxation in its most unjust form because it hit the poor hardest, in the concealed tax on bread. The League thus endeavoured to create against agrarian capitalism a united front made up of the upper middle classes and the middle classes on the one hand and the working and agricultural proletariat on the other. Its propaganda was carried out by typically British methods: petitions, press campaigns and, above all, meetings. It obtained, especially in the urban centres, a success which forced the Prime Minister, Robert Peel, already worried by the Chartists' workers' agitation, to take note of it. In 1842 the Tory Government forced its protectionist majority to vote liberal free-trade measures. Courageously, in order to compensate for the Treasury losses, it re-established Pitt's income tax, but did not dare to abolish the Corn Laws all at once; the sliding scale was maintained but the charges were reduced. From 1843 the price of cereals went down, business recovered, wages were stabilized or slightly increased, and the Chartist movement disintegrated. The League's propaganda redoubled and spread to Europe, forcing it to accept a doctrine admirably adapted to British interests.

*The Foundations of the Power of Industrial Capitalism*

Europe noted with consternation the power of the "British colossus" (Mevissen, 1845). Colossal scale was without doubt the most characteristic feature of British industry and the one which most favoured its rise and assured its prodigious development.

The capital created during the eighteenth century by the great colonial trade did not remain idle. No crisis ever shook the prestige of the old Bank of England (1694): its banknotes were accepted in Europe for their face value in gold. Several powerful joint-stock banks, of which France knew nothing until the Second Empire, marshalled the British funds. "The greatest credit in the world is at the service of the greatest economy of the world" (Labrousse).

The "colossus of credit" was the origin of the "colossus of transport"; roads, canals, then railways, were left to private initiative. At the beginning of the nineteenth century only passengers and the post (the postage stamp originated in England) made use of the road network. The canals, whose era was opened by the Bridgewater canal (1759–61), soon monopolized the transport of goods. Within fifty years the canal companies had constructed almost five thousand kilometres in the mining and industrial regions. The railways, at first, also assured the distribution of coal. Their development was continued for a score of years at a pace more rapid than anywhere else, the United States excepted. The Manchester–Liverpool line, which undertook the transport of goods and passengers from 15 September 1830, began the railway era in Europe. In Great Britain it was first railway "fever" and then, from 1845 onward, railway "folly". The railway companies found on the money market ever more abundant sources of capital, to which French and Belgian constructors also appealed. The length of the network increased from 91 kilometres in 1831 to 1,349 in 1841 and 6,400 in 1848 (the corresponding figures for France were 88, 435 and 1,930). By the beginning of 1848 London was linked to the mining and manufacturing centres as well as to the principal ports.

Great Britain, the leading maritime nation, was admirably adapted to the revolution in the economy created by the steam engine. In 1840 Cunard inaugurated with the *Britannia* a transatlantic line of steamships. "The Victorian period, the apogee of prosperity and power, developed entirely under the aegis of coal . . ." recalls André Siegfried at the beginning of his study *The British Crisis in the Twentieth Century* (1931). The use of steam engines became commonplace after 1820 in the mines, in metallurgy and in the mills, and stimulated production. The railways, also large consumers, assured a reduction in prices. From ten million tons in 1800 the production of the British coalmines rose to fifty-six million in 1850, that is to say three-fifths of world production. From 1840 the consumption of coal per head was 1·11 tons in the United Kingdom as against 0·13 tons in France.

The rapid advance of the metal industries in England more than elsewhere is explained by the abundance of coal. The development of Birmingham, capital of the Black Country and metropolis of the steam engine (Watt founded his factory there in 1776), was prodigious: 15,000 inhabitants in 1700, 73,000 in 1801 and 225,000 in 1850. The appearance of blast-furnaces signalled an even more rapid development in Glasgow; the population increased from 77,000 in 1801 to 345,000 in 1851. At that date the United Kingdom produced half the iron in the world. The growing importance of metallurgy set a limit to the exclusive predominance of consumer goods in the economy.

The textile industry remained, however, as in the eighteenth century, the essential industry of the United Kingdom. With good reason the expression "industrial revolution", sometimes carelessly used, is applicable to the transformation introduced by the mechanical loom and the steam engine. In the first half of the nineteenth century the young cotton industry accepted technical innovations more willingly than the older woollen industry. From 1770 Lancashire was the land of cotton. The mechanization of spinning was a result of the perfecting of Arkwright's waterframe (1771) which by the beginning of the nineteenth century had everywhere replaced the hand loom. Spinning at home disappeared, at first to the advantage of the small craft workshop. Towards 1820 the replacement of hydraulic power by steam was general. The lowering of prices, a European phenomenon already mentioned, forced the manufacturers into mass production. Towards 1830 this process was already far advanced in spinning; it began only in weaving from 1822 onward when definite improvements transformed it at last into a mechanical operation. Like the spinner of the craft workshop, the home weaver became in his turn subjected to the pressures of large-scale capitalist industry. The proportion of factory workers in the cotton industry rose from 4 per cent in 1820 to 70 per cent in 1845. The resistance of the craftsmen to proletarianization was more vigorous in the traditional textile industries. The West Riding tended to become for wool what Lancashire was for cotton. Carding and combing by water and steam power did not become widespread until round about 1830. The opposition of the weavers to mechanization was more effective as it was based on ancient guild rules. It was above all thanks to cotton that British industry dominated the European market. In 1830 the cotton goods of Lancashire represented three-fifths of the exports of the United Kingdom. This enormous industrial power was inseparable from social transformations of which history had never before provided examples on such a scale.

*The Social Consequences of Large-scale Industrialism:*
*Proletariat and Employers*

The increase in the working population meant the growth of all the textile centres. Manchester (20,000 souls in 1760, 250,000 in 1830 and 401,000 in 1851) and Lancashire in general (from the end of the eighteenth century to about 1820 the number of cotton operatives rose roughly from 30,000 to 360,000 in the county where the mills were centred) were the most perfect examples of a new society, divided between industrial feudalism and the factory proletariat. Marx and Engels were soon to describe the insuperable antagonism between them.

History is sometimes ironical; at the wish of his father, a rich cotton-spinner from Barmen and co-proprietor of a Manchester mill, the young Engels went to the mill in 1842 to complete his apprenticeship as a future "exploiter" in this privileged observation post. His first impressions formed the basis of the articles which appeared in the *Rhein Gazette* of Cologne, at that time edited by Marx, collected in 1845 as *Die Lage der arbeitenden Klassen in England (Condition of the Working Class in England)*. They created an immense repercussion in cultivated German-language circles. The review *Gegenwart* of Leipzig, which could hardly be suspected of leanings towards socialism or communism, regarded this work as the most rigorous denunciation of the "industrial society and its consequences".

The increase of the population entailed a rise in rents and the proliferation of slums; in Manchester and Liverpool lodgings were let in cellars. The factory, in which workers and machines were crowded together, was a seedbed of infection; about 1840, 30 per cent of the inhabitants of Derby died of pulmonary diseases. With the spread of gas lighting the working day was extended to sixteen or seventeen hours! This explained the increase in alcoholism, even if certain historians contest its importance, in the world of the disinherited. Wages, usually low, were eroded by the truck system (a part of his gain was paid to the worker in goods at a price arbitrarily fixed by his employer) of which the prohibition was scarcely observed. The workers were, above all, subjected to a double pressure; to the influx of the rural proletariat and the ruined craftsmen was added the competition of cheap labour from Ireland and of women and children.

Important movements towards England preceded the great transatlantic emigrations of the eighteen-forties. More than a million starving Irishmen, whose main food was the potato, an average of ten to twelve pounds per head a day, formed a considerable part of the floating population of the industrial centres. The Irish accepted no matter how low a wage and the worst of living conditions, as Engels discovered when visiting the poorest quarters of Manchester with a young Irish working girl, Mary Burns. His direct observations were the origin of the passage in the Communist Manifesto which links the massive introduction of women and children into the factories with the increase in mechanization: "All are instruments of labour, more or less expensive to use, according to their age and sex." The women's wages, always less than those of the men, were indispensable for the family haunted by the spectre of unemployment. Should there be a crisis, and crises were numerous in the first half of the nineteenth century, thousands of workers had to accept a cut in wages; thousands of others were turned out into the streets. The working population were very sensitive to variations in the price of bread which formed, with potatoes, the essential part of their food. Their diet was unbalanced, for all observers note the progress of rickets, and often of bad quality, since the worker's wife, a worker herself, was a poor housekeeper.

Were the manufacturers the egoistical and indifferent witnesses of this misery? The industrial magnates of the eighteen-forties were in no way a homogeneous group or a restricted caste. In a country where the aristocracy did not limit their activities to the exploitation of their lands, the representatives of the gentry possessed industrial enterprises. Richard Cobden, the great Manchester manufacturer, and Robert Owen, who became, thanks to his mills at New Lanark near Glasgow, one of the largest cotton-spinners, both came from social levels which technical progress had sorely tried. Cobden's father was a poor farmer from the south of England. Owen was the son of a Welsh saddler. In this world of manufacturers of various origins, with enterprises of varying sizes, the workers' complaints, protection of wages, regulation of working conditions and employment (dismissals were at the whim of the employers), did not provoke unanimous reactions.

The puritan spirit which considered wealth to be "a gift of God" led, according to individual reactions, to contrasting attitudes. Some thought to bear witness to their Creator by bettering the conditions of their workers; these were the "good masters". The generous innovations of Robert Owen, founder of the co-operative movement and "father of English socialism", are well known: one willingly recalls the model factory of New Lanark with its workers' city of healthy housing and its school for the children released from the machines. The Robert Owen of that time was still a conservative and his activities followed those of his father-in-law, the very rich manufacturer David Dale. Robert Peel's father was also a "social" master. The anathemas of Engels, the evidence of contemporaries of the most varied tendencies from evangelical philanthropists to antichristian radicals, were at one in denouncing the implacable tyranny of the majority of manufacturers. The old "master and servant" legislation, which the continent also knew, was a formidable weapon. Before the courts, save for proof to the contrary, the master was always in the right. The contradiction between a ferocious egoism and Christian sentiments openly paraded was rarely felt. Such was often the case with the founders of factories with initially modest resources; the capital which offered itself to the great enterprises of assured credit only too often resisted the solicitations of new manufacturers. This explains "the almost total blindness to everything that did not produce a profit and the harshness . . . towards the workers" (Hobsbawm).

Anger against oppression and its symbol, the machine, had at the end of the eighteenth century led the workers to destroy the looms and to burn the mills and the masters' residences. Despite terror legislation, wage claims had been supported by strikes. The workers never hesitated, when conditions were favourable, to make use of this weapon. Their behaviour thus seems consistent with the established idea of the British temperament (priority of material interest over ideological blandishments) although the workers wavered between political and trade-union action until the eighteen-forties.

*The Political Power of the Landed Aristocracy Shaken by the Alliance of the Proletariat and the Middle Classes; the Electoral Reform of 1832*

The crisis of 1815–19 marked among other things by the high price of bread (the Corn Laws had been voted in 1815) created a general dissatisfaction with agrarian capitalism and its mandatory, the Tory ministry. A change of political orientation, conceivable in principle, for the United Kingdom was the only country in the world to practise a parliamentary régime, was impossible in fact as long as the system constructed "for the convenience of an aristocracy" (Maurois) still existed. Every county sent to the House of Commons two members, whatever its population. This unique concession to logic gave a growing advantage to south-east England, rural and in decline, over north-west England, industrial and expanding. Arrangements apparently favourable to the towns reinforced still more the representation of the old England; the counties nominated eighty members, the towns four hundred and five. The so-called towns were in fact boroughs rather than towns, whose loyalty had recommended them to the choice of this or that sovereign. The rotten boroughs with only a few inhabitants, or even deserted, were represented in the Commons whereas commercial and industrial centres such as Liverpool, Manchester or Leeds were without their own members.

The electoral régimes (the singular is a simplification abhorrent to our Cartesian spirit) formulated by chance of circumstances were based on out-of-date economic and social criteria which a charmingly archaic phraseology had alone preserved from oblivion: freeholders, tenants or life-owners of property worth forty shillings (the equivalent of 50 francs in France where the qualification was 300 francs in 1815 and would still be 200 francs on the eve of 1848); pot-wallers (that is those who had enough to keep their pots on the boil). . . . The political supremacy of the landed Anglican aristocracy was less the result of antiquated rules—the more so as until 1828 nonconformists and until 1829 Catholics were ineligible—than of other practices, detestable but efficient.

In the counties the electors had to express their preference on a register in the presence of a representative of the large property-holders. In the rotten boroughs uncontested election was the rule. Elsewhere, the small number of electors favoured the most vulgar forms of corruption. The perverted, coarse and brutal England of Hogarth was silhouetted against the virtuous and respectable Victorian England!

Thus recruited, the House of Commons, supposed to represent the nation, strangely resembled the House of Lords. The interests of landed aristocracy were as well defended by the Tory ministry as they would be by a Whig ministry. At the beginning of the nineteenth century the parties lived out the quarrels of the seventeenth. One was born Whig or Tory as one is born Republican or Democrat in the United States today. It was outside Parliament and outside Whiggism that the radical movement, to which a growing section of the British proletariat was to adhere, developed among the middle classes.

The participation of the masses infused into an ideological trend already ancient, a revolutionary ardour unrivalled on the continent until the Parisian days of 1830. In times of war the governing aristocracy had known how to divert popular passions against France, hostile and "irreligious", and against the English Jacobins who welcomed the French revolution with enthusiasm: James Mill, father of John Stuart Mill, Thomas Paine, whom the Convention had welcomed on its benches, the young poets of the "first romantic generation", Wordsworth and Coleridge. After 1815 the radical party had included not only the survivors of the middle-class Jacobinism of the end of the last century but also men of working-class origin. With William Cobbett, son of a farm labourer and creator of the cheap popular press, and Francis Place, a former journeyman tailor, the radical press reached the proletarians of the country-side and the towns. Formidable slogans—universal suffrage, repeal of the Corn Laws—attracted large crowds: in 1816 at Spitalfields near London thousands of workers cheered a Phrygian bonnet and a green, white and red flag, symbol of a dreamed-of Republic of Great Britain. The agitation persisted until 16 August 1819, the day when fifty thousand workers met at St Peter's Fields near Manchester. The troops charged; eleven dead and hundreds injured was the price paid by the English workers who, the first in Europe, dared openly to demand universal suffrage. The "battle of Manchester", known to the opponents of the régime as Peterloo, evoking Waterloo with bitter irony, was followed by the passing of emergency legislation, the Six Acts. English radicalism had not only panicked the authorities in London, it had evoked terror across the Channel. Commenting on the recent assassination of the Duc de Berry, the *Gazette de France* wrote (27 February 1820): "The axe of the English radicals is the same as that of the French Jacobins." The English workers, however, soon withdrew from a foreign ideology to devote themselves to a specifically British form of activity, trade union action.

Workers' unions had existed in England since the eighteenth century. They were in principle mutual benefit societies and, in fact, trade unions also. In the former case legislation approved their activities; in the latter it forbade them. But the English police force had not the efficiency of that created by Napoleon! The trade union movement, which kept aloof from political agitation, emerged strengthened by the set-backs of the radical party. The economic recovery of 1820–5 facilitated their activities. Strikes multiplied. It remained to give them legal status. Since 1822 the Tory ministry had welcomed new men like Peel and Huskisson, less inclined than their colleagues to maintain the England of the past at all costs. In 1824 a law granted the workers the right of forming unions on questions relating to wages and hours of work. Even though restricted in 1825 its range was considerable. For the first time in history the workers were authorized to defend their right to live by withdrawing their labour. Trade unionism became a force sufficiently conscious of its own power to attempt, in conditions unfavourable to it like in the depression of the years 1825–32, the grouping of the mass of British workers in one vast federation. In 1830 the National Association of United Trades for the Protection of Labour was proposed under the leadership of the Irish worker John Doherty to federate all the textile, metallurgical and miners' unions. The year it disappeared (1831) another was born: the National Union of the Working Classes which, under the leadership of the London cabinet-maker Lovett, proposed to unite all trades.

The appearance of this modern-type trade unionism could not be dissociated from the revolutionary ferment which the Paris days of 1830 had fostered even in England. It was, first and foremost, a political revolutionary ferment; all those excluded from the right to vote demanded electoral reform, the industrial middle classes for themselves and the radicals for the greatest possible number. While the older unions hesitated, as earlier, to become involved in political activities the National Union of the Working Classes concentrated its propaganda on the demand for an annual chamber elected by secret ballot, and universal suffrage. In this Lovett collaborated closely with Place and Cobbett, who had returned to the arena. The obstinacy of the House of Lords unchained the passions of the people; ten thousand workers laid siege to St James' Palace and at Bristol the bishop's residence was burnt. The Lords capitulated: the law of 1832 suppressed the most crying abuses. A hundred and forty-three seats taken from the rotten boroughs were given to the counties and to the unrepresented or under-represented towns. For the first time twenty-one towns, including Manchester, Leeds and Birmingham, were to send members to Westminster. The privileges of the old England of the south-east were reduced but north-west England was still subjected to unjust treatment. All in all, the electoral body grew from little less than 500,000 to 800,000. The industrial and middle classes were the great gainers. The workers felt they had been betrayed. The political unionism of the National Union of the Working Classes had let them down; without abandoning the corporative trade unionism of the old unions they rallied in an atmosphere of social, or socialist, revolution to the Grand National Consolidated Trades Union which was founded by Robert Owen at the end of 1833.

*The Workers' Movement from Revolutionary Trade Unionism to Reformist Trade Unionism by the Chartist Stage of the Struggle for Universal Suffrage*

Robert Owen (1771–1858) enjoyed the prestige of a prophet whom events seemed to justify: he had condemned the agitation for electoral reform which he regarded as a deception. The workers must rely only upon themselves. The Grand National Consolidated Trades Union was intended, as were its two precedents (Lovett, the guiding spirit of the National Union of the Working Classes, had rallied to Owen), to unite all the unions of the United Kingdom. This general confederation of trades, which to-day we should call a Trade Union Congress, was based on an original structure outlined by Owen, a sort of workers' co-operative, a sort of socialism. (Owen's spirit of organization was in contrast to the romanticism of Fourier, who believed in the beneficent role of the passions!) Traditional trade unionism would lead, by way of the workers' co-operative, to socialism. The word appeared about 1825 among Owen's followers. In 1841 Owen's famous booklet *What is Socialism?* gave him an assured place in English literature. The magic word, linked to the idea of an imminent upheaval, unleashed the enthusiasm of the proletariat. The General Union soon counted half a million supporters who were taught that the weapon of the general strike was able to ensure the triumph of the socialist revolution. To the strikes which broke out all over England, the masters replied by lockouts. In the public authorities, terrified by the social agitation, since the Whig ministry was no more favourable to the workers than the Tory Government which had preceded it, they found unconditional support. The failure of the strikes and the subsequent repression explain the disintegration in the summer of 1834 of the General Union, the first example of a revolutionary apolitical trade unionism. The almost unanimous vote of the Commons in August for the inhuman Poor Law led men to question the methods recommended by Owen. The idea gained ground that the fate of the workers would remain uncertain as long as the House of Commons represented only the interests of the owners. Suddenly, with the appearance in 1836 of great economic difficulties, it inflamed a large section of the proletariat and inspired Chartism, "One of the greatest popular movements of modern times" (Labrousse).

This movement was political in principle (the demand for universal suffrage) and social in its aims ("the spoon and the pot") and composition (the workers were the largest element). It was neither socialist (the structural reforms of the General Union were forgotten) nor syndicalist (the unions were at first reserved towards it, as in the great epochs of the agitation for radical reform). British in the full sense of the term, though the Irish had a large place in the motley general staff of the movement, Chartism, linked with the tradition of Jacobinism and the English radicalism of the end of the eighteenth century and the Year XX, opened its arms wide to French revolutionary ideology.

The London Working Men's Association (1836), a society for popular education with a hundred and fifty branches in 1838, put forward a six-point programme drawn up by Lovett and Place: universal suffrage, secret ballot, parliamentary immunity, abolition of property qualification, equality of electoral districts, annual parliaments. The Irish lawyer James Bronterre O'Brien (1805–64) tried to reconcile Owen's teaching and the traditions of the Mountain and Babeuf. In 1837 he translated the work published at Brussels nine years before by Buonarotti: *History of the Conspiracy for Equality Attributed to Babeuf*, and in 1838 wrote a *Life of Robespierre*. Feargus O'Connor (1794–1855), also a lawyer and an Irishman, a truculent orator and a talented journalist, abounded in confused and contradictory ideas.

Despite their divergences all the Chartist leaders were convinced, just as were the rank and file of the movement, skilled workers and master craftsmen, that political democracy was the condition of economic democracy. The two Chartist offensives coincided with the price increases of 1838 when corn reached its record quotation, and the depression of 1842, when unemployment rose and wages decreased. Chartist agitation entered into competition with that of Cobden's League. The Chartists affirmed that reduction in living costs would involve diminution of wages; they added to their political claims a vehement campaign for the repeal of the Poor Law. They attracted a section of the proletariat of the textile mills and the mines but were above all supported by the proletariat in the cottage industries who were more inclined to accept the methods (recourse to "physical force") and the frankly revolutionary objectives of O'Connor: to re-create the England of the past by destroying the machines and reviving the peasant smallholdings! The *Northern Star* was printed in 42,000 copies, more than any French daily. More than 100,000 supporters in Glasgow, Birmingham and Leeds, more than 30,000 in Manchester and Liverpool, acclaimed the movement's programme. The essentially political Six Points of Lovett and Place became the People's Charter. Signatures were collected for a petition to the House of Commons and delegates were

nominated for a Workers' Convention. The enthusiasm of
their supporters incited several unions to take part *en masse* in
the meetings. Rallied in London in February 1839 the people's
parliament stated that the Great Petition had collected only
600,000 signatures. In May the partisans of "physical force"
obtained the agreement of the adepts of "moral force" (Lovett)
to impose by means of a general strike the introduction of
universal suffrage in the United Kingdom. In July the House of
Commons rejected the Chartist petition. The convention, which
had retreated to Birmingham, launched the order to strike in
August. The unions, always hostile to a risky political situation,
defected. Its failure was complete. Repression crashed down
on the rank and file of Chartism. Everything seemed over in
the summer of 1839.

Everything began again at the beginning of 1842. The
renaissance of the movement was a result of the indescribable
sufferings of the winter of 1841–2. The price of bread rose; the
factories closed their doors. The petition of 1842 contained
social, even socialist, demands, amongst others the suppression
of private ownership "of machinery and land". Its success was
unprecedented: 3,300,000 signatures! Nonetheless, the House
of Commons refused to consider it. A section of the working
class reacted spontaneously. Despite the abstention of the
unions and the counsels of moderation from the Chartist
leaders (even O'Connor was to denounce the excesses of the
disciples of "physical force") strikes broke out in an atmosphere
of insurrection. For three weeks in August, the strike was general
in Lancashire, Yorkshire and Staffordshire. Then, with the
recovery of 1843, the flames died down, as in 1820, 1832 and
1839!

The disillusion born of political action did not breach the
authority of the unions, which had remained prudently aloof
from Chartism. The trade unionism of the years 1843–5
broke away from the social and revolutionary trade unionism
of Owen and from traditional and regional trade unionism.
Strictly professional, it endeavoured, as John Doherty had
tried in 1830, to group the unions into powerful centres. In
1842 the Miners' Association of Great Britain and Ireland,

which mustered more than 100,000 members, was founded.
With the National Association of United Trades for the protection of Labour, founded in London in 1845, a fresh step
forward was taken towards united and reformist trade unionism.
This confederation demanded a ten-hour day and higher wages.
It believed that it was possible to obtain by negotiation the
institution of arbitration procedures. These "down to earth"
(E. Halevy) views, far distant from the noble aspirations of the
recent past, were certainly in accord with the state of mind of
the majority of British workers. The most turbulent of the
agitators tried to adapt themselves to the new situation.
O'Connor's daily became, significantly, the *Northern Star and
National Trades Journal*, but far from gaining new readers it lost
those it had. The decline which began after the great fever of
1839 continued. The average circulation fell from 12,000 copies
in 1842 to 7,500 in 1844 and 6,000 in 1846. Everything which
recalled the romance of Chartism seemed as out of date as
Romantic literature.

## Government by the Owners and Social Peace by Philanthropy

The Romantic poets of the "second generation", as liberal,
even as revolutionary, as those of the first, Byron, Shelley and
Keats, had disappeared before 1830. No country in Europe
seemed as far from sentimental effusions as England. The
weakening of protectionism and the electoral reform marked
"the rise of a class of merchants and industrialists, cold and
calculating" (Maurois). Soon power would pass, peacefully and
by the will of God, into the hands of the most deserving: the
manufacturers and the business men. It remained, however,
still in those of the great lords. Doubtless, since 1832, the
enlargement of the electoral body and the redistribution of
seats had strengthened the position of the Whigs. The two
parties were balanced. The Whigs governed from 1830 to 1834
and from 1835 to 1841, the Tories from 1834 to 1835 and from
1841 to 1846. Ministers and men of cabinet mettle still belonged
to the same great families of that aristocracy which knew how
to leave the door open to wealth and talent (the Tory Peel, son

of a manufacturer, is an illustrious example of this prudent liberalism). Thus ideology played a minor role in political struggle. Parliament legislated in the interest of the most worthy, the property owners, and of the weakest, the women and children. The Poor Law of 1834 was the most celebrated instance of egoistic interventionism. The philanthropic interventionism which the evangelical spirit inspired appeared in a series of measures, the first of which dated to the times of Tory hegemony. Inoperative because of lack of control organs they were followed after 1830 by legislative prescriptions to which Marx was to pay homage. In 1833 the Whig majority voted, on the proposal of an evangelical Tory, Lord Ashley, a law applicable to the whole of the textile industry; night work for children was forbidden, and the maximum working day was to be eight hours for those less than thirteen years old and twelve hours for young persons between thirteen and eighteen. As a principal innovation four labour inspectors were created! In 1844 Lord Ashley won from the Tory Government the passing of a law destined to mark an epoch: for workers aged between eight and thirteen the working day must not exceed six-and-a-half hours, and for those between thirteen and eighteen eleven hours. Children less than ten years old could not be employed in the mills or in the mines, and in the mines the employment of women was also forbidden. For the first time in the social history of Europe the State concerned itself with the fate of adult workers. If it was sensitive to the more inhuman aspects of capitalist exploitation, the philanthropic spirit remained deaf, save in exceptional cases, to the demands of nationalist, Romantic and revolutionary Ireland.

### Romantic Ireland against Pragmatic England

English public opinion remained deeply hostile to the Irish, those papists always ready to betray their conquerors. Protestant workers complained of competition from boorish men who, accompanied by their priests, converged on the manufacturing cities. The masters were indignant at finding so many Irishmen among the most fiery advocates of social subversion. The members of the "political class", accustomed to the dull and prosy speeches of the Houses, those closed clubs, were shocked by the violent harangues which Feargus O'Connor delivered to enormous crowds.

In the country of tribunes, the lawyer Daniel O'Connell (1775–1847) had from 1823 led the vocal protests against the most clamant of the inequalities. His Catholic Association succeeded in mobilizing the Irish clergy, ignorant and for long apathetic. For a long time past national sentiment and Catholic fervour had been linked together in the Polish soul, but, thanks to O'Connell, Ireland provided Europe with the first example of a mass party based on a religious confession. Later Lamennais and his French friends were to admire O'Connell and the Belgian and German Catholics were to imitate him. The enlargement of the suffrage was to assure the Catholic parties solid foundations. The public authorities certainly had a presentiment of this at the moment when the Irish agitation forced them to give way. The emancipation of the Catholics in the United Kingdom (1829) allowed the Irish electors to send Catholic members to Westminster. But fair play has its limits! Before 1829 the property qualification was low in Ireland; in 1829 it increased fivefold! The number of electors fell from 200,000 to 26,000! O'Connell had nothing of the revolutionary about him; he did not like either the workers of the trade unions or the tenant-farmers who dreamed of expropriations. In the service of the Catholic Church he obtained, first of all, the suppression of ten Anglican bishoprics and, finally, the reduction of the heavy and much hated (it served the abhorred Church) tithe and its transformation into a tax levied by the State (1938). These successes were due to the power of the Irish parliamentary group, forty-one members in 1832, and to O'Connell's tactics. The proclaimed objective, which was independence by repeal of the Act of Union of 1801, was only a means of exerting pressure on the Whigs who governed, save for a Tory interlude from 1834 to 1835, with the aid of the Irish votes until 1841. O'Connell, ready for a "total and eternal reconciliation", hoped to become the Minister in charge of Irish Affairs. The more advanced elements of the movement denounced the ambitions and compromises of the idol. In the 1841 elections O'Connell lost his seat. The spirit of revolt once again breathed over Ireland.

The Young Ireland group, animated by the Protestant poet Thomas Davis and organized by the journalist Gavan Duffy, became, after the foundation in Dublin (1842) of a weekly paper with the evocative title of *The Nation*, the rallying point of the irreconcilables. Its members were young, for in 1842 Davis was twenty-eight, Duffy twenty-six and Smith O'Brien, the oldest among them, thirty-nine, and all of them intellectuals. To revive the nation one must first restore its soul to the enslaved people. The patriotism of Young Ireland took an original form. It was neither racist nor confessional, scarcely linguistic; being of English culture, the leaders of Young Ireland paid little heed to Gaelic, which was still spoken about 1840 to the west of a line from Londonderry to Waterford. The exaltation of great men, a St Columba or a Duns Scotus, and the publication in English, in *The Spirit of the Nation*, of popular songs and ballads were to forge a community of feeling between the descendants of the Celts and the Saxons, between Protestants and Catholics. These generous views were opposed to the conceptions of O'Connell, defender of the Celts and the Catholics exclusively, views which the birth in 1922 of an Irish Ireland and an English Ireland were to relegate to Utopia. About 1840 opinion began to admit that only a legislative assembly seated in Dublin would be able to resolve at last the agrarian problem; the peasants, precarious tenants of infinitesimal holdings (in 1843 more than a half of them had less than three hectares), felt themselves free to debate their rent-rolls and guarantees against arbitrary eviction without compensation. In order to re-establish a compromised situation O'Connell adopted the slogans of his critics. While Chartism was raging in England a revolutionary movement was shaking Ireland. Enormous crowds acclaimed "the liberator" and led him to predict, in the fire of improvisation, the imminence of independence. O'Connell summoned all the Irish to the Hill of Tara where, on 15 August 1843, more than 200,000 people responded to his appeal. Exuberantly supported by Young Ireland and prisoner of his own oratorical excesses, he proposed to hold, on 8 October at Clontarf near the capital, another popular meeting which the Government forbade. The destiny of Ireland was in his hands. A section of his followers urged him to resist in order to face the English with a difficult choice; passivity would increase the ranks of the supporters of autonomy whereas repression would unleash a popular uprising. But it is one thing to play at revolution; it is another to lead it! O'Connell could not resign himself, and younger leaders were to take the same attitude in 1848, to the responsibility of a bloody confrontation. The meeting was countermanded. Repression struck down O'Connell the opportunist and Duffy the revolutionary. Condemned to prison and a fine, O'Connell appealed to the House of Lords, which annulled the sentence. But liberation finally discredited him! Leader without troops, he went to die in Italy (1847). Young Ireland found the way clear. It ceased to be a state of mind and became a revolutionary movement under the leadership of Duffy; Davis died at the age of thirty-one in 1845.

The spectre of an Irish rising, which any great upheaval would spark off, henceforth troubled the tranquillity of Great Britain. Would this numerous and, till lately, so subversive a proletariat be able, as Engels said in 1845, to emerge from its torpor and crush capitalism? If it finally grew more sober, as the pragmatic Governments hoped, what a paradox would be offered to the wisdom of historians by the country where modern industry had been born with all its grandeur and misery and where the parliamentary régime was reserved for the property-owning classes!

## [ Chapter Two ]

## The Contrasts of Rural France: a Dominant Bourgeoisie, a Revolutionary Capital

THE APPEARANCE of the France of Louis Philippe was no less paradoxical. Industrialization was only at its beginnings; nonetheless, from 1830, the bourgeoisie exercised the power in the shadow of the "citizen-king". The proletariat, unorganized professionally, was dispersed and far from numerous. France was the chosen land of socialist doctrines. These, ignored by the factory workers, penetrated little by little the élite of the workshop artisans of Paris and some of the larger towns. Conspiracies, sudden outbreaks, insurrections not aimed merely at intimidating the authorities in the manner of the English and Irish mass movements but at overthrowing them, were the original manifestations of the democratic, socialist and Romantic currents. The propensity to revolutionary action, in imitation of "the great ancestors", was due to young and ardent men submerged in a prudent and discreet population of slow increase.

### THE SLOWNESS OF DEMOGRAPHIC INCREASE AND THE INSIGNIFICANCE OF URBANIZATION. THE EXAMPLE OF LYONS

Undoubtedly at a time when force of arms primarily depended on the effectives available for mobilization France continued to take the lead. In 1851 with 35,700,000 inhabitants she was (Russia excepted) in first place. However her increase of 30 per cent in fifty years appeared modest compared with that of Europe (50 per cent) and derisory compared with the United Kingdom (71 per cent), the country of transatlantic emigration.

The United Kingdom had not followed the counsels of Malthus; and France forestalled him. The fall in the birth-rate was a well-established and regular phenomenon which owed nothing to the activities of academic circles haunted by the fear of social unrest. The bourgeois minority and the peasant mass had, from the end of the eighteenth century, adopted similar attitudes to life; the desire for social climbing and the wish to reduce to a minimum the effects of partition among heirs encouraged them to birth restrictions. The average annual birth-rate fell from 38·6 in 1771–5 to 31·2 in 1811–15. From 1829 onward it fell below 30, to 28 in 1837 and 27 in 1844. This decline was as striking in the agricultural area of Lot-et-Garonne as in the capital where the preponderance of adults due to immigration led to a high birth-rate. With this birth-rate France was henceforth "sagging".

The death-rate, on the contrary, did not differ from that of most of the European States. The average of the years 1841–5 which preceded the economic and political crisis was almost as low (22·7) as that of England and Wales (21·4) and lower than that of Germany (26·1), the Netherlands (23·9) and Belgium (23·5). Divergence between the morality in the cities and the countryside was, about 1840, a fact. In the unhealthy towns the death-rate was high. The Parisian rate was to be, until 1885, always higher than that of the country as a whole. Nonetheless the wretched and violent Paris of the social enquiries and the novels had a far greater vitality than the modest urban centres scattered throughout the most varied districts; from 1831 to 1851 the death-rate was higher than the birth-rate in Rouen, Caen, Rennes, Orléans, Toulouse, Montpellier, Toulon, Metz and Strasbourg.

The slow French growth had peasant origins. From 1836 to 1851, according to Pouthas who regards the community as rural which has less than three thousand souls, the proportion of inhabitants in the countryside declined from 74·8 to 71·9 per cent. In 1851 a relative decrease of the rural population was noted in all the departments except four (Dordogne, Deux-Sèvres, Cantal and Basses-Alpes). The most marked variations were in the essentially agricultural regions: Pyrénées-Orientales 21·5 per cent, Haute-Loire 33·8 per cent. On the other hand the more industrial regions showed insignificant changes: Rhône 6·4 per cent, Nord 5·2 per cent, Loire 3·9 per cent and Seine 1·9 per cent. "Industrial development, therefore, did not empty the countryside and did not involve a demographic revolution" (Pouthas).

From 1831, as a result of the rural exodus, the towns began to hold a more important place in the total population. From 1836 to 1851 they increased by 13·8 per cent (the increase in the whole country was 9·9 per cent), especially the small towns of from four to five thousand inhabitants (36 per cent), a growth that explains the spectacular decline of the rural population in an agricultural department like Haute-Loire. The archaic character of France in the first half of the nineteenth century is also reflected in the evolution of the very large cities. In 1851 fifteen towns, as against eight in 1801, had more than fifty thousand inhabitants. Their share in the total population (6·5 per cent) was proportionately three times less than in British towns of similar size (in England the link between a prodigious urban increase and an incomparable industrial development was evident). From 1801 to 1851 the workers' towns showed a growth equal to (Amiens 30 per cent) or less than (Rouen 16 per cent) the French average; only one, St Etienne, had increased greatly (193·7 per cent), less however than the military port of Toulon (245 per cent)! In 1845, as always, they were to react under the impetus of Paris.

Lyons, third city of France (177,000 inhabitants in 1851), was in the eighteen-thirties the only provincial revolutionary centre. In November 1831 about twenty thousand workers took up arms, waving the black flag (which the navvies of Rheims had, a few weeks before, unfurled for the first time, over a crowd of workers) with the device: "To live free working or to die fighting". It was "the first purely workers' insurrection in modern times" (Lefebvre). A spontaneous reaction of workers in defence of their wages, it was inspired by no ideology. Unlike the English workers, the workers of Lyons did not yet claim the right to vote.

But the year 1834 was to see a sensational event: a workers' insurrection with undeniable political origins. Lyons with its Society of the Rights of Man and of the Citizen which had two thousand members became at the beginning of 1834 "the first republican town of France". When the Government decided, at the end of February, to modify Article 291 of the Penal Code which the Society of the Rights of Man held in derision, it examined methods of outwitting the authorities. (Meetings of more than twenty persons were forbidden; it therefore broke up into sections of from ten to twenty members!) The Parisian leaders, divided, consulted. On 9 April a great demonstration against the government was staged at Lyons. A shot was fired. The workers took up arms. The troops opened fire. The fighting went on for four days (9 to 12 April). On 13 April Paris learnt of the Lyons rising; barricades were set up in the Marais. The next day the massacre of the rue Transnonain sealed the defeat of the rioters. The April insurrection was only an episode in the revolutionary history of Paris. The second Lyons insurrection of the July Monarchy presents, as also the first but for different reasons, some exceptional traits; it was, firstly, the consequence of a link never before realized in France between the workers' aspirations and the republican ideal; and it provided the unique model for a provincial and autonomous armed movement whose example impressed the capital.

After 1834 the revolutionary spirit was to decline with the appearance of a factory proletariat. At the beginning of the reign of Louis Philippe the silk industry employed manual workers dispersed in tens of thousands of small workshops; their bosses, who were skilled in several crafts, together with one or two associates, wage-earners like themselves, worked on materials supplied to them by from three to five hundred "manufacturers". More educated than their fellows, they showed themselves able in 1831 and in 1834 to indoctrinate

them and lead them in the struggle. When, from the eighteen-
forties onwards, new factories were set up in the suburbs, the
rough and docile peasants, who had formerly worked side by
side with the old-style workshop bosses and were now cut off
from them, formed a new type of proletariat whom misery and
ignorance prevented from thinking.

PARIS, CAPITAL OF THE REVOLUTION IN FRANCE

*The Parisian Paradoxes*

It was from Paris alone that France and also Europe hoped or
feared to see the flash of the revolutionary spark.

With its 1,053,000 inhabitants in 1846 and in 1851 (the
economic crisis and the political tension were the origin of a
stagnation that lasted five years) the capital remained, as at
the beginning of the century, the only town with more than
200,000 souls. In 1851 it represented about 3 per cent of the
total population. But London had more than twice as many
inhabitants (2,363,000) and a higher proportion of the population (more than 8 per cent of the inhabitants of the United
Kingdom and 10 per cent of that of Great Britain). The
"demographic peculiarity" of Paris should not, therefore, be
exaggerated.

On the other hand its importance in national and international political life was evident. Of the great popular movements (radicalism, Chartism, free trade) London felt only the
echo, all agitation ending with the solemn presentation of a
petition to the House of Commons. In France, save for the
Lyons insurrection of 1831 and 1834, everything began in Paris,
in violence, and everything ended there. The barricades, which
had disappeared from the Parisian streets since 25 and 26
August 1648, were to rise again on 19 November 1827 to
"salute the fall of Villèle" (Duveau). On 27, 28 and 29 July
1830 they played a decisive role in the accession of Louis
Philippe. After the fruitless and bloody attempts of 5 and 6
June 1832, 13 April 1834 and 12 May 1839 they forced the
"king of the barricades" to flight and stirred up "chain

revolutions". The inclination of the Paris populace to insurrection and the extraordinary repercussion of the February
days throughout Europe conferred exceptional originality on
the French capital. This was the result of many causes, geographical, democratic and spiritual.

## Workers' Paris Faces Bourgeois Paris

The Paris of the eighteen-forties still resembled the Paris of the
end of the eighteenth century. It was still surrounded by a
circle of the tax gatherers. Between it and the fortifications
completed in 1844 stretched the "little suburbs", a region which
was becoming industrialized in certain parts: Belleville, La
Villette, La Chapelle. The concentrations of workers there were
still too sporadic to relieve the congestion of over-crowded
Paris; the average density of 1846 (30,655) was roughly equal
to that of 1970, the area of the city having doubled since 1860.
Never were the demographic contrasts more marked. Of the
forty-eight quarters (four for each of the twelve arrondissements)
two had a density of less than ten thousand (Invalides and
Champs-Elysées) and eight more than a hundred thousand
(Les Arcis, Les Marchés, Bonne-Nouvelle, Lombards, Montor-
gueil, Banque, Saint-Avoye, Porte Saint-Denis). These formed
the kernel of a zone of over-population, limited on the north
and south by the Louvre and the Porte Saint-Denis, on the
west and east by Les Halles and L'Hôtel de Ville. It was the
Paris of narrow winding alleys which might be said to have
been made by and for the builders of the barricades. It was the
Paris of the labourers, the beggars and the thieves, depicted
with professional indifference in the police memoirs of Vidocq
(1828) and Canler (1862) and with pitying sympathy in *The
Mysteries of Paris* by Eugène Sue (1842-3). The Île de la Cité
was like a "*cour des miracles*" (Hugo) enclosing fences, thieves,
pawnbrokers, released or escaped convicts, exploiters of stolen
children, prostitutes and vagabonds. It welcomed and contaminated newcomers.

Immigration is a constant feature of Parisian history;
economics had scarcely any influence on it, at least up to the

census of 1846. By necessity, the immigrants at first lived as "nomads" (Chevalier) for in this city of working classes and menial jobs (the water-carrier from the Auvergne was a part of the scene) employment was only available to this over-abundant labour force in the building trade. Thousands of men arrived in the spring and went back to spend the winter "in the country", like the Creusot masons, portrayed from nature by the most famous amongst them, Martin Nadaud (*Mémoires de Léonard, ouvrier garçon maçon*, 1895). From 1840 onward, the employment offered by the construction of railways and stations and the completion of the fortifications contributed to the decline of nomadism. The habits thus acquired stabilized the new residents, who crowded into tiny sordid lodgings in the centre. (The foreign labour force is adopting under our own eyes this gregarious behaviour, characteristic of rootless, famished refugees.) Landlords did good business converting century-old buildings; unfurnished, a room could be let to these outcasts, with no fixed income, for twelve francs a month; wretchedly furnished, if such were to be found, for twenty francs a fortnight. Thus, little by little, the worlds of the labourers and the thieves met in the same surroundings and they succeeded one another in the same slums. But a double movement began; a section of the workers and almost all of the bourgeois families moved out of these over-populated quarters of ill repute.

The workers moved towards the arrondissements of the "cross" of Paris: the VIIIe (Marais, Popincourt, Faubourg Saint-Antoine, Quinze-Vingts) on the right bank and the XIIe (Saint-Jacques, Saint-Marcel, Conservatoire, Jardin des Plantes) on the left bank. These quarters, whose names appear at every great moment of revolutionary history, were inhabited by artisans (carpenters, cabinet-makers in the Faubourg Saint-Antoine, tanners on the banks of the Bièvre) deep-rooted in an environment open to subversive propaganda. Here, coming into contact with fellow-workers of more advanced ideology, the provincial would eventually find himself merging with the local populace, however much this meant a change in his mental outlook.

The distressing sensation of becoming a "foreigner" in the heart of a Paris thus invaded forced the wealthier classes to move away. This segregation was only to be completed under the Second Empire. However, the contours of a Paris of the poor to the east and a Paris of the rich to the west were beginning to be apparent. In June 1848 the zone of the barricades was bounded by a line which followed the suburbs Poissonière, Saint-Denis, Saint-Martin and Saint-Antoine, the Île de la Cité and the rue Saint-Jacques. It was "the frontier between bourgeois Paris and the workers' Paris" (Duveau).

Bourgeois Paris was afraid of the Paris of the "nomads" and the "wild ones". *The Mysteries of Paris*, which appeared by instalments in the very Orléanist *Journal des Débats*, revealed to a wide public (the common people and the upper classes alike followed passionately the adventures of Fleur-de-Marie and the Grand duke Rudolph) the growing degradation of a large section of the populace. The lesson of the novel with its countless vicissitudes, that extreme destitution engenders crime, entered the domain of accepted ideas. Liberal-minded people demanded a struggle against misery, the hard-hearted well-to-do called for a stop to the invasion of the "vile mob" which Thiers was to denounce in 1850. The great study of Chevalier (*Working classes and criminal classes in Paris in the first half of the nineteenth century*, 1958) confirms the impression felt by contemporaries of an inevitable social opposition, moral and mental, between two peoples. It made the tempests of Paris more comprehensible but the calm of London more mysterious.

## The Power of Myths: Jacobinism and Bonapartism

London and Paris can be painted with the same palette. "Residents and vagrants ... established city-dwellers and recent immigrants met ... The source of social fears, lack of balance between the mass of the people and the small minority of property-owners weighed continually on the mind" (Bédarida). Similar tensions within the two agglomerations, as misery increased on the banks of the Thames and of the Seine, were not capable of provoking similar movements. The depression of 1825–32 struck the United Kingdom more severely than France. However, it was Paris which rose in revolt and overthrew a king in 1830. The London cabinet-maker Lovett did not dream, like his fellows of the Faubourg Saint-Antoine, of setting up barricades to obtain universal suffrage! Revolutionary in principle, since it rejected the very foundations of the régime, the Parisian working-class republican opposition accepted, in an atmosphere of passionate feeling, the risks of revolutionary action; memories of 1792 were reborn and with them the dream of a new republic won, for France, by Paris. Revolutionary history cast its shadow over Paris, but not London. We know this today, but the best informed contemporaries were unaware of it at the time and in particular the court and the middle classes of London, which were to be haunted in April 1848 by the spectre of Jacobinism and the troubles of the seventeenth century. A hundred and forty-four years before Louis XVI, Charles I had been beheaded and a hundred and forty-two years before Charles X, James II had lost his crown. The dictatorship of Napoleon, indifferent or hostile to Christianity, egalitarian and expansionist, had helped to weaken the idea of revolution in England. The cult of Robespierre and Babeuf, introduced to London in 1837–8 by James Bronterre O'Brien, rallied only a handful of the converted to its cause. It enjoyed a growing enthusiasm among the Parisian republicans and workers at the moment when Guizot invoked the English precedent of 1688 to halt the course of French revolutionary history in 1830. (The period 1789–1815 was the tremendous first act of this drama.)

Before 2 December 1851 Frenchmen in all walks of life confounded in nostalgic admiration Empire and Revolution. Committed writers, addressing themselves to a restricted circle of readers, painted in legendary colours events still recent but little known. At the end of the Restoration, Thiers (1823–7) and then Mignet (1824) published a *History of the French Revolution*. In 1845 the former tackled a *History of the Consulate*; in 1847 Michelet and Blanc began the publication of important works devoted to the *History of the Revolution* and Lamartine published the seven volumes of the *History of the Girondins*, a monument to the glory of the Revolution. These works were not the origin either of the barricades of February 1848 or of the imperial cult which Thiers was reproached with having "very imprudently" (Jullian) broadcast. Among the lower classes, they influenced only the readers of the democratic press, few in number, for the benefits of the Guizot law on primary education were not to become evident before the Second Empire. (Moreover, fifty years after the scholastic legislation of Jules Ferry a Parisian railway station still provided the astonishing spectacle of a busy public letter-writer.) At the end of the eighteen-forties and at the cost of arduous and touching efforts an infinitesimal section of the working class had acquired the ability to read and even to write. *The Atelier, organ of the moral and material interests of the workers,* founded by Dr Buchez in 1840, counted on its staff jewellery workers and tailors. But its few readers, the monthly circulation fell from 1,000 copies in 1840 to 500 in 1846, were members of the upper classes, curious to know the demands of the workers. The working-class élite of the eighteen-forties read *The National* (3,000 subscribers) and above all *The Reform* (2,000) which was bolder from the social viewpoint.

Daily exalting the France of before 1815, this press was in accord with the deeper sentiments of unlettered men who dreamed of a return of the Mountain dictatorship and the Napoleonic era. The paradoxical link between love of the tricolour (Republicanism) and the cult of the "little corporal" (Dictatorship) were to lead to the stupefying results of the presidential election of 10 December 1848. The "flight of the eagle" had aroused the spirit of 1793 for several weeks. Agricol Perdiguier in *Mémoires d'un compagnon* had touchingly evoked his father's rallying to the Emperor though a peaceable carpenter and a former captain in the revolutionary wars. Under the Restoration, propaganda against "the usurper" did not have any effect on the popular masses; the "growlers" (Napoleonic veterans) were many among the Parisian workers. In contrast to London, where the English had provided only small contingents to the armies of the anti-French coalitions and had ignored the great colonial expeditions, Paris had remained a city of ex-soldiers. From 1830 on, the conquest of Algeria added young ex-soldiers to the veterans of the Revolution and the Empire, whose ranks were brightened up by this addition. In this way the techniques which the people from the working-class quarters were to use for the last time during the Commune of 1871 were handed down. In June 1848 Tocqueville was to discover with wonder and admiration the skill with which barricades were built!

The memories of the "growlers" and also those of the old Jacobins (the men of the generation of Michelet (born 1798) had, in their youth, received the confidence of the contemporaries of Marat, Danton or Robespierre) spread an ambiguous ideology made up of aggressive nationalism and Messianic emancipation: the defeat of perfidious Albion, of barbarous Russia and the Austria of Metternich would give the left bank of the Rhine to France, once again the "great nation", and would liberate the Italians and above all the Poles from foreign and reactionary oppression.

### The Workers' Insurrection of 1832; for the Republic and for Poland

The Polish cause was popular everywhere: Vienna, Brussels and London were to welcome as friends the defeated of the 1830 insurrection. But what about the delirious welcome of the French? Like the Greeks before them, the Poles had in 1830 partisans among all classes. Madame Adélaide, sister and confidante of the King, longed for the victory of the insurgents! The legitimists reacted as Catholics and denounced the oppression exercised by a "legitimate" but Orthodox sovereign! The liberal Catholics grouped around Lamennais and demanded armed intervention. So too the bellicose *Globe*, which had become, since 27 December 1830, the *Journal de la doctrine de Saint-Simon*. Certainly the audience of the liberal Catholics and the followers of Saint-Simon was limited: the *Avenir* and the *Globe* lasted two years. The former had 1,200 subscribers, three quarters of whom were ecclesiastics, the latter 500, all members of the "enlightened classes" (Charlety). Insignificant minorities (*The Tribune* of Marrast, then the only republican journal, which had a mere 1,500 subscribers, and *The National*, organ of the *Movement*, were, naturally, savagely pro-Polish) would hardly have been able to mobilize the working class areas on 5 June 1832 had not the myth of liberated Poland, linked to the exalted memories of the Revolution and the Empire, the glorious history of the Polish legions incorporated in the French armies, exercised its attraction.

Doubtless circumstances were favourable to a popular explosion. The economic difficulties of 1828 had been worsened by the political troubles of 1830 which they had in part provoked. The rise in the cost of foodstuffs and in unemployment engendered a permanent unrest. It was in Lyons, as we have seen, and not in Paris that the social crisis unleashed an insurrection. In the spring of 1832 a cholera epidemic broke out in the capital. It did not spare the rich (Casimir Périer was an illustrious victim) but it was the undernourished populace huddled in the "Paris cross" that it struck especially. It created in the deteriorating social atmosphere the psychological tension which sometimes precedes uprisings. The funeral of Evariste Gallois (today a communist cell bears his name), adorned with all the charm of youth (he was twenty-one) and with the double halo of a *savant* and a revolutionary, took place peacefully. Some days later, that of an old general was the cause of the first great revolutionary battle in Paris since 1795 (Labrousse). A volunteer during the Revolution, a General and Count of the Empire, Lamarque became, during the Hundred Days, once again a man of 1793 in order to crush the Vendeans, an insurgent against Napoleon transformed into a Jacobin. His popularity dated from his entry into the Chamber of Deputies where he denounced the peace established by the treaties of 1815! Irreconcilable enemy of England, ardent friend of Poland, he had strongly criticized the passivity of the Government in face of Russian repression, not long before he died. The majority of the organizers of the ceremony, the Orléanists Barrot and Laffitte and the republican Arago, were known for their Polish sympathies. The presence of the Marquis de la Fayette gave, it is true, a certain ambiguous tone to the obsequies of the republican general risen from the ranks. Despite the unfortunate publicity of a biographical notice in the *Dictionary of Weathercocks*, this versatile and timorous aristocrat had become a legend in his lifetime. An almost religious respect surrounded the old man of eighty-five who was associated with two revolutions: the American, which created that republic which the pro-American, advanced European circles regarded as a new Arcadia; the French, of which the "hero of two worlds" symbolized the mission of emancipation. The sight of this patriarch holding one of the traces of the hearse, the spectacle of the flags of the oppressed nations, the Polish as well as those of the future Italy and the future Germany, reawoke the anger against a régime which was unfaithful to the mission of France. Finally, the appearance of the red flag, for the first time in a worker's procession, borne by a mysterious horseman, added to the emotion. Some cries of "Long live the Republic!", doubtless shouted by members of the secret societies, unleashed the riot which quickly turned into an insurrection. The working-class quarters (Marais, Arcis, Les Halles, the Faubourgs Saint-Denis, Saint-Martin and Saint-Antoine) were covered with barricades. At the first shot La Fayette went home; Arago, like Laffitte and Barrot, spoke and then disappeared. The united front presented by the property-owning classes against the disorders was almost total. The National Guard vied in ardour with the troops. The insurgents had as sole allies a few students and polytechnicians (students at the Military Academy of Artillery and Engineering). Their desperate resistance ended on the sixth. The memory of the heroic combatants of the Saint-Merri cloister was to become an example for the revolutionaries of 1848.

Regarded from its causes and its development, the insurrection of June 1832 was, in contrast to the riots of April 1834 and May 1839, a real prelude to the days of 1848. Its "moral root" was the same as that which was to produce the attack on the National Assembly on 15 May 1848: the Polish question. In its proletarian character, the explosion of June 1832 foreshadowed the great workers' insurrection of June 1848, sixteen years later the republican leaders deserted, while the builders of the barricades fought recklessly against the National Guards who were united in the defence of order.

Polytechnicians and students finally became part of the Parisian Revolutionary scene. The École Polytechnique was a specifically French institution. The Faculty of Arts and Sciences was vegetating aimlessly. Student life only existed around the Faculties of Law and Medicine which prepared students for the liberal professions. But in this regard the supremacy of the capital was shattering. Its Faculty of Medicine had more than eight thousand students in 1835; that of Montpellier, the second in France, less than six hundred in 1837. Polytechnicians and students were concentrated in the Latin Quarter, where they could overhear the rumours of old Paris. At the sound of a riot they ran to take part, for subversive doctrines enchanted the sons of the bourgeoisie (the École Polytechnique provided the church of Saint-Simon with many adepts following in the footsteps of "father" Enfantin; Considérant, the most eminent representative of Fourierism, was a polytechnician). As well as turbulent students, young men subjected to the military hierarchy admired the "democratic triumvirate" of the Collège de France—Michelet, Quinet, Mickiewicz. Romantics, bored in a France where nothing ever happened, despised the prosaic and pacific July Monarchy. Their longing for change was fed on memories and dreams.

## PARIS CAPITAL OF THE REVOLUTION IN EUROPE

Louis Philippe's threat in 1840 to "unmuzzle the tiger" was not serious but it was based on a psychological reality; a part of the Parisian press laid claim to the left bank of the Rhine, and Quinet published a booklet with the suggestive title: *1815–1840*. If the Germans were indignant, the Poles and the Italians awaited the liberation of unification of their countries from a European war.

### Cosmopolitan Paris

The reaction in their countries after the setbacks of 1830–1 had transformed the liberals and the democrats into wanderers, who sought the opportunity of coming to Paris or dreamed of returning there after they had been chased out by police harassments. The "capital of European liberalism" (Pouthas) of the eighteen-thirties was to become "the capital of the revolution" (Fejtö) of the eighteen-forties.

For the élite immigrants Paris was not merely "the new Jerusalem" as the young Heine imagined it, even before knowing it. It was also the city of enchantment because of its brilliant and cosmopolitan society. The salons of Mme de Girardin, a successful author under the name of Delphine Gay, of Mme d'Agoult (Daniel Stern in literature) of the fecund pen, of George Sand, incarnation of feminism and who received dressed as a man, were open to foreign artists (Liszt, Meyerbeer and Chopin became Parisians) and poets. Herwegh and Mickiewicz appeared as the disciples of Lamartine, Hugo and Michelet. The "foreign salons", another example of the international character of Paris, were at the same time propaganda centres and meeting places for refugees. Germans, Italians and Poles thronged the salon of Mme de Circourt, a Russian married to a French diplomat; that of the beautiful Princess Belgiojoso (1808–71) (whose arrival in Malan at the beginning of May 1848 at the head of a corps of volunteers equipped at her expense was to make a sensation) served as a post office for the emissaries of Mazzini. Prince Czartoryski used his international credit to prepare for the liberation of the Poles.

The activities of those members of society, who supported "nationalities" (this word was used by writers in all countries from this point) and helped exiles, must not obscure the fact that there were many foreigners in both Paris and the provinces of whose presence society was completely unaware. Those proscribed were a minority which the police considered, according to their spy de la Hodde, as a "virus with which France had been inoculated". In the workshops of the old trades thousands of manual workers were indoctrinated with revolutionary ideology. Political refugees of every class and immigrant workers preserved their national cohesion. The largest number of these were Poles and Germans.

## *The Messianism of the Polish "Pilgrims"*

The Polish colony was not the most numerous, but it included the highest proportion of political refugees. In its overwhelming majority the "great emigration" of 1831 chose France, where so many faithful servants of Poland and of Napoleon had found asylum after 1815. It was continually being reinforced from the Prussian and Austrian provinces as the King and the Emperor did not delay on the example of the Tsar in carrying out a policy of repression. For the exiles France was not merely a second country, it was their only real country. With its name, Poland had lost its lands, but its soul had been saved by the creation, by the actions of refugee writers, of an ideal Poland.

This Poland had Paris as its capital and Adam Mickiewicz (1798–1855) as its spokesman. Since 1834 he had been "the spiritual leader of the emigration and, by extension, of the Polish nation" (Wilczkowski), despite the presence in Paris of the two other members of the "great romantic triad", Krasinski and Slowacki and of the historian Lelewel who had been Mickiewicz's master at Vilna. In his *Books of the Polish nation and of the Pilgrimage* (1832) Mickiewicz had formulated the doctrine of a crucified nation called upon to give Europe an example of sacrifice! "Everything in Europe where there is oppression of liberty and the struggle for liberty ... all the Poles must join the struggle." Preaching this example, he was to form a Polish legion which he placed at the disposal of the Lombard patriots in May 1848. Poland remained the privileged ally of a France which, renouncing its expansionist nationalism in the general atmosphere of romanticism, was more than ever desirous of waging wars of liberation. A reign of brotherhood would of necessity be set up among the liberated peoples, under the guidance of France. The simultaneous presence at the Collège de France of Michelet, Quinet and Mickiewicz was the symbol of a deep accord between French Messianism and Polish Messianism.

The former could, in the expectation of inevitable disorders, indulge in dreams. The latter was forced, as Mickiewicz demanded, into action. But in action the mystique of the "pilgrims" became dissipated; the dissensions of the past were reborn and grew greater. The Whites had as their chief Prince Czartoryski. He wanted to restore, with the diplomatic support of France and the United Kingdom, a monarchical Poland; his adversaries called it aristocratic. The sympathies of the majority of the refugees were with the Reds, partisans of a democratic but also social Poland, for they had learnt in 1831 that the support for the national liberation movement of the most numerous class presupposed that first of all the essential problem of the Slav world, the agrarian problem, should be settled. Good and decisive speakers, the Reds too displayed their divisions. Lelewel at one time succeeded in reconciling the factions, but had to take refuge at Brussels. The most advanced elements in March 1832 were grouped in the Polish Democratic Society which relentlessly fought the Whites and affirmed the primacy of the Polish people among the Slavs. The Democratic Society organized secret societies against the oppressors which foreshadowed the "resistance movements" of World War II. From 1833 to 1850 the Russian police were to uncover thirteen subversive groups and to arrest more than five hundred patriots. In 1838 the Austrians in Galicia destroyed the network of Major Konarski, whom the Russians shot in 1839. While still in France, the Democratic Society prepared a general rising in Poznania against the Prussians, Russians and Austrians; at the beginning of 1846 Mieroslawski was arrested at Posen (Poznan) even before the rebellion had broken out. Son of a Polish father and a French mother, born in France and brought up in Poland, Louis Mieroslawski (1812–78) personified Polish nationalist Messianism and French emancipatory Messianism. For more than thirty years his life was that of a paladin, always defeated, never disheartened. The Berlin revolution of 18 March 1848 released him from a Prussian gaol; he rushed back to Poznania to command a group of insurgents which laid down its arms in May. Fifteen years later he appeared again in Russian Poland, only to return to France beaten and discouraged. The glory won in 1849 at the head of the Magyar armies by General Bem, a White, overshadowed the extraordinary popularity of Mieroslawski in the Europe of 1848. It was, however, under his orders that the rebellious Sicilians fought their last battles in 1849. A month later envoys of the insurrectionist Government of Karlsruhe came to Paris to beg him to take command of the Baden insurgents who attempted, with a handful of German volunteers such as Friedrich Engels, to oppose the penetration southward of the Prussian troops.

The presence of a Mieroslawski in the Democratic Society explains the poor success of the propaganda of Young Poland, a branch of Young Europe, among the Reds of Paris. The proud exaltation of the Italian mission aroused the susceptibilities of touchy patriots. The Poles took part in only one of the numerous insurrections fomented by Mazzini: that was the unfortunate escapade against the Savoy then Sardinian (1834) of General Ramorino, one of the leaders of the insurrection of 1830. On the other hand the links formed by the Reds with the German democrats after the brotherly welcome reserved for the vanquished of 1831 were continually strengthened. In 1832 Poles took part in the manifestation of unity at Hambach, and in 1833 others led the rioters who tried to overthrow the Germanic Diet at Frankfurt. The same love of liberty, the same hatred of tsarism, created a feeling of concord difficult to imagine now, in the last third of the twentieth century. Herwegh, in his *Poems of a Survivor* (1840–1) had preached a coalition of the west against Russia "to avenge Poland and banish Asiatic tyranny from the face of Europe" (Fleury). In Paris, in the spring of 1848, he thought up an adventurous project for armed co-operation between German and Polish emigrants with the hoped-for aid of republican France.

## The Revolutionary Education of the German Proletariat

The proximity of Germany and the linguistic community had drawn many refugees to Strasbourg, the provincial capital of the German political emigration. The population was won over to liberal ideas; the republican party looked on the German democrats as "brothers". Pamphlets published by

Strasbourg printers kept up the agitation among the people, and the uneasiness of the rulers. In 1834 the prefect of the Bas-Rhin observed that the Governments of the South "were more concerned about what was happening in Strasbourg than in Paris". A native of Darmstadt, Georg Büchner (1813–37) chose to study natural sciences at Strasbourg. On his return to Hesse he founded a Society of the Rights of Man and incited the peasants to revolt. The appearance of his famous pamphlet *Peace to the Cottages! War to the Châteaux!* as well as his drama *Danton's Death* (produced in Paris in 1968), showed the influences to which he had been subjected in Alsace. Threatened with arrest in 1835, it was in Strasbourg that he sought refuge! However, his case was an isolated one; for the more notorious Germans Strasbourg was but a step to Paris.

At the end of the eighteen-forties the fifty to seventy thousand Germans there formed the most important foreign colony in Paris. The preponderance of workers was overwhelming. The German towns and countryside poured out a continual stream of apprentices seeking work or journeymen wishing to complete their technical knowledge in the capital of taste. Others took root in Paris, such as the cabinet-makers of the Faubourg Saint-Antoine, admirers of the Napoleons.

Paris was also the capital of the Germany of liberalism, democracy and socialism. Boerne and Heine ended their lives there in 1837 and 1856. Ruge transferred the *German Annals* (*Deutsche Jahrbücher*) the organ of the Hegelian Left, from Dresden to Paris which there became the *Franco-German Annals* (*Deutsche-Französische Jahrbücher*). This review, of which a single number (February 1844) appeared, owes its posthumous fame to the articles of Karl Marx who also collaborated in the *Vorwärts* of his friend Börnstein. It would be tedious to give a list of the Germans who, in Paris, were ready to play a role, even a modest one, in the movements of 1848–9. An élite, rich in strong personalities with decisive opinions and theoretical views of astonishing complexity, deprived the German emigration of the ideological unity so characteristic of the Polish emigration. Despite their dissensions the Poles were more or less unanimous on the main aim: the reconquest of their lost country. The Germans too were in agreement about improving the lot of the workers and rejecting the institutions imposed in 1815. But how many variations when it came to envisaging practical reforms! The intellectuals had mixed feelings towards the French; they despised them on the plane of thought and admired them on the plane of action. The former students of the renowned universities scattered throughout the Confederation, nourished by the teachings of Kant, Herder, Fichte and Hegel, cast scornful glances at the puny French provincial universities and on the eclecticism, the fragile structure, which led to Victor Cousin being promoted to the rank of a national philosopher. It is known with what disdain "doctor" Marx was to treat the self-taught Proudhon. Many were the refugees to whom the judgement of Mehring on Grün, author of *The Social Movement in France and Belgium* (*Die sociale Bewegung in Frankreich und Belgien*, Darmstadt, 1845) could be applied: "He has the pride of the German writer and the German philosopher." Nonetheless they were attracted to Paris. It was not a question of the pilgrimage of a Boerne or a Heine, but of a study trip. Von Stein had, in *Socialism and Communism in Present-day France* (*Der Socialismus und Communismus des heutigen Frankreichs*, Leipzig, 1842), made known in Germany the doctrines "which he had been told to study". Marx also wished to make contact with socialism and communism,[1] "French products" (Halevy) and observe the class to which he had confided the mission of accomplishing the revolution, the German bourgeoisie having shown its faint heart. It mattered little if the German proletariat which Marx wished to awaken to class consciousness and the Parisian proletariat so spontaneously revolutionary still had nothing in common with the proletariat of large-scale industry envisaged, after the British example, in the *Communist Manifesto*. The important fact, which Marx stated between 1844 and 1845, was the adoption by the German artisans of

[1] Even the names were launched in France, the former by the Saint-Simonist Leroux in 1833 at the time when it was being born in England, the latter by the leaders of the Parisian secret societies about 1840. They were not yet completely Germanized; von Stein wrote *socialismus* and *communismus*, not *Sozialismus* and *Kommunismus*. Despite the *Communist Manifesto* these two words retained their French flavour until the eighteen-fifties.

socialist and communist republican ideas and methods of combat suitable for the Parisian situation.

The Germans, and this must never be forgotten when evoking the French ideological progress, had a higher level of education than that of their companions in the workshops. In 1848 school attendance rose to 93 per cent in Prussia, 80 per cent in Bavaria. The German proletariat was thus an apt pupil of the élite of the Paris workers. The history of the Federation of the Just (*Bund der Gerechten*) is unimpeachable proof of this. The Federation of Exiles (*Bund der Geächteten*) united in 1834 intellectuals and several hundred artisans. In imitation of the Society of the Rights of Man it was a secret organization with a hierarchy of its own, its two main tendencies, were firstly animated by Venedey (1805-71), a Rhineland anti-Prussian republican who placed political questions (unity in liberty) first of all, and secondly by Schuster, a young revolutionary from the university of Göttingen, a follower of Saint-Simon and an admirer of Lamennais, who insisted on the priority of the social question. Sensitive to Schuster's preaching the workers founded clandestine groups in Mainz, Frankfurt, Munich, Hanover, Bremen, Leipzig and Berlin, which recognized the authority of the Parisian centre.

The return of the proletarian elements to Germany on the orders of the Diet made it possible for the purely political trend to prevail. In 1836 the dissenters had founded the Federation of the Just. Its leaders belonged to those trades which provided opportunities for reflection or day-dreams and thus supplied the workers' movement with so many militants at its beginning: Schapper (1813-70), a former student and Mazzinian, soon to be the faithful companion of Marx and Engels, became a compositor; Bauer, also a future collaborator with the authors of the *Manifesto*, was a shoemaker; Weitling a tailor.

Of all the social reformers (Grün, Marx, Engels, Hess, etc.) only Weitling (1808-71) was not a philosopher. The first theoretician of German communism, he was one of those self-taught artisans often to be met with in the alleyways of old Paris. His work is inseparable from French socialist thought and the Babeuf-Blanqui persuasion. His first pamphlet *Humanity as It*

*Is and as It Should Be* (*Die Menschheit wie sie ist und wie sie sein sollte*) was a manifesto drawn up in 1838 in the name of the Federation of the Just. Weitling carefully copied the *Livre du peuple* which Lamennais had published the year before. Unable to admit the graded society that the Saint-Simon school envisaged, he felt more sympathy with Fourier, the little clerk who disappeared in loneliness in 1837. He knew him through the innumerable booklets of the *Petite Bibliothèque phalanstérienne* edited by Considérant. From these teachings he had retained the romantic assumption of the excellence of the passions, but he was not at ease with certain aspects of the doctrine: the denunciation of the "egalitarian chimaera" and the repudiation of violence.

From 1838 Weitling was the prophet of a communist society arising out of a revolt of the working class, with a core of artisans. The Parisian revolutionaries looked forward to a future starting from a legendary reconstitution of the revolutionary past. Alongside the "Bonapartist myth", more discreet but always vigorous, the "Jacobin myth" was reinvigorated by the activities of Buonarotti (1761–1837), the old Tuscan revolutionary who was also perhaps the principal leader of the Carbonari. His *Histoire de la conspiration pour l'égalité dite de Babeuf* (1828) had an enormous influence on the already politicized members of the French working class; in the prisons, the workers held there for their participation in the insurrections of June 1832 and April 1834 were indoctrinated by the disciples of Buonarotti. The craftsmen of the Faubourgs Saint-Antoine and Saint-Denis would henceforward have two "brotherly demigods", for Buonarotti had, towards the end of his life, managed to reconcile Robespierre and Babeuf: the holding in common of all means of production, preached by Babeuf, would be realized by the dictatorial methods of the "sublime Committee of Public Safety". The programme and above all the method was to seduce the republican secret societies who were recruited for the most part from among the workers. In 1837 the Society of Seasons replaced the Society of Families, the former led by the compositor Martin Bernard and two bourgeois, Barbès and Blanqui. A fig for doctrinal discussions!

There must first of all be a rising which would liberate the poor!
This specifically French communism was adopted by Weitling
and the Federation of the Just, the German associate of the
Seasons. Its members participated in the insurrection of 12 May
1839. Schapper and Bauer were, like Barbès and Blanqui,
thrown into prison. Expelled, they left for London. In 1847 the
London Group was to take the name of the Federation of
Communists and receive as members Marx and Engels. At the
end of 1845 the Babeuf cult was extended to the New World.
Borrowing its title from the *Tribun du Peuple*, *Der Volks-Tribun*,
edited by the exiles united in a new Federation of the Just, was
to appear in New York at the beginning of 1846. Surrounded
by a few disciples, amongst whom was the physician Ewerbeck
(1816–60), and soon converted to the philosophy of Cabet
(who had just translated *The Voyage in Icaria*) which was
hostile to the mystique of the barricades, Weitling in his turn
left Paris in 1841. He founded in Switzerland another Federation of the Just whose activities in Germany were based on the
revolutionary breviary conceived in the atmosphere of the
Parisian secret societies, printed secretly and first published in
two thousand copies. Yet such a publicist was to declare in
1852 that it had passed unnoticed!

In attributing such inordinate importance to a leaflet which
had attracted little attention but had been publicly distributed,
the Prussian and French Governments committed an error of
judgement; the former demanded and obtained from the latter
the expulsion of the editors of the *Vorwärts*. The influence of
Börnstein, Ruge and Marx, weak in Germany, was nil in
France. The Parisian revolutionaries did not know either
German or philosophy; the men of the opposition were dis-
concerted by the atheism of the neo-Hegelians. Lamartine,
Lamennais, Blanc and Leroux, when approached to collaborate
in the *Franco-German Annals*, declined.

### The Italian Intellectuals

At the beginning of the eighteen-thirties fortuitous
circumstances gave credit to the myth of a revolutionary

committee working to hatch conspiracies in Germany and
Italy. Arrested in 1830, Mazzini was exiled to Marseilles in 1831
and there founded the Young Italy movement. Member, to
use his own expression, of the "nation of outlaws", he too went
to the "capital of the revolution". However, in 1834, he chose
Berne for the creation of his Young Europe and in 1836
transferred the centre of the Italian and international movement
to London. Like Alfieri, the reactionary late eighteenth-century
poet, and his rival Gioberti, the liberal and patriotic priest, the
republican, anti-clerical Mazzini belonged to the anti-French
current of Italian thought, nourished on the great memories of
the Rome of the Caesars and the Popes. Its prodigious past
corresponded to the future of Italy. The Italians alone were
the chosen people. The departure of Mazzini for London had
the sense of a retroactive condemnation of the persecuted
Italians who had fled to Paris. But Paris preserved its attraction.
Silvio Pellico who had spent eight years in Austrian gaols (his
book *Le mie prigioni* was to have a tremendous moral influence
in Italy and in Europe) was given a triumphal welcome in
Paris when he was released in 1830. Compromised in the
agitation of Young Italy, Gioberti first took refuge in Paris
before settling in Brussels where the book which immortalized
him was to appear. The central theme, unity in the form of a
confederation under the control of the Papacy, had been put
forward seven years earlier in a pamphlet of limited circulation
published in Paris; its author was Tommaseo, novelist and
philologist, who was to share in March 1848 the control of the
revolutionary movement in Venice with Manin, also a refugee
in France. In 1844 it was Balbo who, from Paris, replied most
vigorously to Gioberti. In 1841 the jurist and philosopher
Mamiani had launched an appeal from Paris for the liberation
of Italy. Favourable to the supremacy of the King of Sardinia
and supporter of the secularization of the Papal States, he
became, paradoxically, in 1848 the prime minister of Pius IX.
His successor, Rossi, who was to be assassinated in November
1848, had to flee Bologna. He began an astonishing career as
French citizen and Italian patriot which led him, by way of the
Chamber of Peers and the Embassy of the Holy See, from the

Collège de France and the Faculty of Law to become head of the Roman Government. The Lombard Ferrari, who arrived in Paris in 1836, represented the minority group of Italians won over to French Messianism. A number of Mazzini's friends waited in France for Paris to give the signal to the Italians to liberate themselves. Faced with a mass of immigrants whom illiteracy and habitual acquiescence prevented, in contrast to the Germans, from borrowing from the French working class its forms of political organization and its social aspirations, the Italian political elements formed an élite. The Parisian atmosphere was merely embellished by their dreams.

## The Intellectuals of Eastern Europe

The cultivated circles of eastern and south-eastern Europe, rural lands subject to serfdom and absolutism, were still more restricted. A section of the nobility and the middle class were infatuated with the French Romantics and were consumed with a desire to admire those writers who preached the liberty of man and the brotherhood of peoples. "Who has not dreamed of Paris in his youth?" demanded the Magyar Eötvös in 1839. In 1846 the Wallachian Bratianu took a new interest in the formula of the young Heine and recalled the accents of Mickiewicz: "The pilgrims no longer go some to Mecca and others to Jerusalem . . . they all come to France . . . the Holy Land of all." The Magyar colony included artisans who were to fight on the February barricades. The students of Moldavia and Wallachia heard in the Collège de France the prophecies of Quinet and Michelet on the emancipation of peoples. At the beginning of the eighteen-forties the Latin Quarter sheltered young men destined to fame: Kogalniceanu, historian of language and literature and emancipator of the peasants; the historian Balcescu, who took part in the February struggles; the brothers D. and J. Bratianu, founders of a dynasty of politicians. After the victory of the revolution in Paris, they wanted to take it all back with them; for the most part social moderates, they demanded with a certain snobbism a Parisian imprint, that of the "Reds". The ascendancy of France was even felt in the Principality of Serbia, only just emerged from ignorance, which hoped to get from Paris an active framework on which to build a still embryonic administration. On their return the former students would bear for a long time the laudatory cognomen of Parisian; the Serb poet Nenadović was to handle a gun in February. From the vastness of Russia, finally, came two of the most representative persons of the enlightened classes opposed to tsarist autocracy: Bakunin and Herzen scarcely knew the people of Paris, save through their friend Proudhon. Bakunin, the future theorist of anarchism, was then a fervent admirer of Marx. Collaborator on the *Vorwärts*, he was forced to leave Paris in 1847. That year the liberal Herzen obtained authorization to go there.

The myth of a France holding out her hands to Europe at the appeal of her capital was common to most of the democrats, the "communists" and the patriot refugees. Could a Parisian revolution sweep away the institutions of a centralized State, as in 1830, as in 1792? In such a case would Frenchmen lend themselves to warlike adventures so that myth might become reality?


ECONOMY, SOCIETY, POLITICS

*The Advance of the Economy and its Limits*

The economic crisis of 1846–7 relegated to oblivion the period of expansion which in its turn had followed the depression of 1828–32. From the increase in the number of qualified electors and the greater yield of the taxes, contemporaries assessed the enrichment of France; but those who observed the difficulties of the peasants and the misery of the working classes were convinced that the sole beneficiary of economic progress was the bourgeoisie, whose unlimited power and egoism had been stigmatized by Tocqueville. The July Monarchy suffered from inevitable comparisons; a still archaic economy was timidly making its first steps towards modernization, steps which the Second Empire was to follow resolutely. France was, nevertheless, the greatest industrial State of the continent. The French, even before the Germans, had with all their energies begun to learn from the English.

The road network which had, at the beginning of the eighteenth century, excited the admiration of Arthur Young, had been enlarged. Canals begun long before 1830—the Rhône–Rhine canal had been in abeyance since 1795—had been completed and work on others started (the Marne–Rhine canal). The State, and local administrative bodies, financed these works (the Ministry of Public Works was created in 1831) largely by recourse to loans, according to the procedure of the *ancien régime*. The usual custom was to apply to the great financial houses (out of 900 millions of State loans, Baron James de Rothschild had taken up 800 millions). It was "High Finance". This "France of the Jews of the Bourse" (Marx) dominated the Bank of France with its fifteen sub-offices. The cautiousness of capital and the amount of red tape were the main obstacles to the development of the railways. The French bourgeoisie, which never demanded for itself the exploitation of the roads and canals, could have accepted, without renouncing its principles, control of the railways by the State as in Belgium or Prussia. It did not believe in the future of a revolutionary means of transport (in this matter the republican savant Arago reacted in exactly the same way as the Orléanist Thiers) and considered it impossible for the State to collect the enormous sums of capital demanded by the programmes conceived by the enthusiastic Saint-Simon polytechnicians. From the failure of the private companies in 1842 a compromise was born: seven main lines were conceded for ninety-nine years to the companies, the State assuming the acquisition of the land and the erection of the necessary buildings and stations. After British finance, "High Finance" began to interest itself in the French railways; in 1845 James de Rothschild formed the Northern Company with the English banker Blount. The network in 1848 amounted to 1,930 kilometres. This balance-sheet, modest if compared with that of the United Kingdom, Germany or Belgium or with the brilliant results of the Second Empire, reflects the mentality of a society with no taste for taking risks.

Rigorous protectionism was another expression of this state of mind. The last Chamber of the régime, like the last of the Restoration, contained three times more great landed proprietors than industrialists, business men or bankers, and these, as those, considered land the most certain investment for capital and the most visible sign of success. This agreement among the notables was the major factor in the parliamentary history of France between 1815 and 1848. The law of 1819 broke with the *ancien régime*'s policy of cheap bread, which had been maintained through the Revolution and the Empire. The protectionist régime was again reinforced in 1821. Courageous ministers could not, under Louis Philippe, do more than modify it. Historians rightly denounce the egoism of the representatives of landed property. However, the "qualified electors" were also, as the Left-wing deputies stressed, the spokesmen of millions of smallholders excluded from the vote. The return to agricultural protectionism (1892) after the free trade interlude of the Second Empire was to satisfy the wishes of the peasants, and its instigator Méline was regarded as the "Saviour of French agriculture".

The industrial protectionism which Napoleon III's desire for innovation momentarily interrupted went back to the *ancien régime* and served as a pledge of agricultural protectionism. English competition justified measures of protection. The period when the great landed proprietors were dominant at the Palais Bourbon was a golden age for the industrialists. The struggle against the English textile industry was transformed into a blind prohibition. The Bourgeois Monarchy tried gently to loosen the prohibitionist choker. The publicists and professors who in 1841 founded the *Journal des Économistes* at first met only with an amused indifference. But when Bastiat took it into his head to create, in imitation of the Manchester organization, a Free Trade League, the Chamber resounded with indignant speeches. The adversaries of free trade had at their disposal an apparently irrefutable argument: the French economy was developing at a pace never before achieved. From 1825 to 1847 agricultural revenue had increased by 38 per cent and industrial revenue by 66 per cent.

This soaring flight was, in fact, due to the failure of protectionism. Customs duties not having succeeded in eliminating the inexorable trend towards lower prices, agriculture, so slow to change, in certain regions adapted itself in order to survive. Cultivated areas increased; fallow land diminished. A larger and larger part of the commons was leased out; the area devoted to wheat and, above all, to potatoes was extended. The advances in stockbreeding were remarkable; from 1812 to 1852 the number of sheep increased by a fifth, and from 1830 to 1850 that of cattle by almost a third. Maintenance of meat prices, due to protection and also to more frequent consumption by the lower classes, contributed to this "spurt of cultivation".

To the British "challenge" French industry tried to respond by finding inspiration in the British example: the concentration in the large factories of workers using machines driven by steam. Against this industrial revolution a banking system which was unadapted to a modern economy, the spirit of red tape proper to a rural society and the weakness of heavy industry acted as a brake. France was poor in coal (the rich basin of the Pas-de-Calais discovered in 1841 was not to be exploited until after 1847) and in iron (the Lorraine ores were then little in demand). The duty on British coal and iron held up the modernization of the metal industries and the development of the steam-engine. As in the United Kingdom, the textile industry was the first to mechanize. Mechanical methods triumphed in the mills of Mulhouse, Lille and Rouen, but in the Elbeuf region wool was still carded by hand. In Alsace and in Normandy the mechanical spinning of cotton was still only half the production. The insignificance of urban growth was in correlation with the dispersal of factories employing a small number of workers: in 1845 only 3,200 enterprises employed more than fifty persons; of these 135 employed at least five hundred. The family character of the enterprises of the Nord and Haut-Rhin departments, which was to survive until our own times, was an obstacle to the formation of the "monopoly-capital" which Ledru-Rollin denounced in 1847. This phenomenon in reality only affected the coal industry and the railways. It was to a great extent the work of the bank (the exploitation of the Anzin mines was one of the foundations of the Périer family) and of "High Finance". Marx was not wrong to stress in his *Class Struggles in France, 1848–1850* the economic predominance of the "financial aristocracy" over the "industrial bourgeoisie" and the feeble numbers of the factory proletariat. Despite the transformations which took place under the July Monarchy, the France of 1848 remained a nation of peasants and artisans.

## A Society of Peasants and Artisans

*The Lower Classes.* The peasants formed the mass of "the lower classes", excluded until 1848 from political life. What was their proportion to the whole population? Michelet estimated it in 1846 as 68 per cent. This estimate pays more heed to social reality than the statistic of 1851 (56 per cent of adult males had agricultural employment and 27 per cent were employed in industry or commerce) which ignores those peasants who were occasional industrial workers.

Instead of expanding, as in England, the large estates diminished; from 1815 to 1850 the number of landowners rose from six-and-a-half million to seven-and-a-half million. Nonetheless, over-population explained the existence of a large proletariat. In the Côte-d'Or, an essentially agricultural department, out of a hundred peasants there were forty-five day-labourers or domestic servants, five tenants or *metayers* and five countrymen who were only in part cultivators. The rise in agricultural revenue benefited only a minority. Smallholders often had less than five hectares of land. In a good year the sale of excess produce encouraged them to rent or to acquire coveted allotments. Without credit institutions, they contracted mortgage loans at usurious interest. The French peasant, "self-seeking and shrewd", painted sympathetically by Michelet, was, on the eve of 1848, staggering, under the burden of his debts. He already had the feeling of having become the victim of progress.

The administration would have liked to suppress at once the common rights and the use of common lands. In the Côte-d'Or it succeeded bit by bit in turning over 1,600 hectares to cultivation between 1843 and 1847. Justified economically, this policy in fact favoured the interests of the great landed proprietors and harmed those of the mass of the peasants.

The mechanization of the textile industry accentuated the rancour of the smallholder and the journeyman, badly paid and under-employed. In winter in many provinces work at home was the main activity in the countryside. About 1845 hand-spinning represented nine-tenths of linen production, but as far as cotton was concerned it was gradually disappearing. Rural weaving declined. The peasant, who trembled at the thought of losing his secondary occupation, earned less than the factory worker; in 1847 in the Rouen region the total income of the home workers was less than the total wages of the factory workers, three times less numerous.

On the morrow of the February outbreak the Norman peasant craftsmen were to smash the machines. In Alsace the country people attacked the persons and properties of the Jews, accused of usury. Almost everywhere the forests were laid waste and the rights of use restored. Finally, it was believed that by destroying the tax registers they would also destroy the indirect taxes! The universality of these disconnected outbreaks made it impossible to establish who were the leaders. The effect of the republican propaganda in the countryside was often over-estimated. The Creusot masons and above all Martin Nadaud who is always cited were exceptional cases. The illiterate peasants were not aroused by theories completely foreign to them. In 1848 the Government Commissioners were to discover with astonishment country people who did not understand "the difference between a republic and a monarchy". We know that the names of two of the ministers of the new régime were to become the names of two women of easy virtue—Marie and Martine! Napoleon, on the other hand, was a well-known person. In a self-contained world, folded back on itself, the only means of efficient communication was oral tradition. At wakes and vigils the memories of the veterans of 1815 was infused with a rough tenderness for the image of "the little corporal", friend of the peasants. By voting massively for his nephew in December 1848 the country electors were to make a shattering entry into history.

In France and in Germany the phrases "working classes", "labouring classes" or "toilers" were used indiscriminately. The famous Luxembourg Commission was to be called officially: "Government commission for the workers". The constant use of the plural bears witness to the heterogeneity of the workers' world.

The industrial proletariat was still, at the dawn of mechanization, a minority. About 1848 the factory workers were only a million and a quarter, whereas the workers in rooms or small workshops were as many as four million. To describe the formation of the new class and to evoke its conditions of life and work would entail many repetitions. For France, like all the continental countries which were to follow her on the path of industrialization, copied, though on a lower scale, the English "model". Enquiries by Catholic societies revealed, between 1834 and 1840, the appalling situation of the textile workers. In Lille the cellars of the Saint-Sauveur quarter had been let out as lodgings. The scandal forced the Chambers to control the work of children. Inspired by the English legislation of 1833, the law of 1841 provided no means of enforcement. There was nothing, in fact, comparable with the Ashley law of 1844 in favour of women workers. The hope of a rise in wages or a reduction of the working day (the claim for a ten-hour day appeared, as in England, about 1840) could goad the workers in the great enterprises into sudden action; thus in 1844 there was a great strike in the Loire collieries with incidents such as Rive-de-Gier harshly repressed by troops, and as in Lyons in 1831 and 1834. Class consciousness was an intermittent sentiment. Any idea of overthrowing the social order was absent.

The artisans formed the backbone of the workers' movement under the July Monarchy. The trade-guilds, the centuries-old custom of the building trade in France and in the Germanic countries, were perpetuated in anachronistic forms. The members of the "noble" trades (stonemasons, carpenters and locksmiths) were divided by rival disciplines (the *Duties*) and behaved as aristocrats. It is enough to quote the opinion of Agricol Perdiguier, carpenter of the Faubourg Saint-Antoine,

whose *Book of Guilds* (*Livre de compagnonnage*) (1839) inspired
George Sand's *Le Compagnon du Tour de France* (1841): "I
respect an honest baker and an honest shoemaker as much as
a carpenter or a stonemason, when they too are honest." The
dissension which the guilds perpetuated among these men who
had risen from the working class, together with their basic lack
of political affiliation, guaranteed the tolerance of the authorities towards their organizations, which were illegal in principle.
However, the guild system was declining. In the shadow of the
mutual benefit societies, which grouped workers of the same
trade on a local level, the resistance societies were born. Their
real aim was to cover the risk of unemployment during strikes.
Coalition with the aim of obtaining a rise in wages being a
crime, they broke up, like the republican associations, into
groups of less than twenty members. The Friendly Society of
Lyons organized, together with the Society of the Rights of
Man, the insurrection of April 1834. The resistance societies
played a leading role in the Parisian strikes of 1840, 1843, and
1847. Save for the mechanics and the compositors, they were
recruited only from the old trades. The similarity of origin
between them and the British unions is striking. The sudden
development of trade unionism in the United Kingdom was
the result of the long standing and large number of the unions
and of the conciliatory attitude of the State; the right of
coalition granted to the British workers from 1824 would be
refused to the French workers until the time of Napoleon III
(1864). Forced to indulge in secret activities, the resistance
societies, not numerous, belonged to the pre-history of French
trade unionism, whose real history began under the Third
Republic. Concentrated to a great extent in Lyons and, above
all, in Paris, they saw their most ardent members working
actively in the heart of the revolutionary organizations for the
advent of a social, even socialist or communist, republic. A
political not a trade union élite was to recruit the insurgents of
February who were to overthrow the Bourgeois Monarchy.

*The Bourgeoisie.* Seen from Paris the revolution of 1848 seemed
like the victory of the "working classes" over the bourgeoisie.

This class had reached its apogee in a predominantly rural and craftsman's France, without banking institutions and scarcely ruffled by industrialization. Since Tocqueville most authors, accustomed to the paradoxical aspect of its rise, over-estimated its numerical importance and cohesion.

The two hundred thousand privileged who were permitted to elect deputies formed the "qualified bourgeoisie". This unambiguous expression was applied in fact to diversified social groups whose incomes differed widely in amount and in origin. A minority of a few hundred families included the financiers of the Parisian "High Finance", the shipowners of Bordeaux, Nantes and Marseilles, the great merchants who were also at the head of small dispersed enterprises (the Lyons "manufacturers") and finally the manufacturers themselves.

The "middle bourgeoisie" included other merchants and manufacturers, lawyers, solicitors, attorneys, senior civil servants, owners of real estate and town properties. Since the basis of the qualification, at a time when income tax was unknown, was professional licences and estate tax, landed proprietors made up the mass of the electoral body. In their ranks were open enemies of the Bourgeois Monarchy. Members of the former aristocracy pursued with the same hatred the usurping Monarch and his allies. They did not dread the reforms (though the social Catholics were drawn from the legitimist nobility) which affected the interests of the industrialists. Some of them were far-sighted enough to appreciate the advantages of a less restricted suffrage. When they took part in the functioning of a régime which they execrated, it was with the intention of destroying it.

On the other hand, those excluded from the electoral system wanted to take part in it. The vague expression of "petty bourgeoisie" first applied to those who had the feeling of not belonging, or no longer belonging, to the working classes— professional men and civil servants. The small tradesmen, shopkeepers and property owners with several employees formed a marginal category. The feeling of class was changing; thus the hosier of the Faubourg Saint-Denis who took up arms against the rioters in June 1832 and against the troops in

February 1848, in June 1848 turned his arms against the insurgents. Why had the "petty bourgeoisie" become revolutionary in February?

*The Parliamentary Régime in the Service of the King and the Middle Classes*

The "petty bourgeoisie" had lost hope of participating, even indirectly, in the conduct of affairs. However, the first months of the reign had seemed rich in promises.

Reformed in 1831, the National Guard was an institution envied by liberal Europe. In 1848 it was to serve as a model for all revolutionary movements. In principle, all Frenchmen between the ages of twenty and sixty could be called upon to serve in it; in fact, only those subject to personal taxation were enrolled. This "bourgeoisie militia" had a basis as wide as the legislative electoral body. It included the immense mass of small property holders. The much beribboned "grocer janissaries" bravely supported the July régime up to the moment when they understood that they would never choose their deputies. By giving the French the right which Napoleon had taken from them of electing their local administrators, Louis Philippe seemed to have set off along the path of reform. Without doubt the municipal law of 1831 accorded the right of suffrage to most ratepayers; but as the proportion of electors was fixed at one tenth of the population in the communes of less than a thousand inhabitants, its application was very liberal for the times. The law for the recruitment of the Chamber which was to contribute so greatly to the downfall of the régime had been well received in 1831. The property qualification was reduced from 300 francs to 200 francs and even to 100 francs for certain "qualified people" (members of the Institute and some retired officers). The number of electors almost doubled: 168,000 as against 94,000. Montalembert had, in the tradition of realist legislation, demanded that the qualification be reduced to 50 francs but his proposal had been judged demagogic. Ten years later, the excluded who paraded at the reviews of the National Guard and took part in the municipal elections lost patience;

legislative electoral right was less a political privilege than a social ratification. The increase in the number of qualified electors (247,000 in 1846) made the immobility of the régime even more intolerable to one who had done his utmost to follow the famous advice of Guizot: "Enrich yourself!" A feeling of frustration drove the small property holders to lend a complacent ear to the attacks of the parliamentary opposition.

The questions of electoral reform and parliamentary reform were linked. Both were to help to maintain the ferment whence the republic would arise, to the great fear of its antagonists. The parliamentary system, according to the British model admired by the leaders (Guizot, Borglie, Thiers) was introduced in France. But it was changed. The peers, nominated for life as a reward for services rendered to the sovereign, did not enjoy the credit of the Lords. In the Lower Chamber, the individualist spirit, rebellious to party discipline, became accentuated about 1830. France had the experience of ministerial instability: fifteen cabinets in ten years. In 1840 the game came to an end, Louis Philippe having succeeded in outwitting the politicians who had aimed at confining him to a decorative role. Up till 1848 he governed in association with Guizot. But the façade of the parliamentary régime was saved. Like the leaders of the totalitarian States of today, Guizot was supported by men whom he himself chose. A part of political custom in England in the eighteenth century and practised in France since the Restoration, electoral corruption became a system. Constituencies of only a few hundred electors facilitated this. The loyalty of deputies elected by corruption is assured by corruption; the granting of fatly remunerated sinecures or promotions preceded important polls. In 1846 the elected Chamber was made up of 142 landowners and *rentiers*, 16 men of letters, 52 lawyers, 7 doctors, 34 bankers and industrialists—and 185 civil servants! Guizot's party was not a class party; it was a clientèle of officials desperately anxious for advancement. But ministerial stability, born of an appeal to egoistic sentiments, covered over the speculations of the businessmen and the "deals" of the higher administration. The Government "took on the appearance of an industrial company where all operations were carried out with a view to the profit of the shareholders" (Tocqueville). Legitimist and radical (from 1835 the name "republican" was prohibited), the parliamentary opposition, reduced to a few individuals, was essentially composed of about sixty deputies of the dynastic Left. These Orléanists from the higher levels of the middle bourgeoisie were political moderates who reproached the ministry for its administration without brilliance and—its longevity! Guizot's enemies then proposed to destroy the machinery which made him invincible. They demanded untiringly but in vain from a Chamber dominated by civil servants a law which would forbid civil servants to sit there! Morally justified, parliamentary reform scarcely affected public opinion for it only concerned those privileged few who paid 500 francs in direct taxes. The electoral reform demanded in 1840 and then in 1847 had a clear significance for the minority whom the opposition could count on mobilizing. The proposal of Duvergier de Hauranne had nothing democratic in it; foreseeing the reduction of the property qualification to 100 francs and the increase in the number of "special qualifications", it was put forward as an adaptation of the principles set out in 1831 to the spirit of the times. The electoral body having been doubled by the addition of 200,000 new members, the property holders could no longer rally around the throne as in July 1830. Guizot had not wanted it. When he opposed the anodyne project of Duvergier de Hauranne ("it is not yet time for universal suffrage!") his enemies, who were also the enemies of democracy, had to play for a diversion. Was it unreasonable to foresee that a modification of the legislation of 1831 would involve other modifications which, by stages, would lead to universal suffrage? Such were without doubt the opinions of the radical parliamentarians tired of insurrections, always defeated, which committed those of the reform party.

The greater number of the workers in the countryside and in the towns were unaware of, or did not understand, a conflict which was above their heads. The craftsmen élite of the Parisian secret societies, better informed, did not believe in the virtues of representative institutions, unlike the English working class. Deprived of freedom of assembly, of the right of coalition, they associated the parliamentary régime with the policy of reaction in internal affairs and treason in foreign affairs.

But for the reader of *Reform* the word "reform", launched by the adversaries of Guizot, awoke dreams of a democratic and social régime. To the astonishment of the sorcerers' apprentices of the Chamber of Deputies, some thousand of Parisians manned the barricades and overthrew Guizot, the King and the monarchy and the parliamentary system.

[ Chapter Three ]

# The Constitutional Régimes of France's Neighbours

In a europe where liberal and national aspirations were for the most part intermingled, the unrest on the French frontiers was exclusively political and religious. Despite its brief existence, the Belgian State, troubled today by quarrels between Flemings and Walloons, enjoyed a remarkable stability in an atmosphere of liberty. A long history in common assured an undeniable national cohesion to the Swiss Confederation, at least until 1845, despite its linguistic divisions, and to Spain and Portugal, despite dynastic wars and pronunciamentos.

## THE IBERIAN PENINSULA: CIVIL WARS AND PRONUNCIAMENTOS

Spain and Portugal seemed to develop in every way along parallel lines. After the loss of their empires in central and southern America (1824–5) they passed, almost without transition, from absolute monarchy to constitutional monarchy, entered an era of civil wars and pronunciamentos, and finally attained, on the eve of 1848, a precarious political stability; dictatorships were set up behind a façade of liberalism.

The liberalization of institutions was not, as in the United Kingdom or in France, a consequence of the rise of the middle classes. Archaic economies (the first railways were to be opened in Spain only in 1851) just managed to maintain, at a very mediocre level, the living standards of millions of peasants with limited horizons. Demographic growth in the first half of the nineteenth century was below the European mean (50 per cent); in 1850 the populations of Spain (15 million) and of Portugal (3·5 million) had increased by 43 per cent and 25 per cent respectively. Social authority was in the hands of the nobility and the clergy, holders of vast estates. In ardently Catholic countries absolutism could only be fully exercised in accord with the Church, which always had the Inquisition at its disposal. Its traditional adversaries were recruited from the commercial middle classes and the working classes of a few urban centres: Lisbon and Oporto in Portugal, Corunna, Barcelona, Valencia and Cadiz in Spain. They would doubtless have long remained impotent had not revolutionary elements appeared in the army. Many officers who had collaborated with the Italian Carbonari and with freemasons in Italy, Spain and Portugal to conspire against the domination of Napoleon remained after the departure of the French. Their activities are not without a certain similarity to the participation of young officers in the revolutionary movements in the "under-developed" countries of the contemporary world.

This union between the bourgeois liberals and a part of the army took place in similar circumstances; the king was absent (Ferdinand VII of Spain had been imprisoned in France and John VI of Portugal had fled to Brazil) and military operations hindered the working of civil institutions. In Spain, the 1812 constitution, inspired by the French constitution of 1791, had suppressed feudal rights and proclaimed that "sovereignty resides essentially in the nation". Abolished in 1814, it was re-established by a military *coup d'état* in 1820. In Portugal John VI was forced to accept the constitution of 1822, a replica of that of 1812 and an object of the veneration of Mediterranean liberalism. Had not the military conspiracies of 1820–1 proposed to introduce it into the Kingdoms of the Two Sicilies and Sardinia? Constitutional problems were the origin of the formation of parties. The absolutists, relying on the support of

the clergy, aimed at abolishing the constitutions which the
Spanish Progressives and the Portuguese Septembrists wished
to maintain or to restore. Partisans favouring a compromise
put forward solutions (the Portuguese Charter, the Spanish
Statute of 1834) which exacerbated the quarrels. The same
sonorous languages lent themselves, as in Latin America, to
solemn affirmations of doctrine. To invoke the law did not
prohibit recourse to violence or illegality; one joyously destroyed the constitution of a rival or deliberately violated one's
own. For deputies on the lookout for a portfolio, for ambitious
officers or civil servants, for badly paid soldiers or under-
occupied civilians, the conquest and preservation of power
took the place of a political programme. Very soon the
Governments in power discovered the art of winning elections
or gaining control of the Chambers, the opposition parties the
means of overthrowing them. Pronunciamentos became the
favourite weapon of professional politicians.

The people, however, only began to take an interest in the
party struggle when the stake was no longer a scarcely comprehensible document but a person of the royal family. In 1826
and 1833, children, Maria (seven years old) in Portugal,
Isabella (three years old) in Spain, came to the throne. Miguel
and Carlos tried to oust their respective nieces. In the two
countries the liberals supported the queens, the absolutists the
uncles. By proclaiming himself king in 1829 Miguel unleashed
a civil war which went on until 1835. The "Carlist war", begun
in 1834, came to an end in 1839. These cruel dynastic struggles
assumed both an Iberian and an international character.
Miguel and Carlos were allied, as were their adversaries: they
received subsidies from the conservative powers, while Great
Britain and France supported Maria and the Queen-Regent,
Maria Christina, mother of Isabella, whose final succession
they were to assure. In Portugal and in Spain Septembrists and
Progressives enjoyed the favours of London, supporters of the
Charter and of the 1834 Statute the favours of Paris. The
prestige of the two Governments was in question, but also the
interests of their citizens; traditionally masters of the Portuguese
market, the British obtained from Madrid the reduction of

protectionist customs dues. The manufacturers of the United Kingdom and to a lesser degree those of France competed dangerously with the young Catalan textile industry.

Catalonia, which in 1640 and 1714 had championed its regional interests brilliantly against Madrid, did not react despite the appearance of a cultured bourgeoisie and a turbulent proletariat. Catalan remained the language of the people, Castilian that of the upper classes and the writers. Stifled national sentiment would appear again only at the close of the century. Its beginnings, here as elsewhere, would be literary and of romantic inspiration. In this regard the *Ode to the Fatherland* by Carlos Aribaud (1798–1862) was a precocious but timid forerunner which his editor of 1833 declared he had published with "patriotic pride". The violence of the Basques was in marked contrast to the passivity of the Catalans. These rough peasants, accustomed to administering their mountain villages democratically, defended their privileges (*fueros*) and only laid down their arms on the promise of being freed from the intervention of Madrid civil servants. Portugal remained, amid internal troubles, unruffled by "regionalist" temptations.

In both States the end of the civil wars marked the beginning of the era of dictatorships. The pronunciamento was inspired by a political clique; but its principal executor, most often a high-ranking officer, was often its beneficiary in the end. His opposition to the coalition of the parties was dependent on the loyalty of the army and the support of Paris or London. General Espartero (1793–1879) and General Narvaez (1800–68) founded a system in Spain which was to take root in the former American possessions. General Espartero enjoyed English friendship. For three years this so-called "progressive" treated the constitution of 1837, a watered-down version of that of 1812, with the most complete disdain. The army abandoned it in 1843. In 1844 Narvaez took over power; in foreign affairs alliances were reversed and the conclusion of the famous Franco-Spanish marriages (1846) was resented in London as a provocation; in internal affairs the moderates were hoodwinked as efficiently as formerly the Progressives. Narvaez governed by decree, had recourse to the state of siege

and gaily shot his opponents. Despite the efforts of London,
Portugal too moved towards a dictatorship. A civilian, Costa
Cabral (1803–89), and a soldier, Marshal Saldanha (1791–
1876), alternated in power. The former was a moderate in the
manner of Narvaez, the latter, erstwhile companion of the
reactionary pretender, was a Progressive of the Espartero
type.

When, at the beginning of March 1848, Europe entered the
era of revolutions, a Parisian journalist felt that he would not
be committing himself if he foretold "events which cannot fail
incessantly to disturb Spain and Portugal". He considered that
the dictatorships would be swept away, but that constitutional
monarchy, symbol of national unity, had nothing to fear from
the petty republican minorities.

## SWITZERLAND: UNION OF NATIONALITIES AND POLITICAL UNREST

Until 1848 Switzerland lived under the régime of the Federal
Pact of 1815 which tended to regard the revolutionary and
imperial period as an unfortunate incident. It had not dared,
however, to restore the tithes and the feudal dues. The Restoration was purely political. The maintenance of neutrality
afforded the five powers guaranteeing the territorial inviola-
bility of Switzerland pretexts for interfering in internal affairs.
The Federal Pact was less a constitution than a treaty of
alliance between the sovereign cantons to assure their internal
and external security. They could still conclude agreements
between themselves "on condition they should not be pre-
judicial to the Pact" and, as in the good old times, sign military
"capitulations" with foreign States; democratic Europe was
to learn with pained stupor the news of the victory of a Berne
regiment over the Neapolitan rioters of 15 May 1848! The
Swiss Diet, like the Germanic Diet, was made up of envoys of
the Governments. Without fixed seat, it met alternately every
two years in one of the principal cantons of Zurich, Berne or
Lucerne. The Governments of these three cantons, in turn,
took the place of a federal Government; it appointed diplomatic

representatives and succeeded in equipping an army, but was unable to establish an organization comparable to the *Zollverein*. The cantonal tolls and customs dues continued to exist.

With the exception of Neuchâtel, which was both Swiss canton and German principality, the twenty-two cantons were republics. Each had its own constitution. The three little mountain cantons (Schwyz, Uri and Unterwalden), whose alliance in 1291 was the origin of Switzerland, had been able to preserve their medieval democratic institutions; once a year the people appointed their heads of Government. Taken as a whole, these constitutions established or re-established in 1814–15 were inspired by the spirit of reaction which at that time breathed over the continent. In the new cantons (Saint-Gall, Aargau, Vaud, Ticino) the system of qualified electors in the French manner assured that the rich were in control. In the old cantons, at Berne, Lucerne, Fribourg, Solothurn, Neuchâtel and Geneva, the "bourgeoisie" had again assumed power. This word has preserved in Switzerland its medieval political sense, while at the same time beginning to acquire its present meaning. A "bourgeois" was still a member of a family which held the "bourgeois right" which conferred the privileges of voting and of being eligible for election; he was already an eminent personage whose ancestors had grown rich by exploit-ation of the soil or by commercial or industrial activity. The oligarchs of the main towns had, by shameless manœuvres, extended their dominance to the countryside. Political oppres-sion was everywhere the rule (the press was subject to censor-ship, the right of political assembly was prohibited) and also religious intolerance; Protestantism was forbidden in the Valais, Catholicism in the Vaud. The awakening of 1830 which paved the way to the movement of the eighteen-forties would have been impossible in a country divided into egoistic republics, had it not undergone profound economic trans-formations and shown a remarkable development of national sentiment.

The return of peace favoured the recovery of activity. The strict financial management of prudent bourgeois provided the means to undertake great public works, like the fine Saint-

Gothard carriage road. On the other hand the parish-pump mentality prevented Switzerland from entering the "railway era"; in 1848 the rail network was only twenty-five kilometres! Moreover, continuing a development which had started in the eighteenth century, stockbreeding had taken precedence over agriculture. The rural exodus to the New World diminished slowly; the population (2·4 million in 1850) rose by only a third in half a century. It was modern industry which provided the solution to the difficulties of an over-populated countryside. The textile industry adapted itself with prodigious speed to technical innovations; by 1840 Switzerland was, with regard to gross consumption of cotton per inhabitant (3·7 kg.), second in Europe after the United Kingdom (7·3 kg.). Mechanical spinning used water power; it was mainly concentrated in the canton of Zurich. The advance of the textile industry led to the birth of the machine industry, soon to become one of the foundations of Swiss prosperity. The precocious industrialization of a country handicapped by lack of coal was exclusively the work of the great commercial capitalists and the banks. The "will to win" of these Protestant bourgeois of Germanic culture was to drive some of them, at the time of the *Zollverein*, to extend their activities across the Rhine, especially in Baden. The idea soon took root that the material interests of the Swiss would only be protected against foreigners by a strong Federal State, replacing an obsolescent and inert Confederation.

Such ideas could not prevail until the feeling of nationality was established. The lack of national feeling among the Swiss of 1848 in no way embarrassed the historians. Without referring to the social clashes in the industrialized cantons, they had at their disposal a varied repertory of explanations: the political divisions of the country, the antagonism of religious and, above all, the language difficulties. With the exception of the Romansch (2 per cent), the Swiss spoke and wrote (in the land of Pestalozzi primary education was organized in most of the cantons after 1830; from 1832 it was obligatory in Zurich) the "noble" languages: German (70 per cent), French (20 per cent) and Italian (7 per cent). As in all Romantic Europe, history and linguistics, whose role we know in the awakening or re-awakening of national consciousness, were honoured and old legends lovingly collected. But far from leading to the disintegration of a weak State, the use of French and German helped to reinforce it. Love of the tiny homeland (*Heimat*) was always associated by the writers who used German with the cult of the great *Vaterland*. The *Idiotikon* of Stalden, the first dictionary of Germanic dialect expressions, bears witness to the care taken to clarify the differences from *hochdeutsch*. The Vaudois Bridel (d. 1845), who collected the traditions of French Switzerland, worked indefatigably to bring French and German speakers together. Gotthelf (d. 1854), gentle portrayer of Bernese customs, Keller (1819–90) and Meyer (1825–98) held a leading place in German literature. In 1848 Keller was to be "the bard of democracy", liberal and unitary. Meyer, after long residence in French Switzerland, in France and in Italy, was to represent the most perfect synthesis of "the Swiss spirit". The progress of national feeling, in conditions the most unfavourable for its flowering, is the most important fact in the history of the Europe of the nationalities. It disproves the prophecy, so often justified, of Martin, who in 1847 announced the devastating effects of the principle of nationalities ("States which do not draw their reason for existence from this principle will either be transformed or dissolved") and illustrates the definition which the French example was to suggest to Renan in 1882: "A nation is a soul, a spiritual principle . . .".

From the time of the Restoration, the soul of Switzerland was expressed by associations without apparent political aims but which disregarded cantonal fontiers: the Society of Swiss History (1811), the Students' Society of Zofingen (1819) which united Swiss youth under the federal banner, the Swiss Society of Carabineers which from 1824 organized the famous federal shooting matches, etc. Men from all classes, of differing religions and languages, supported the intellectuals and industrialists who proposed to create a State strong enough to shake off the "protection" of the great powers and to abolish internal customs duties. As a reform of the Federal Pact required the assent of the majority of the cantons, federal regeneration developed out of cantonal regeneration. Thus in 1829 the Liberal party was created, which demanded a constitutional revision in each canton, stressed the extension of suffrage, civic equality, freedom of the press, freedom of opinion and a strict limitation of the influence of the Church in public affairs. The Conservative party wanted to preserve the political monopoly of the privileged, the dominance of the churches and the sovereignty of the cantons. The struggle of the Liberal party for the conquest of power was therefore necessarily preceded by a trial of strength.

The Switzerland of today, the "witness to democracy" (Siegfried), the model of constitutional stability and political wisdom, was to know a time of trouble and civil commotions between 1830 and 1847. The backlash of the July Revolution was more intense and more lasting there than in Germany or even in Italy. From 1830 to 1831 Switzerland carried out, on the cantonal level, its own "1848 revolution". Huge mass meetings foreshadowed the great meetings of March and April 1848 in favour of the liberalization of institutions in the German States. Most of the oligarchic Governments, terrified, granted constitutional assemblies. In the most populous cantons (Zurich, Berne, Lucerne, etc.; Fribourg and Vaud; Ticino) new constitutions suppressed privileges based on birth, wealth or residence, proclaimed the sovereignty of the people (an elected Great Council nominated the Government) and conceded the "basic freedoms". The resistance of the former authorities provoked the insurrection of Neuchâtel (1831) and the civil war of Basle (1832–3). The special political status of the canton of Neuchâtel gave rise to conflicts in the manner of 1848; the local republican party proposed not only to overthrow the bourgeois rule but also to withdraw the canton from the authority of the King of Prussia. The Diet avoided international complications by aiding the conservative Government to suppress the republican uprising. Its intervention in the canton of Basle was powerless to restore the *status quo*. Here political rivalries concealed social antagonisms. Not obtaining equality of rights from the Basle bourgeois, the peasants formed a dissident government. The civil war was ended by splitting the canton into two half-cantons: Basle-Ville and Basle-Campagne.

The Left wing of the Liberal party imputed the set-back at Neuchâtel as well as the fruitless attempt at a timid revision of the Federal Pact (1833) to the faint-heartedness of its leaders. In most of the cantons it founded a new party which adopted the epithet "radical" as a challenge. In the United Kingdom the word had acquired an undeniable respectability since the eighteen-twenties. Imported to the continent, the reaction used it to describe a mysterious conspiracy which aimed at destroying the social order. Ardent patriots, the radicals insisted even more than the liberals on the unitary characters of the future constitution. Democrats enamoured of fraternity, they resisted even more stubbornly the pretensions of the Governments which demanded the expulsion of the German, Polish or Italian refugees; Protestants or rationalists, they denounced the influence of an Ultramontane Church and took issue with all religious institutions: convents, the Jesuits. The political struggles which divided the social classes (if the peasants of Basle-Campagne were radicals, those of Lucerne were Christian-democrats) masked the inexpiable character of the wars of religion. Thanks to the freedom of the press, every quarrel in the interior of a canton stirred up the whole country: the Radical party and the Conservative or Catholic party became national parties. In 1841 the government of Aargau suppressed, despite the terms of the Federal Pact which guaranteed their existence, the eight convents of the canton. Catholic Switzerland obtained from the Diet the re-establishment of four of the convents. This demi-victory did not satisfy it, but exasperated radical Switzerland.

With the installation of the Jesuits at Lucerne in 1844, one of the "principal cantons", the period of cantonal troubles came to an end, while the period of countrywide civil war was imminent. On two occasions (December 1844 and April 1845) the radical minority rose against the government at Lucerne. It received, with the connivance of the authorities, the support of volunteers from Berne, Aargau, Solothurn and Basle-

Campagne. The seven Catholic cantons (Lucerne, Uri, Schwyz, Unterwalden, Zug, German-speaking: Fribourg and Valais, French speaking) concluded in December 1845 a separate union (*Sonderbund*) intended to preserve the sovereignty and territorial integrity of its members. The religious conflict was crystallized into an opposition of constitutional character: the *Sonderbund* was against the Federal Pact which the Catholic cantons wished to maintain! This violation was denounced by the radicals who dreamed of giving Switzerland a new constitution! A serious internal crisis therefore threatened to break up a State till then preserved, despite the dominance of the German language, from Germanic ambitions. Would the Swiss give the signal for vast popular upheavals even before the Parisian proletariat? Did not civil war run the risk of provoking international conflicts?

BELGIUM: NATIONAL UNITY AND "DEMOCRATIC" PARLIAMENTARY MONARCHY. APPEARANCES AND REALITIES

In the eighteen-forties the liberals of the small German and Italian States saw in the kingdom of Belgium the exemplary constitutional monarchy. The German, Italian and Polish refugees appreciated the tolerance of the new State and the extraordinary freedom granted to the press. It was at Brussels that Karl Marx was to draw up the *Communist Manifesto* and it was from Brussels that the pamphlets of the political exiles against the Second Empire were to come.

The history of the Belgian State, national and liberal, began on 25 August 1830 in a theatre auditorium. The presentation of Auber's *The Dumb Girl of Portici* at the Paris Opera in 1828 had not shaken the throne of Charles X; but at Brussels it unleashed the rancours accumulated against the enlightened despotism of William I. In the great patriotic chorus which French domination in Europe and then the defeat of Napoleon had aroused, the voice of the Belgians had been extremely feeble. By the end of August 1830 the idea of nationality had not yet been expressed. Catholics and Liberals united to demand guarantees against an authoritarian régime under Calvinist influence. The intransigence of the King, the extension of the unrest beyond the borders of Brabant, the transformation of a municipal and provincial movement into a national movement through the activities of the working classes, the offensive of the Netherlands' troops and their defeat by the volunteers from the proletariat (at the end of October they held no more than the citadels of Antwerp, Maastricht and Luxembourg), changed the nature of the conflict. In a few weeks a demand for reforms became a demand for autonomy and, finally (4 October), a declaration of independence.

The nomination of a king, the demarcation of frontiers, even the survival of the new state depended on the powers which had signed the treaties of 1815 which the Belgian revolution clearly violated. Nicholas I dreamed of restoring order on the Senne, but the Polish insurrection kept him tied to the Vistula; Frederick William III was also in favour of armed intervention. In a personal union with William I the Grand Duchy of Luxembourg had entered the Germanic Confederation in 1815; the federal fortress of Luxembourg harboured a Prussian garrison. Luxembourg deputies, however, had taken their seats informally at the National Congress. The desire to chastise the Belgians gave way before the threat of a French counter-intervention. Louis Philippe, only a few weeks after his own tumultuous advent, could hardly do less to appease an ardently bellicose public opinion. The Belgian cause, as that of the Poles, brought together the Catholics of *L'Avenir* (Felix de Mérode, father-in-law of Montalembert was a member of the Provisional Government) and the men of the Left: Dupont de L'Eure and Louis Blanc dreamed of reviving the revolutionary tradition. The Dutch invasion of August 1831, the insistence of William I in 1832 on keeping the Antwerp citadel, permitted national sentiment to arouse feelings outside the country. Behind the tricolour flag, the soldiers of Louis Philippe got the impression, shared by the public, that they were carrying out an act of symbolic restoration. Liberating France made, for the first time since 1815, an attack on the statute decreed by the absolutist powers. But it in no way shattered the universal peace; relying on the wisdom of Louis Philippe the Government in London tolerated the operations of the French armies.

For Belgium was to a great extent an Anglo-French "co-production". The understanding between London and Paris, London playing the leading role, had imposed upon Europe the recognition of Belgian independence, upon the new State the choice of a sovereign and upon the recalcitrant adversaries the demarcation of its frontiers. The National Congress, which had chosen as king the Duc de Nemours, second son of Louis Philippe, had to choose a German prince instead. The uncle of Queen Victoria, Leopold of Saxe-Coburg, did his utmost to calm French resentment; he married Louise, one of Louis Philippe's daughters. He had, however, to tack an uneasy course between the verbal exigencies of his parliamentarians and the decisions of united Europe in London. Perpetual neutrality, guaranteed for a State not yet completely formed, placed Belgium in a situation even more uncomfortable than that of Switzerland in 1815, France, and above all the United Kingdom, refused to exasperate the Dutch or annoy the Germans. Belgian nationality as it was expressed in the speeches of French-speaking politicians was founded on the self-determination of peoples. The French revolutionary thesis legitimized, in the name of the former theory of "historic rights", claims on Zeeland Flanders, Limburg and Luxembourg of which Belgium received the western part. Since William I refused to approve the treaty until 1839, the Belgians continued to occupy the territories which they had lost by law! In 1839 the Chamber, at the end of a debate which has been compared by some with that of the French National Assembly at Bordeaux on the cession of Alsace and Lorraine, resigned itself to the inevitable. The Diet of Frankfurt, which had been thought so weak, obtained in compensation for the amputation of Luxembourg the entry of Limburg into the Confederation.

The Dutch menace had preserved the alliance concluded in 1828 between the Catholic and Liberal parties. The pro-clerical press, enemies of Jacobinism, and the anti-clerical press, admirers of the revolution, got together under the influence of the current emanating from France. Won over little by little to the ideas of Lamennais, the Belgian Catholic party, the only European politico-religious organization save for the Irish party, became the great party of reform, of which the founder of *L'Avenir* had dreamed for his country. On the one hand freedom of religion was conceded, on the other that of education. The Constitution of 7 February 1831 registered, for the first time in Europe, a voluntarily agreed compromise between political Catholicism and Voltairean liberalism: priority of civil over religious marriage, separation of Church and State, which continued none the less to pay the salaries of the clergy. Voted before the election of Leopold, it erected solid barriers against a return to arbitrary rule. The individual enjoyed the freedoms customary in the United Kingdom. "All power is from the nation." The sovereign, in the manner of "the King of the French", was "the King of the Belgians". Ministers were responsible to a parliament made up of a Chamber and a Senate recruited by the same electors. Like all the monarchies of the continent, the new State considered the right to vote as a social function linked to a certain income, but the qualification was not uniform; it varied, according to the presumed economic standard of the province, between a maximum of 100 florins (211·60 French francs), slightly higher than the French qualification, and a minimum of twenty florins. The Abbé De Foere had fought for the immediate extension of the figure of twenty florins to the whole country but his proposal suffered the same fate as that of Montalembert at the same period. The notables, in Belgium as in France, placed their interests above their principles. However, the existence of a constitutional minimum provided a means of yielding to popular pressure without endangering the foundations of the régime. Meanwhile the electoral body was, after that of the United Kingdom following the 1832 reform (one elector for every twenty-six inhabitants), the largest in Europe (one elector for every ninety Belgians, as against one for every hundred and seventy Frenchmen). It contributed, together with the peaceful enjoyment of freedoms contested elsewhere and a succession of Governments "of national union" co-operating with the King, to confer on the Belgium of Leopold a reputation of being a State gallicized but national, more liberal and more active than the France of Louis Philippe.

In the 1846 census 57 per cent of the Belgian people were Flemings. However, they seemed divorced from public life. Only a single article of the constitution, proclaiming the equality of languages, indicated their existence. The Flemish districts had been, in principle, equitably represented in the National Congress (115 deputies out of 200). In fact, the combination of electoral qualifications and eligibility tended towards the election in the Flemish constituencies of leading Francophones. The gallicization of the bourgeoisie, begun curiously enough in the seventeenth century by the centralizing activities of the House of Austria, was continued in the times of the Revolution and the Empire had had not been checked by the Netherlands régime. After 1830 the Belgian "political class" was in agreement to ensure the triumph of the French language throughout the country; in Flanders it was not only the language of the social élite but also that of the administration of the courts and of the army. Many Flemish bourgeois regarded the Netherland dialects as boorish idioms. Uneducated (in 1846 50 per cent of the troops were illiterate), excluded from political life, the people seemed incapable of formulating their demands. The awareness of nationality was, in central and eastern Europe, the work of peaceful intellectuals, whose disciples were to become aggressive nationalists. But in Flanders the task was at first easier; it was not a question of forging a literary language but of putting an existing language into the service of national regeneration. The Romantic movement, by its taste for the past, incited Flemish historians and philologists to reveal once again the literary heritage of the people and exalt the grandeurs of the nation. The most outstanding of these pioneers of the "Flemish movement" were nostalgic for the Dutch régime, and admirers of German erudition which very soon showed an interest in the Low Countries of Germanic speech. The archivist Willems (d. 1846) and the Abbé David founded a Flemish Society in Ghent in 1836 for an apparently limited public. By his historical novels Conscience (1812–83), the son of a French sailor, appealed directly to a section of the working classes. His *Lion of Flanders* (1838) is a romantic evocation of the victory of Courtrai (1302) won by the Flemish "craftsmen" over the French knights. The appeal of these "awakeners" of national feeling was underestimated. However, when Willems organized a petition with the aim of granting Flemish a place equal to that of French in the provinces of Netherland dialects he received from a largely illiterate population a hundred thousand signatories! Would gallicized Belgium resist the introduction of universal suffrage?

Would not a Flemish Belgium endanger an economic prosperity apparently founded on the misery of a despised community? The boldness of Belgian financial capitalism was well known, especially that of the Société Générale which, following the example of the British bankers and in association with them, favoured the prodigious expansion of the railway network. The name of John Cockerill (1790–1840), son of an English immigrant and founder of the Seraing factories, was soon famous throughout the world. The first locomotive built on the continent appeared in 1835 from these workshops. The recent calculations of Bairoch confirm the astonishing economic progress of Belgium. In 1840 it held, proportionate to its population, the second place in Europe after the United Kingdom for the consumption of steam-coal, the proportion of horse-power per head and the extent of the railway network, and the third place for the consumption of raw cotton and the production of pig-iron (Switzerland and Sweden shared second place). The Walloon country, with its coal and its metallurgical industries, grew in power. The business classes and manufacturers increased their dominance. The misery of the workers seemed to have reached its culmination in Flanders, once so prosperous. The soil was of high yield and great attention was paid to making waste land productive. But the fractioning of holdings, consequences of a high birth-rate, involved the regular increase of rents and the cost of land, so that the mechanization of the linen industry ruined the cottage industries which were linked even more closely than in France to the position of land tenure. In 1834 more than 200,000 Flemings, part-peasants, part-craftsmen saw their existence menaced by the development of factories (Ghent, whose population doubled in half a century, 103,000 inhabitants in 1846 as against 55,000 in 1801, became the great textile centre and also by the entry of English cotton goods. To resist this competition the Ghent manufacturers enforced a working day of from thirteen to fourteen hours, with low wages. The workers of the expanding regions (the provinces of Hainaut and Liège had in 1846 41 per cent of the workers in the kingdom, the two Flanders 31 per cent) had a less tragic destiny. Although not represented in the parliament, the Belgian working classes found defenders, thanks to the freedom of the press, without resorting to violence (the Constitution took no account of freedom of assembly).

Kats founded in 1835 papers and reviews which depicted, in the Netherlands dialects, the moral and economic distress of a people deprived of their right to their own culture and their own way of life. Bartels, a Calvinist convert to Catholicism, was the moving spirit of a French-language press with democratic and socialist tendencies. In this Belgium which gave a welcome to outlaws, Buonarotti lived in the times of Dutch domination; his egalitarian theories won over a small group of intellectuals. From 1838 Considérant went there frequently to try to win over the progressive bourgeoisie to Fourierism. Bartels seasoned the Saint-Simonian doctrine in his own way in his *Essay on the Organization of Labour* (1842), whose title reveals a knowledge of the booklet which Louis Blanc had just published in 1839 in the *Revue du progrès*. Democrats hostile to the régime of electoral property qualifications and a tyrannic social order were in touch with the romantic revolutionaries like Lelewel, or Marx and Engels who arrived in Brussels at the beginning of 1845. The subversive doctrines preached in Switzerland and above all in Paris began to be known to a backward working class through the German workers numerous in the capital.

The extreme Left, democratic and socialist, was too weak to undertake anything against the political and social institutions. Would not a European upheaval, especially if it came from France, be a temptation, as in 1830? If this hypothesis had been formulated about 1846, perspicacious observers would have hesitated to take for granted the perpetuity of the young State, for the revival of the former quarrels between the two great Government formations menaced political stability, while a food crisis transformed the Flemish areas into another Ireland, source of misery and hatred.

## [Chapter Four]

## Northern Europe: Aristocratic and Absolutist

AT THE CLOSE of the eighteen-forties authoritarian sovereigns governed the Netherlands, Sweden and Denmark with the support of the Church (Calvinist in the Netherlands, Lutheran in Sweden, Norway and Denmark) and the great landowners. The British model of a Protestant and liberal monarchy and the example of the revolutionary upheavals of 1830 seemed incapable of shaking the institutions of the old régime. The legislative assemblies, where they existed, represented not the nation but the "orders", based on out-of-date distinctions. Only Norway, a dependency of Sweden, provided the astonishing spectacle of a society of smallholders who had imposed upon a foreign king political institutions in harmony with transformed social structures.

The Conservative forces were supported by the personal activities of Tsar Nicholas I and encouraged by reactionary Austria, the inspirer of the Frankfurt Diet where the delegates of the sovereigns of the Netherlands and Denmark sat. The question of Holstein and Schleswig, which ranged Danish nationalism against German nationalism, would have as effect the reinforcement in Copenhagen of the liberal and patriotic trend and the increase in the Scandinavian countries of a public for writers whose works evoked the common past of long-separated peoples.

### HOLLAND: A NATIONAL STATE OF THE OLD RÉGIME

Holland acquired its present frontiers in 1839. A little larger than Belgium (32,600 square kilometres against 29,500) it was at that time less populous (in 1850, 3·1 million as against 4·3 million).

The decline which began in the eighteenth century was continued. The spirit of enterprise of the bourgeois of the seventeenth century had deserted their descendants who stagnated in a cult of "the golden age". After the loss of Belgium, William I tried to shake his subjects out of their torpor. With the co-operation of the men of Ghent, anxious to preserve their markets in Java, he encouraged the setting up of cotton mills. The results were mediocre. Railway construction, more sluggish than in Belgium (Brussels was linked to Malines in 1835, Amsterdam to Haarlem in 1839) was continued at a slower pace: the line from Rotterdam to The Hague was opened only in 1847. The Dutch flag was seen less and less in the Dutch ports (42 per cent in 1831, 28 per cent in 1850), to the advantage of the English. With the exception of a handful of audacious cynics who went to Java to make their fortunes through starving the local people by substituting industrial for food crops, the Dutch seemed to have become a people of timorous and resigned shopkeepers.

This resignation was shown in their attitude towards a despot and the institutions of another age imposed in the atmosphere of national unanimity of 1813. The republican institutions which had formerly allowed the bourgeois to govern were manipulated to the profit of royal absolutism and the aristocracy. The Fundamental Law of 1814 had envisaged, alongside an Upper House nominated by the sovereign, a Lower House elected by the provincial Estates and made up of deputies of the nobility of the towns and countryside. The parliament which voted the budget every ten years was without any control over the ministers. Under such a régime Holland remained unaware of the freedoms which, in the eighteenth century, had made the United Provinces an asylum for free-thinkers. The press was strictly supervised. It was only in 1828 that the first great Amsterdam newspaper, the *Handelsblad,* was founded.

The weakening of absolutism was due less to political opposition than to religious discord. In a nation "impregnated by theology and nourished on the Bible for two centuries" (van Gelder) the incorporation of Limburg, of Netherlands speech but Catholic religion, revived the furies of the past. The majority of Dutchmen noted with resentment that the State, born of the revolt of Calvinism against Spanish Catholicism, had lost the essential element of its greatness—its moral unity. Faced by Catholics who now made up a third of the population and who were demanding the rights enjoyed by the Protestants, the Protestants adopted an attitude of total rejection. William I did not dare to grant to his Catholic subjects the re-establishment of the bishoprics abolished since the early days of the Reformation. If his inaction deprived him of the support of the Catholics, his intervention in the life of the reformed Church alienated the traditional allies of the House of Orange; he demanded the union of all the sects. The "orthodox", hostile to the liberal interpretation of dogmas, seceded and created a lively agitation among the mass of the people against the reformed Church and against the King. Disheartened, he abdicated in 1840.

With the advent of his son, William II, who had the reputation of a reformer, a small and very moderate liberal party under the leadership of Thorbecke (1796–1872), a professor of Leyden University, demanded freedom of the press and elections to the Lower Chamber on a property qualification basis, thus breaking with the idea of representation by "orders". The realization of a Dutch 1789 met with the resistance of the nobility and the fanaticism of the pastors, and led to the reserve of the new king, whom his brother-in-law Nicholas I urged to inaction. The attempt at constitutional revision of 1844 failed.

But, as in Belgium on the eve of 1830, an alliance was sketched out between Liberals and Catholics. The fear of being swept away by a growing revolutionary wave prompted the King to make concessions. Would not a liberalization of the régime be, after all, the best method of resisting the appetites of a Germany then forging its unity on a basis of linguistic affinity and memories of the Holy Empire?

## AN ILL-ASSORTED PAIR: AUTOCRATIC SWEDEN AND DEMOCRATIC NORWAY

The centuries-old contest between Sweden and Denmark for the domination of Scandinavia ended in 1814 to the advantage of Sweden. A loyal ally of Napoleon, Denmark had to cede Norway to Sweden which had entered the Great Coalition, under Bernadotte, the heir presumptive. From 1818 to 1844 Charles XIV reigned over Sweden and Norway but whereas he governed aristocratic Sweden as a despot, he had to allow a rural democracy, of which there was no other example in monarchical Europe, to be installed in Norway.

Sweden (450,000 square kilometres) which in 1800 had fewer inhabitants (2·3 million) than Holland, had more in 1850 (3·5 million). This growth (52 per cent) was the result of the low death-rate (20·2 between 1841 and 1845) peculiar to the Nordic countries and of a birth-rate (31·1 for the period 1841–50) scarcely lower than that of England and Wales. The economy was prosperous. Sweden was an exporter of cereals and was to remain so until about 1870. The timber of its immense forests and its mines of proverbial wealth were the foundations of its export trade. Despite the substitution of coke for wood in metallurgy, it was in 1840, proportionate to its population, the second largest producer of pig-iron. This economic progress had as consequence an increase in the numerical importance of the bourgeoisie.

At the beginning of the century the mass of the population was made up of poor peasants, fishermen and miners. The nobility, holders of vast estates, maintained their power, with the Lutheran Church their monopoly. They dominated the *Riksdag*, divided into four *curias* (nobles, clergy, bourgeois, peasants), endowed with derisory powers. The army, coddled by the former marshal, and the bureaucracy were the pillars of a system of oppression. Stockholm, however, perceived a feeble echo of the July revolution. This was the period when Swedish romanticism, hostile to French influences and filled with admiration for German literature, reached its apogee and began to abandon the conservative camp. An example of this evolution is given by the poet Geijer (1783–1847). The *Aftonbladed* of Stockholm, organ of the more daring bourgeois and intellectuals, was campaigning for freedom of the press and the repeal of laws against non-Lutherans. After 1840 the King made a few formal concessions to liberalism. The accession of his son in 1844, who was said to be liberal, awakened the hopes of the adherents of the modernization of institutions. But, allied to Russia since the end of the Napoleonic Empire, Sweden, like the Netherlands, could not disregard the warnings of Nicholas I. Moreover the propaganda of the Liberals could not stir a people deeply attached to the young dynasty.

In Norway the people placed their trust in a constitution imposed on the King. Over its immense territory (320,000 square kilometres) Norway had in 1800 less than a million inhabitants (in 1850: 1·3 million), fishermen, sailors, merchants and, above all, peasants. The nobility, few in number, was on the defensive; between 1814 and 1835 the number of small-holders doubled. When the threat of annexation by absolutist and aristocratic Sweden became evident, peasant Norway had already drawn up (1814) the most progressive constitution in Europe: the *Storthing*, elected by the smallholders and those having an income of from 750 to 1,000 francs, could not be dissolved. In matters of legislation, the King had only a suspensive veto. The Assembly could also, against the will of the former Jacobin, abolish titles of nobility. Charles XIV did not manage to acquire either the absolute veto or the right of dissolution. Even more, from the eighteen-thirties onward, he was the object of fresh demands.

This advance of the democratic spirit was allied to the rebirth of national feeling. To an instinctive distrust of Sweden was added an awareness of nationality. Between the educated bourgeoisie and the peasants there existed, as in Flanders, a linguistic barrier of social significance; the former spoke Danish, the state language for five centuries, the latter spoke the despised dialects. Norwegian romanticism, the most national of the Scandinavian romanticisms, waged a twofold struggle; political, against Sweden, and cultural, against Denmark. Wergeland (d. 1845), liberal poet and journalist, was in 1830 "the typical example of Norwegianism" (Bjurström). He recruited among the students of Christiania the first bourgeois opponents of the "Danophiles". Together with the national language, romanticism exalted the ancient kingdom of Norway, which disappeared in 1397, and the peasantry, symbol of the nation.

The peasantry was still more or less untouched by an eclectic literature (the *Peasant Tales* of Björnson, disciple of Wergeland, only appeared in 1857), but, master of the *Storthing*, it sought doggedly to slacken the ties with Sweden which the King was trying to reinforce. Residing in Stockholm, Charles XIV wanted in 1836 to impose the presence of a Swedish viceroy at Christiania. The *Storthing* forced him to nominate a Norwegian and to promise, in the latter part of his life, a revision of the Act of Union of 1815. Under Oscar I, Norway obtained the recognition of its flag and the suppression of the vice-royalty, the final stages towards an apparently imminent secession.

## DENMARK FACED BY GERMANIC NATIONALISM

Situated outside the Scandinavian peninsula, Denmark was more closely linked to German Europe since 1815. Hereditary sovereign of the duchies of Schleswig and Holstein since the fifteenth century, the crown had acquired the little State of Lauenburg, a member, like Holstein, of the Germanic Confederation. The actions of Copenhagen in the duchies risked an intervention by the Diet, that is of Austria and of Prussia.

At the time of the Restoration in France the two great powers had, it is true, no motive to disturb Frederick VI (1803–39) who governed on absolutist traditions. The social structure and the demography of Denmark and the duchies were similar to those of northern Germany. The landed aristocracy exercised considerable powers over the peasantry; the bourgeoisie, few in number, were concentrated in Copenhagen. Seven times less extensive (43,000 square kilometres) than Norway, Denmark had almost as many inhabitants (0·9 million) in 1800 and more (1·5 million) in 1850; furthermore the population of the duchies was about 900,000 souls. The growth of Denmark (66 per cent) exceeded that of Sweden despite an almost exclusively agricultural economy, which was stimulated by the reduction of British protectionism. Principal benefactors of this expansion, the Danish nobility demanded, with the aid of the liberal agitations of 1830, representative institutions.

In the duchies this had been demanded by the nobles, the bourgeoisie and a majority of the members of Kiel University for the previous fifteen years; it had above all a national significance. German was both the language of the majority of the population and of the educated classes. Danish, in continual decline, was spoken by one third of the inhabitants of Schleswig, in fact only by the peasants of the north. The historian Dahlmann (1785–1860), then a professor at Kiel, shrewdly combined juridical and historical arguments; he relied on the Germanic Federal Act applicable to Holstein alone to demand the institution of provincial Estates for the whole of the duchies, on the pretext of their "indissoluble union".

The reform which came into force in 1834 treated the kingdom and the duchies alike; four purely consultative assemblies were created: in Jutland, the islands, Schleswig and Holstein. In the capital, already of a size disproportionate to the smallness of the State (Copenhagen had more than one tenth of the Danish population), the bourgeoisie and the members of the universities voiced their disappointment. A Liberal party was formed which demanded a constitution and a chamber elected on modern lines and endowed with real powers. Without a hearing among the rural masses and opposed by the nobility, the Liberal party was quite unable to overcome the resistance of Frederick VI. Under Christian VIII (1839–48) agitation in the duchies resembled more and more the patriotic, even nationalist, liberalism of an absolutist State threatened by secession.

In the Schleswig Estates the presence of Danish deputies

raised the tone of the debates. To satisfy them Copenhagen had introduced Danish as the language of administration in northern Schleswig in 1840. This measure aroused violent protests from the Germans. Schleswig became ungovernable. A reasonable solution would have been a partition on a linguistic basis. It was, in fact, about the languages spoken in Schleswig that the worthy philologists of Copenhagen and Jena disputed in the war of the lampoons. Each of the antagonists cherished the hope of appropriating all Schleswig for itself. Appeals were made to History, even more docile than philology, for the suggestions of expansionist nationalism. The liberals of Copenhagen proclaimed that History had fixed the frontiers of Denmark on the Eider, that is to say the southern border of Schleswig. Thus the "Eider Party" was born. As the University of Kiel saw it the Danish pretensions were in flagrant contradiction to three principles: that the duchies were independent States, inseparable, and inherited through the male line. Adopted in 1844 by the Estates of Holstein, these theses were henceforward the platform of the separatist movement.

The last of these theses was, in the circumstances, a direct threat to Danish sovereignty. As Prince Frederick, son of Christian VIII, had no children the succession passed to his nearest relative, Christian of Glücksburg, great-grandson of Frederic V (d. 1766) on his mother's side. His coming to the throne would unleash a long-prepared secession of the duchies. Repudiating an heir on the female side, the Estates of Schleswig and Holstein rallied to another member of the royal family, the Duke Christian Augustus of Augustenburg, who had won the support of the anti-Danish movement. Christian VIII in his "open letter" of July 1846 had declared Schleswig subject to the same rules of succession as Denmark, but reserved for further study the decision on Holstein. The University of Kiel, led by Dahlmann, protested at the "affront" to the "rights" of the Augustenburgs and the declared intention of separating Schleswig from Holstein. The Estates of Schleswig and Holstein refused to sit. Won over by the complaints of the subjects of a "German" prince, the Diet of Frankfurt, contrary to its custom but under pressure from an overheated public opinion, declared

itself in their favour: the fate and the rights of the duchies could
not be altered by the "open letter". The historian Sybel was
not wrong when he recalled in 1892 that the feeling of nationality had crystallized in the duchies from 1846. The war-
mongering attitude of the parliament in Frankfurt at the time
of the Prusso-Danish armistice of August 1848 would be
incomprehensible if one were not aware of the fevered
enthusiasm of the German people for "the cause of Schleswig-
Holstein" (only the Danes and the diplomats still spoke of
Schleswig and of Holstein!). Composed in 1844 the *Lied
Schleswig-Holstein meerumschlungen* (sea-surrounded) echoed at
the mass meetings whose size and spontaneity surprised and
disturbed the sovereigns who thought they had been ruling
over apathetic and indifferent subjects. There were few
Germans who escaped the infection, the "madness" of which
the disrespectful philosopher Bruno Bauer wrote, of Schleswig-
Holstein! The Prussian conservative Radowitz published a
study against female inheritance in Schleswig in 1846. Engels
was not embarrassed by juridical considerations: "These lands
obviously German by nationality, by language and by mentality
. . . are necessary to Germany" (1852).

But Denmark could count on the support of Russia and the
United Kingdom, equally interested in the maintenance of the
*status quo* in Kiel and in the Straits. In Scandinavia Denmark
no longer seemed alone. The feeling of belonging to the same
community was beginning to draw together these peoples of
similar languages and civilization, these neighbours separated
by memories of centuries-old quarrels. Scandinavianism was
at first a literary movement, closely linked to Romanticism.
Danes, Swedes, even Norwegians, delved in the common store
of popular poetry and Scandinavian mythology to find there
an inspiration which went far beyond the framework of the
nations. Oehlenschläger (1779–1850) was leader of the Danish
Romantics. His rival Grundtvig (1783–1872) was the adapter
of old legends. Without doubt Norwegianism was an obstacle
to a Scandinavianism which took the form of Danophilia. But
the poet Welhaven (1807–1872), the adversary of Wergeland,
opposed it. In Sweden Romanticism placed itself at the service

of Scandinavianism; in Lund, Oehlenschläger was proclaimed "king of the Nordic poets".

Faced with Prussia, the trustee of Germanism, would a movement of intellectuals be able to mobilize the peoples of Sweden and Norway? That was to be the problem posed to Scandinavianism in 1848.

# [ Chapter Five ]

# Germanic Central Europe

AT THE TIME of the Rhine crisis of 1840 the outburst of popular passions indisputably proved that the ideal "German nation" to which Fichte addressed himself 1807–8 (*Reden an die deutsche Nation*) did not belong to the realm of dreams. It based its "rights" on language and on grandiose memories of the Holy Empire. These linguistic and historical arguments (which in 1848 were to shock the French democrats who were accustomed to see in the nation the result of a contract consented to by free individuals since 1789) were to be made use of, in imitation of the Germans, by peoples ("peoples" and "nations" were at that time used indiscriminately) who were admirers of the French Revolution. It was the ideological reflection of situations which, if not identical, were at least more or less similar; men who had become aware of their national origins resented with more or less bitterness the total or partial absence of the existence of a State which should be the surety of their aspirations.

Between parliamentary "bourgeois" France and rural and autocratic Russia stretched, from the North Sea and the Baltic to the Adriatic on the one hand and from the Rhine to the Vistula on the other, countries which only geographers were able to distinguish. The vague term *Mitteleuropa* was applied to this Europe in transition: essentially agricultural economies

founded on the servitude of the peasants were typical of eastern
Europe, the existence of smallholders and also of cultured
intellectuals and bourgeois enriched by trade and the exploitation of modern factories recalled western Europe. All the forms
of political régime existed together; the most retrograde
absolutism fell back before the rise of constitutional monarchies,
some of which began, under the pressure of resolute opposition,
to develop towards a real parliamentarianism. The religions
of the west and the north (Catholicism, Calvinism,
Lutheranism) confronted and fought with the religion of the
east, Orthodoxy. The fanaticism of the wars of religion was
mingled with political and national conflicts. In the former
the influence of the clergy was exercised in favour of the forces
of conservatism; in the latter it played its part in favour of the
revolutionary ideology of the nationalities.

### GERMAN POLITICAL PROBLEMS: AUSTRIA AND PRUSSIA AGAINST UNITY AND FREEDOM

The German people and Germany summed up the complex
problems of central Europe. That the Germans formed the
most numerous linguistic group was an evident fact; that it was
impossible to demarcate a country whose extent and political
system varied according to the chances of the battlefield was
another. The Germany of 1848, born in 1815, lived until 1866,
longer than the Germany of Bismarck (forty-seven years), of
Weimar (fifteen years) or of Hitler (twelve years). At the close
of the eighteen-forties the thirty-eight States of the German
Confederation (*Deutscher Bund*) represented, by comparison
with the three hundred and sixty sovereign territories of 1789,
a remarkable simplification. There were the four ancient Free
Cities of Bremen, Hamburg, Lübeck and Frankfurt, and
thirty-four monarchies (a part of the Austrian Empire, the
kingdoms of Prussia, Bavaria, Saxony, Hanover, Wurtemberg,
with duchies, grand-duchies and principalities). Certain
provinces of the Prussian State, to us the symbol of Germanism
launched for the conquest of the Slav world, were repudiated
by the German organization: Poznania, peopled by a Polish

majority, and also East Prussia and West Prussia, land of the uncouth Teutonic Knights. Königsberg, that tremendous fortress still redolent of memories of the royal coronation of an elector of Brandenburg (1701), did not figure on the list of towns juridically considered German, which included Prague, Laibach (Ljubljana), Trento and Trieste! For the Hapsburg possessions integrated with the *Bund* were made up of German Austria and the greater part of those other lands of the Empire which did not belong to the Crown of St Stephen. Finally, two foreign kings (up to the advent of Victoria in 1837 this was also the case of the English sovereign of Hanover) were members of the *Bund* for a fraction of their territories—the kings of the Low Countries and of Denmark.

This strange composition of the *Bund* was bound to influence the unifying efforts of the Frankfurt parliament towards an aggressive nationalism of which the Schleswig-Holstein affair provided a foretaste. It would have still further contradicted the French principle of nationality if the diplomats meeting at Vienna had listened to the German patriots. In a romantic atmosphere of medieval fervour the aspiration towards a strong State able to impose itself upon the outside world was based on an ancient and imprecise notion. The idea of restoring the *Reich*, which had disappeared in 1806 after eight hundred and forty-four years, impressed itself on the élite. The word Empire of the famous formula, the Holy Roman Germanic Empire (*Das heilige römische Reich deutscher Nation*) is the insipid translation of a word which usually means "kingdom" (animal, vegetable, etc.) and never "empire" except when it is a question of purely German creations. (*Kaiserreich* designates the Austrian Empire, like Napoleonic in the Napoleonic Empire.) The *Reich* was to materialize successively in the great enterprises of 1871 (the Second Reich) and of 1933 (the Third Reich). The *Reich* as conceived in 1814-15 went beyond the limits of the one which Napoleon had destroyed and which had included the Austrian Netherlands. While the hotheads demanded a Germany extending from Switzerland to Schleswig, from Alsace to Latvia, the "moderates" claimed in the name of "historic rights" a return to the situation existing prior to the treaties of Westphalia (1648). The Pomeranian Arndt (1769–1860) claimed "Germanic" Flanders, Alsace and Lorraine. Stein, from Nassau (1757–1831), approved. In his *Rhine Mercury* published at Koblenz, Goerres (1776–1848) limited his ambitions to Alsace and Lorraine, inseparable from the *Reich*. Strasbourg, Worms, Speyer, Trier, Mainz, Cologne, were so many holy cities over which "the ancient Mecca" of Aachen, city of Charlemagne, ruled and "the modern Mecca", Frankfurt, where in its *Römer* the Emperor was elected and, from 1562, crowned! Arndt's booklet with its provocative title: *The Rhine, German River but not German Frontier (Der Rhein, Deutschlands Strom aber nicht Deutschlands Grenze)* was not merely an admonition to the Germans. It was, above all, an exhortation to the "brothers" of Alsace. Like Arndt the Lutheran pastor, the Catholic Goerres stated that "the population of Alsace, which felt itself German even while Goethe was still a student, has been won over to France by the political order and the new social currents created by the Empire". Since history can correct history, these peoples who were forgetful of their past must be reminded of their allegiance to *Deutschtum* (a noun launched by Goerres), that is to say to Germanism. A few years after the death of Herder (1744–1803), the "father of German Romanticism" and of the Slav Romanticism, his disciples turned his thinking into a formidable weapon. Herder considered the nation as a living being animated by the *Volksgeist* (literally: spirit of the people), "the unconscious collective spirit" (Minder), which was spontaneously revealed in folk stories and songs, in customs and, above all, in language. A strictly aesthetic doctrine! Friend of the Slavs, partisan of the emancipation of the Jews, he found the conception of a chosen people aspiring to the domination of central Europe alien to him. With Fichte (1762–1814), whose considerable influence on the universities was after 1815, Herder's ideas took shape in the claim of a state which should unite the scattered members of the uncontaminated *Urvolk* (primitive people)! Even before 1815 they were popularized by two men of mediocre talent who were to live long enough to assume the role of patriarchs in Frankfurt: in the song *What is the German's Land? (Was ist*

*des Deutschen Vaterland?*) Arndt replied that it was "everywhere
where the German language and the songs of God in the
heavens resounded . . .". A typical representative of pan-
German Romanticism was Jahn (1778–1852), the *Turnvater*
(he was the inventor of the noun *Turnen*—gymnastics). He was
filled with the desire to create specifically Germanic expressions;
for *Nationalität*, too obviously inspired by the French *nation*
(*nationalité* only appeared in French dictionaries in 1823) he
substitued *Volkstum* (from which Arndt derived the adjective
*volkstümlich*), without equivalent in any other language. The
*Volkstum* was primarily the sum of the manifestations of the
*Volksgeist*. It was also a moral and ethnical community superior
to the will of individuals. The explosive character of this vague
term reappeared in the use made of it during the Third Reich.

Armed from 1815 onward with its ambiguous ideology and
its equivocal vocabulary, German nationalism was too far in
advance of its times not to clash with Governments enamoured
of independence, order and peace. Its campaign to recreate a
*Reich* united around an emperor met with the opposition of
princes hostile to a strong central power which would alienate
a portion of their sovereignty. Everything finally depended on
the attitude of Austria. Historians are doubtless right to say
that Prussia in 1815 was already the most powerful of the
German States. Contemporaries judged otherwise. As in the
eighteenth century, French opinion was inclined towards a
weak but enlightened Prussia and dreaded a strong and
reactionary Austria. None of the many combinations elaborated
in 1815 to restore a head to Germany envisaged the exclusion
of Austria and the accession of the king of Prussia to the
imperial dignity.

Stein, the reforming minister of the Prussian State, was
willing in 1813 "to make Austria the mistress of Germany".
By holding an elective crown, almost without interruption, for
nearly four centuries, the Hapsburgs had built up an incontestable authority. The dynasty was the personification of
anti-French sentiments and the symbol of the *Reich*. But the
Rhinelander Metternich considered that the imperial Germanic
crown would weaken the activities of the emperor of Austria

in the Danubian monarchy. In order to hold a mosaic of peoples in submission, the State must be vigorous enough to curb liberal aspirations and reduce the provincial assemblies to a figurative role. The patriots held the view that the creation of representatives of the German nation would be something to dread. In the regions incorporated in the *Reich* it would put an end to the omnipotence of the Vienna bureaucracy; it would incite the other provinces of the Empire to demand elected assemblies which would become the fields of battle first of the political parties and then of the nationalists. Metternich would always fight against representative institutions which he judged to be fatal to the Hapsburg monarchy.

The Federal Act (*Bundesakt*) of 8 June 1815 was the Austrian solution to the German problem. This unitary organization concerned the princes and not the peoples. In the free city of Frankfurt, haunted by memories of the *Reich*, sat the Diet. Like the United Nations, it was a permanent conference of Government delegates, subject as far as essential problems were concerned to the rule of unanimity, without an executive and without its own financial resources, the States paying their contributions more or less regularly. Under the permanent presidency of Austria, it had to keep watch on "the maintenance of internal and external security and the independence and integrity of individual States". Officially, it had no external policy (in contrast to the Swiss Diet, it did not accredit envoys); in fact German diplomacy was identical to Austrian diplomacy. However, with a majestic slowness, the Diet carried out its task for the defence of the *Bund*, a task often underestimated but considerable enough to arouse the criticisms of the liberals, admirers of the French "citizen militia". On the eve of 1848 each State maintained a force equivalent to one hundredth part of its population. The federal contingents formed ten army corps placed under the control of representatives of the Emperor of Austria and the Kings. Other than the Slavs of the Austrian troops, in the 9th and 10th corps were men from Luxembourg and Limburg, soldiers from Holstein and from Lauenburg, who could quite legally be called upon to fight against their own sovereign. The quandary of having to choose between Austria and Prussia impeded both the nomination of a commander-in-chief and the organization of manœuvres outside the sphere of activity of individual army corps. However, the construction of federal fortresses in the west, accelerated by the Rhine crisis of 1840, was entrusted to professional soldiers who paid no heed to the necessity of preparing a united force to resist a French invasion and confirmed in a most striking manner the Germanic character of the Hapsburg Empire; in 1848 the Austrians had garrisons in Mainz, Ulm and Rastatt.

The disregard of particularisms was not limited in principle to the exigencies of national defence. Article 13 of the Federal Act implied the obligation of according certain liberties to all subjects: "There will be in all the Confederated States an organization of Assemblies of Estates." Mixing the modern notion of elected legislative assemblies guaranteed by a constitution (*Verfassung*) and the medieval notion of Estates (*Landstände*) without great powers and composed of the traditional "orders", this ambiguous article allowed the princes to do whatever they pleased. Those of northern and middle Germany eagerly followed the example of the two great reactionary powers. In the Austrian provinces incorporated in the *Bund* (9,700,000 inhabitants as against 29,400,000 in 1822) as in the rest of the Austrian Empire the centralizing policy of Joseph II was continued. The governor was its agent, the German nobility and the Catholic clergy were its instruments.

Absolutism displayed its most retrograde forms in that State which German historians were later to depict in the seductive colours of liberalism. For more than thirty years the essential task of the Hohenzollerns would be to unify the kingdom and not Germany. Prussia, Protestant, agricultural and feudal, had acquired in 1815, together with the Rhineland province, Westphalia and the Saar, Catholic lands already partially industrialized, with social structures and mentalities modified by the influence of revolutionary and imperial France. Like Metternich, Frederick William III (1797–1840) believed that centralized absolutism was the most efficient method to weld disparate human groups into a single body. The army and the bureaucracy were entrusted to the energetic Prussian nobility.

Only in 1823 did Frederick William III agree to create provincial Estates after the Austrian model. Dominated by the nobility, purely consultative, convoked at the discretion of the sovereign, they did not risk imitating those of the South which, to the indignation of Frederick William III and of Metternich, propagated subversive doctrines.

At the beginning of the eighteen-twenties the south was a liberal enclave in the Germany of the Holy Alliance. The Grand duke of Nassau (1816), the King of Bavaria and the Grand duke of Baden (1818), the King of Wurtemberg (1819) and the Grand duke of Hesse-Darmstadt (1820) had "bestowed" constitutions on their peoples. These principles had benefited greatly under the French régime from the suppression of countless principalities and free towns and from the secularization of numerous bishoprics. The idea had come to them that political institutions common to the whole of their Estate would contribute to its cohesion. This view was confirmed when the Lower Chambers, which were elected on a much wider basis than in the United Kingdom or in Belgium (with its million electors Baden in 1830 had more electors than France), grew bold. Very soon they demanded a reduction of police powers, the institution of a jury system, complete freedom of the press and the introduction of a parliamentary régime. Taking into account the nature of the electoral body, this liberalism of the intellectuals was apparently paradoxical; the majority of the electors were smallholders freed from serfdom, enjoying the benefits of the Civil Code but sometimes subjected to feudal restrictions which the Diet had set out to maintain; in 1825 85 per cent of the rural properties in Bavaria were burdened with dues to the mediatized princes (*Standesherren*) and to the nobles (*Grundherren*); in 1830 the privileged classes in Baden controlled more than 34 per cent of the territory and 29 per cent of the population. Even where legislation had foreseen a representation by the nobles, civil servants were the most numerous group (in 1830 fifty-four seats out of a hundred and twenty-four in Bavaria). In the Grand duchy of Baden, they sometimes almost attained an absolute majority (thirty-one or thirty-two seats out of sixty-three). A high property qualification eliminated or considerably reduced the candidature of really representative elements of society; peasants, artisans, even tradesmen. This, on the other hand, was not demanded from the many holders of public office. From this omnipotence at the time of the *Aufklärung*, the functionary (he was still pompously known as a "State-servant") still had, in the eyes of the populace, a prestige which was preserved in Germany up to the twentieth century. In 1818–19 the Bavarian and Baden functionaries, having achieved permanence of employment and the possibility of anticipatory retirement linked to a comfortable pension, had an almost complete liberty of vote. At this time the docility of a Chamber was not assessed, as in France, by the number of functionaries. Deliberating in the smaller towns (in 1850 Stuttgart had 50,000 inhabitants, Karlsruhe 26,000) where rumours circulated rapidly, the deputies talked at the tops of their voices "in the name of the people". A sort of vertigo assailed cultured men, assiduous readers of the French and British liberal press. From the humble platforms of assemblies without great powers, they broadcast a message of freedom to oppressed Germany. At their head, the most respected and most independent of these functionaries were the professors (the masters of higher education alone had the right to the tremendous title of professor) who condescended to teach history and law to their colleagues, and even to ministers.

Irritated by the diatribes against absolutism of these professor-deputies, Metternich indignantly remarked that freedom of speech kept the students in a perpetual ferment against the federal institutions. Since 1815 the national idea had taken deep root in the universities. When demobilized, these young men had taken up their studies again with the mentality of ex-soldiers who had been betrayed. At a time when a wind of reaction was blowing from Berlin and Vienna, the University of Jena became the centre of German patriotism. The Grand duke of Saxe-Weimar, a friend of Goethe, had made his tiny state (257,000 inhabitants in 1846) an oasis of liberalism. In the summer of 1815 the *Burschenschaft* was formed there. From Jena this student movement spread to fourteen other universities. Its inspiration was at the same time national, religious and revolutionary. Like the Parisian students, but for quite different reasons, the *Burschenschaft* condemned the work of 1815; division and partition, a condition of Russian hegemony and the basis of the British economic prosperity, was established in the *Bund*. The three colours, black, red, gold, flown during the "wars of liberation" by Lutzow's "free corps" symbolized unity. The revolutionaries claimed Luther as an authority. The struggle against Rome seemed like a fight against the spiritual *ancien régime*. 1517 became, for the Protestant intellectuals, the equivalent of 1789. Held at the Wartburg, the revered asylum of Luther, on 18 October 1817, to commemorate both the third centenary of the Reformation and the fourth anniversary of the victory at Leipzig, the famous meeting of the *Burschenschaft* dangerously inflamed young people. In 1819 the assassination by the student Karl Sand of Kotzebue, a writer connected with the Tsar, provided Metternich with the opportunity of unleashing a general offensive against the forces hostile to particularism and absolutism—the press, the universities, the assemblies of the constitutional States.

In the towns of the Confederation but under the jurisdiction of the Emperor (Teplitz, Münchengrätz, Karlsbad, Vienna) Metternich's proposals received the approval of Prussia and Russia (the Federal Act and its interpretation were under the guarantee of the Great Powers) and they were then put into force in the German Estates which Austria wished to convoke. The Diet emerged from its torpor. In 1819–20 newspapers were censored and trustees supervised the universities; not only was the *Burschenschaft* dissolved but its former members were forbidden entry into the public service. The Diet would aid sovereigns in trouble with their assembly members. The federal commission of Mainz empowered to enquire into revolutionary intrigues crowned this first stage of unification by repression. Jahn was thrown into prison. Arndt was dismissed from Bonn. Goerres was forced to seek refuge in Strasbourg which he had formerly dreamed of annexing! Henceforward those in opposition knew that the triumph of liberty was a condition for German unity.

The July revolution, the Polish insurrection (the admiration of the German liberals for these brave people, enemies of the hated Russia, was well known) and the unrest in Italy at least provoked activities which foreshadowed, though on a lesser scale, those of 1848. Some meetings, summoned by university leaders, students and members of the liberal professions, were enough to make absolutism tremble. The kings of Hanover and Saxony, the Duke of Brunswick, the Elector of Hesse-Cassel, all granted constitutions. In the south the Chambers of Munich, Stuttgart and Karlsruhe accomplished in a few months political reforms (freedom of the press) and social reforms (partial abolition of feudal dues) which deliberately violated federal legislation. Abandoned by Metternich, who was then occupied in maintaining Austrian predominance in Italy, the Diet did not react. A minority of intellectual democrats allied to "foreign brothers", mainly Poles, chose the moment when Louis Philippe's desire for peace had restored freedom of action to Metternich to organize a noisy manifestation of unity (Hambach, May 1832) and to attempt a putsch against the Diet (April 1833). Each of these ill-considered moves was followed by measures increasing the repression of 1819–20. The Six Acts voted by the Diet in June 1832 forbade elected assemblies to involve themselves in all-German affairs (at Karlsruhe Welcker had proposed in 1831 to replace the representation of the princes by a parliament elected by the peoples of the Confederation). The greater number of the liberal laws adopted since 1830 were abolished. In 1833 a new and unified repressive institution was created in Frankfurt, and charged with keeping a watch on the German liberals and the exiles in Switzerland and France. In 1834 the Vienna conference drew up common regulations for press censorship and decided to ban former members of the *Burschenschaft* from becoming physicians or lawyers. Professor Jordan, principal compiler of the Hesse-Cassel constitution, was suspended; seven professors of Göttingen (including the brothers Grimm, Gervinus and Dahlmann) who protested were dismissed. In the south, fortress of liberalism, the Conservative Governments hypocritically refused to grant leave to those opposition deputies who were civil servants to take part in the work of the Chambers. Here, as in northern Germany, reaction made the bureaucracy its tool.

The Chambers abolished or reduced to impotence, the masters and their students silenced, Metternich, at the end of the eighteen-thirties, seemed to have triumphed completely. But he had ruined the reputation of the Diet, which had now become an institution both despised and ignored. The Diet found no more defenders than Metternich himself in 1848. Once the head of the anti-French resistance, Frederick William III had betrayed the liberal idea and the national idea by his alliance with the Junkers and with Metternich.

### THE ZOLLVEREIN AND ITS LEGENDS: ECONOMIC, SOCIAL AND POLITICAL PROBLEMS

Closely allied politically with Austria, Prussia had nonetheless created between 1818 and 1836, without serious opposition from Metternich, a vast "common market" of twenty-five States totalling twenty-six million inhabitants. The work of Marxist bureaucrats before Marx, the *Zollverein* had, according to a long-lived legend, been created by the desire to prepare the way to political unity under Prussian hegemony in order to satisfy material interests. Even if they reject this thesis, the majority of authors consider that the *Zollverein* engendered a state of mind favourable to the foundation of the *Second Reich*. But what, for the Germans of the eighteen-forties, were the financial, economic, social and political consequences of the *Zollverein*?

Even the least favourably disposed of the Governments had to recognize that the *Zollverein* was a good thing financially. The cost of collection of customs dues fell from 44 per cent to 9 per cent of the receipts of the States as a whole, since the length of the frontier to be guarded was diminished. The receipts shared *pro rata* according to the population of the States increased between 1834 and 1843 by 71 per cent. Opponents of the *Zollverein* recognized that it was the source of the reduction in direct taxation.

Its effect on the economy, on the eve of 1848, was less evident. Many authors considered the eighteen-forties in the light of the eighteen-sixties. The advantages of freedom of trade are stressed, as if the abolition of internal customs dues brought about the suppression of the taxes on goods using the Elbe, the Weser and the Rhine. It is true that some industries, sheltered by the protective tariff, had begun to make progress. The old cotton industries of southern Baden owed their revival to it; the prospect of being excluded from the German market incited the dynamic capitalists of German Switzerland to invest beyond the Rhine. Nonetheless, industrialization only really affected the Saxony textile industry and the textile and metallurgical enterprises of the Rhine-Westphalia region, which used nine-tenths of the steam power within the *Zollverein*. All in all, the results attained by 1848 were modest. The recent studies of Bairoch measure the gap that still divided German from French industry in 1840. France was dominant in all representative sectors; she consumed more raw cotton per inhabitant (1·5 kg. as against 0·9 kg.), coal (130 kg. against 110 kg.). She produced more iron (12 kg. against 5 kg.). Twenty years later only the situation as regards coal consumption was reversed (390 kg. against 449 kg.).

However, in an environment essential for the transformation of living standards and the acceleration of the exchange of ideas, the German superiority was overwhelming. In 1841 the German railways (1,138 km.) were longer than the French (435 km.); on 1 January 1849 they still maintained their advantage (5,500 km. as against 2,000 km.). Later on the railways were greatly to contribute to the decline in particularism and were to achieve, according to Treitschke, "what the *Zollverein* had only begun". Even if they got little from it, a number of princes wanted to have a railhead in their capital. It seems tortuous to discern in the railway expansion of 1848 a particularism which "betrayed a discipline". The work of the Berlin bureaucracy tended to link the old provinces of the centre and east with the recent acquisitions in the west. In 1849 1,600 kilometres of track were in service; thirteen times less populous, the district of Baden had 350. Apart from the *Zollverein*, Austria participated in the general movement. Vienna was in railway communication with Prague, Prussian Silesia and Pressburg (Bratislava). The interests of an empire which wished to be both Germanic and Mediterranean were stressed in the south; in 1850 the railway reached Trieste which was henceforward to divert the Indian mail from Marseilles. The almost unanimous encouragements of the sovereigns were not theoretical; the States were induced to finance the track laying, either partially (Prussia) or totally (Saxony, Bavaria, Baden).

For capital was scarce. Because of the extreme diversity of currencies, the main activity of the modest banks was money-changing, as in the Middle Ages. The Rhineland province provided the unusual spectacle of bankers (Camphausen and Mevissen at Cologne, Hansemann at Aachen) giving their support to industry. The most important banks perpetuated the German tradition of the "Court Jews" of the eighteenth century. The pressing needs of States, which intervened more and more in economic life, imposed recourse not to a distant public but to friends who were financiers, primarily to the Rothschild family of Frankfurt, or Anselm and Salomon of Vienna.

A banking organization dominated by a few financiers (at Frankfurt only the house of Bethmann competed with the Rothschild bank) and an industry left to fend for itself assuredly constituted obstacles to the formation of a vigorous bourgeoisie. Rhineland bankers and industrialists, the great merchants of the major distribution centres (Frankfurt, Bremen, Hamburg, Lübeck) represented this far from numerous class. Ever since Marx the German bourgeois had not ceased to be on trial. The accounts of the events of 1848 provided an occasion for denouncing its class egoism and its incapacity. In fact, however, the bourgeoisie which was to hold the centre of the stage for less than a year had nothing in common with the capitalist bourgeoisie. Marx had felt the need to introduce into the German language the French nouns *bourgeois* and *bourgeoisie*, for their equivalents *Bürger*, *Bürgertum*, and *Bürgerstand* were extremely imprecise. In 1845 Blittersdorf, an aristocrat, began to associate *Bürgertum* with the property-owning class. The same year a journal of Konstanz saw in *Bürgerstand* the small trading

and artisan bourgeoisie whose studies had ended in the primary
school. The *Bürger* was first and foremost the holder of the right
of communal citizenship and only incidentally a man of means.
About 1848 he was a somebody, very different from the simple
bourgeois of Daumier. His prestige lay less in his wealth than
in his culture. He belonged to the class of the *Akademiker* (those
who had attended a university), a pedantic élite revered by a
people respectful towards every form of learning (in the
eighteen-thirties primary education in most of the German
States had reached a stage of development unknown in the rest
of Europe). With the extension of the constitutional régime,
political authority was added to moral authority. The rich
manufacturer who had started at the bottom hesitated to follow
onto the rostrum the talkative *Akademiker* who overwhelmed his
opponent with a flood of quotations from Kant, Herder,
Fichte and Hegel! Bourgeois liberalism was in Germany even
more than in the United Kingdom or in France a liberalism of
intellectuals. The apparent disdain for the social consequences
of mechanization at its beginnings resulted both in the formation of a group excluded from technical skills, and the insignificance of the industrial proletariat.

Lacking federal statistics, the number, even approximate, of
the factory workers of the *Bund* is unknown. The statistics of the
*Zollverein*, notably those of 1842, confuse the wage-earners in
the factories with the peasant homeworkers. Kuczynski's
estimates for the territory of Germany in 1914 (600,000 factory
workers and 100,000 miners), populated more or less like the
France of 1848 (thirty-five million), seem reasonable. The
advantage to France was in the ratio of 3:2. There was in the
Confederation a single textile factory employing more than
eight thousand workers at Reichenberg (Liberec) in Bohemia!
In Berlin the Borsig factory, with twelve hundred workers,
which built the first German locomotive, and the spinning-mill
of Ettlingen (Baden) were exceptional cases. The firm of Krupp
at Essen had in 1841 only two hundred and fifty workers. Even
if one adds the home-weavers, numerous in Silesia and in Baden,
the heterogeneous class of industrial workers was pushed into
the background by the numbers of the traditional craftsmen.

On the whole, the oppressive and Malthusian régime of the guilds (*Zünfte*) existed in the towns; the countryside escaped it, as did also the more recent enterprises, that is to say the factories. Rare (probably less than a hundred from 1791 to 1848) were the strikes unleashed by these tailors, book-binders or compositors who were always in the van of the workers' movement. In 1840 the Diet crowned its work of unifying reaction by co-ordinating measures of social repression; henceforward every guild member condemned in a State other than his own for participation in an illegal organization or in the preparation of a strike would be sent back to his own country and compelled to reside there. Thanks to his own spies and those of the federal commission of Frankfurt, Metternich followed very closely the infiltration of "anarchist doctrines". He regularly had sent to the princes carefully compiled lists of members of the Federation of the Exiles and the Federation of the Just. On their return such men were placed under the surveillance of the police. The peril which Metternich dreaded was by no means imaginary. Marx and Engels, though far from tender towards "utopian socialism", recognized its influence on the German artisan in their articles for the *New York Daily Tribune* (1851–2). The novels of Eugène Sue, amongst others *The Mysteries of Paris* and *The Wandering Jew*, found, unlike the learned works of Stein and Grün, readers in every social class. From 1838 they were continually being republished, often in very cheap editions; they appealed to a wide public receptive to the diffusion of Parisian ideologies by those other wanderers who were members of the guilds. The rigidity of the German guild system conspicuously favoured, it seemed, the antagonisms between classes even in the sphere of work. Engels has depicted with humour the "masters" (tailors, cobblers, cabinet-makers) of the princely residences eager to ingratiate themselves with their clientèle of aristocrats, officers, higher civil servants, by professing ultra-conservative opinions. In fact, the difficulties of the mass of the craft guild professions brought patrons and workers close together. From 1830 onward the effectives were considered superabundant. According to Fr. Lütge, the urban and rural craftsmen amounted to 59 inhabitants in every thousand in 1861 as against 30·8 in 1816! The guild members, proud of their qualifications so dearly earned, were reduced to the status of manual labourers and the "masters" felt themselves rejected by the *Bürgerstand*. They imputed the responsibility for their degradation to free enterprise. In 1845 the Baden republican Fickler led a fervent campaign against rich men who were authorized to found breweries, printing-works, bakeries and the like, even though they had not passed through the guild channels. The guild workers for their part were jealous of the factory workers whose conditions were in every way comparable to those of the United Kingdom or of France (the Prussian legislation of 1839 regulating the labour of children was in no way better observed than the French law of 1841). But they noted that the real wages of the workers in the mechanized industries had resisted the recession of 1820–1850 better than theirs. Between the "masters" favourable to the maintenance of their dynasties and the partisans of the united social republic preached in the workshops of the Faubourg Saint-Antoine there were only shades of difference on the economic plane. Reinforcement of the guild system was the panacea envisaged to break the first timid offensive of capitalism; it is true that the guild member expected the suppression of the subtle regulations which had transferred, little by little, the mastership into a family monopoly.

Contrasted to the unreality of the aspirations of the craftsmen and artisans, a majority in the towns, were the dreaded demands of an important section of the peasants, a majority in the nation. The Germany of the *Zollverein* was a vast rural area with structures scarcely modified by the activities of the French occupiers or the German reformers. In Prussia, where the agricultural east and the industrial west were balanced, the percentage of the rural population only declined from 72·73 to 72·45 between 1834 and 1843! Demographic causes aggravated the difficulties of the peasantry of an "under-developed" nation; a high birth-rate (36·1 as against 27·4 in France between 1841–50) and a high death-rate (26·1 as against 22·7 in France between 1841 and 1845). Every year young proletarians were added to the mass of former cultivators which the administration of the feudal régime had turned into starving journeymen. East of the Elbe the reforms of the "Jacobin" Stein had paradoxically involved the proletarization of a section of the peasant class. In thirty years the number of agricultural workers had almost doubled. There was thus developed on the twelve thousand (in round figures) estates of the Junkers an agriculture of modern type copied from the English landlords. Silesia had not known even a hint of peasant reform; the weavers whose spontaneous uprising in 1844 had aroused profound echoes in Germany were subjected as serfs to the exploitation of the seigneurs or as casual workers to the exploitation of the capitalists. Like the proletarians of the Prussian countryside they were to play no part in the great events of 1848-9. On the other hand, the peasants of the south were to take their destinies into their hands in March 1848. Whereas the French Revolution and the Empire had abolished the social *ancien régime* in the Rhineland, the seigniorial régime had continued to exist in the southern states. The redemption of taxes and dues were, despite state assistance, heavy charges on smallholders practising a backward agriculture. Even more than in France, the absence of credit institutions delivered the peasants into the hands of the usurers, for the most part Jews. Fear of the proletarization was openly expressed in demands at the same time progressive and reactionary. Exploiting the extraordinary contradictions resulting from the co-existence of modern political institutions and medieval social institutions, the peasants of Baden protested by voting against the price fixed for the redemption of the feudal rights which had been abolished and at the same time demanded the suppression without compensation of others, especially hunting rights. At the same time they refused political equality to the Jews. The liberal deputies of Karlsruhe up until 1846 adopted as keynotes of their electoral programme: for peasant emancipation, against Jewish emancipation.

The persistence of medieval anti-Semitism, the complacent admiration for the guild régime of former times, expressed the deep disarray of social categories numerous enough to threaten the established order. Their misery (*Armut, Not, Elend*) became

a literary theme. Between 1822 and 1847 it inspired almost
two hundred works; from 1834 onward interest began to be
concentrated on the factory workers. New terms, borrowed
from French or English (*Pauperismus, Classe* or *Klasse, Proletarier,
Mittelstand*) depicted a society of earlier type; on the one hand
ease and culture, on the other misery and lack of culture.
Attempts were made to instruct the "lower classes" and above
all to educate them; thus in the eighteen-forties under bourgeois stimulus associations were created for "encouraging the
advancement of the labouring classes". Shrewd observers who
had revealed the deep causes of social unrest and the lack of
harmony between the increase of the population and economic
development denounced the illusions of philanthropy.

From 1830 works devoted to the problem of over-population
in the countryside became more and more frequent. The remedy
proposed was emigration. Governments formerly "popula-
tionists" accepted it with relief. The great migratory flood of
the eighteen-fifties towards the United States had been
prepared for, psychologically, since 1820; the number of
German emigrants had increased from 52,000 (1821–35) to
329,000 (1846–50). On the eve of 1848 emigration was considered as a "national duty". Friedrich List (1789–1846),
precursor of the idea of a *Mitteleuropa*, vainly recommended
would-be emigrants to move to the Hapsburg Danubian lands.
He relied, in fact, on industrialization to resolve the problem
of over-population, but a society dominated by the *Akademiker*
did not understand him. The literature of the time was hostile
to the factory, source of undeserved profit for the scarcely
cultured proprietors and place of perdition for the disorganized
workers. The works devoted to socialism or communism relied
on French or English examples. As for the "organization of
labour" so dear to Louis Blanc, it was vague enough to become
integrated with the German conception of the proletariat.
Wage increases, the reduction of working hours and the
tightening of corporative bonds were demanded (Rodbertus
was in this matter a notable exception). Finally, many authors
imputed the sufferings of the "working classes" to the *Zollverein*
and to Prussia, the moving spirit of its customs policy.

It was admitted that the *Zollverein* was, in many States, imposed on a reluctant opinion; but by the end of the forties its outstanding advantages were recognized to the greater glory of Prussia. This gave rise to a belief which counteracted the growing irritation against the Berlin Government. The partisans of adhesion to the *Zollverein* had promised a powerful protection against British competition, but the wish to humour the English and the desire to win over the Hanseatic cities, those fortresses of free trade, had meant the maintenance of moderate tariffs. Prussian bureaucracy was accused of sacrificing German interests to "the British giant". Far from being a preparation for union, the *Zollverein* appeared as a foment of division. The spinners of the south had the support of "the apostle of the industrial revolution"; in his *National System of Political Economy* (1841) Fr. List began an ardent campaign in favour of a vigorous protectionism. Nebenius, from Baden, who was with List one of the first supporters of the idea of a German customs union, demanded high duties on British iron in 1842. In 1845 Mevissen, a strong upholder of the *Zollverein* and of German unity under Prussian direction, demanded, in the name of the Rhineland Chambers of Commerce, a modification of the customs policy. At the secret *Zollverein* conferences tension rose. Despite the censorship, the press kept the public on tenterhooks. Public opinion was, in fact, convinced that British competition was not only damaging to the greater number of German factories (weaving excepted) but a death-blow for craftsmanship and rural home industries. The very slight changes in the tariffs of 1846 were regarded as a betrayal. Prussia appeared to many as the United Kingdom's Trojan Horse in Germany. The *Zollverein* had in no way contributed to the unifying task of Prussia. In 1866, on the eve of the Austro-Prussian war, almost all of the German States were in favour of Austria.

## THE NATIONAL IDEA AND LIBERALISM IN THE EIGHTEEN-FORTIES

In Germany the growing force of national feeling and the awakening of liberal ideas were characteristic of the period

which began in 1840. In that year Frederick William IV
became King of Prussia, and Thiers thoughtlessly unleashed an
international crisis. The former event should not be over-
estimated; the advent of the new king, who roused to enthusiasm
those intellectuals who were already won over to the Prussian
cause, deluded few of the liberals, with the exception of the
Rhinelanders.

The effects of French claims to restore France's natural
frontiers were, on the other hand, deep and lasting.

### The Rhineland Crisis of 1840 and its Effects

In a Germany reduced to silence the spirit of 1813 was reborn.
Sovereigns wrapped up in their particularism, prudent
journalists, peaceful professors and students, all reacted with
surprising vigour. The anti-French current reached its
maximum of intensity in the west and south, regions that were
liberal but exposed to the risk of a possible invasion. Its force
was such that the democrats, friends of revolutionary France,
contributed (with various nuances, it is true, but they contributed) to the polemic literature of which Arndt was the
forerunner. The immense success of the *Rheinlied* of the Rhinelander N. Becker and the witty riposte of de Musset are well
known. In similar vein to the *Rheinlied*, the *Wacht am Rhein* (*The
Watch on the Rhine*) by the Wurtemberger Schneckenburger was
to become the most popular patriotic hymn from 1870 to 1914.
Another Rhinelander, M. Hess (1812–75), future leader with K.
Grün (1817–87) of 'true socialism', was the author simultaneously of an apologia for France, and of a melody for the Francophobe *Rheinlied*! "The Rhine must stay German" repeats a
refrain by the Wurtemberger Herwegh, the most Francophile
of the German republicans of the eighteen-forties. In Paris,
Venedey, a member of the Federation of Exiles and author of
an indictment against the Prussia of Frederick William III,
denounced the French chimeras. His friends Quinet, Michelet,
Arago and Lamennais were aroused. Venedey then published
in Paris, one after the other, *France, Germany and the Holy
Alliance of Peoples* (in French) and *Der Rhein*. Let the French

democrats renounce the Rhine and the German democrats
renounce Alsace! Only the little group of the Hegelian Left,
animated by Ruge (1802–80), kept cool heads. Ruge feared
lest national enthusiasm might become a welcome diversion
for the régimes of oppression. The *Annales de Halle* (transferred
to Dresden, then to Paris, where they were to become the
*Annales franco-allemandes*) published in reply to the *Rheinlied*
another *Rhein*, one of the few Rhineland poems which did not
conform. The anti-French current which swept away a section
of the extreme Left of the Chambers of the south, traditionally
admirers of the principles of 1789, led level-headed persons
about 1845 to accept the absurd rumour of an alliance between
France and abhorred Russia as possible. To the phantoms of a
barbarous and bellicose Russia ready to loose her hordes upon
a cultivated and peaceful nation and of an England exploiting
a people abandoned to its own resources with the complicity
of Prussia was now added that of a France thirsting for conquest.
Against the French, the English and the Russians, patriots
appealed to the brotherhood of Germans and not to the brotherhood of peoples, a diabolical French invention! The *Deutschland
über alles* (1841) preached a "brotherly union ... from the
Meuse to the Niemen, from the Adige to the Belt ...".
Hoffmann von Fallersleben, its Saxon author, was, moreover,
from the national viewpoint a moderate, from the internal viewpoint a democrat. Professor at Breslau, he was dismissed in 1842
from the University because of his sympathies with the Poles and
his criticism of the Prussian Government. He had done no more
than popularize ideas already familiar to the university world.

## The Universities

Strong in prestige which stretched far beyond the frontiers of the
Germanic world, German professors and students embodied
the unifying aspirations of the German nation more and more,
even if they did not participate in active political life, quite
naturally, the Frankfurt parliament was to become, on the
model of the Chambers of the constitutional states, a "parliament of professors" and ex-*Burschenschaftler*.

In a particularist Germany where the suffocating atmosphere
of the eighteen-thirties was slackening, professors subject to
dismissal at the whim of the authorities paved the way to the
limitation of princely sovereignties! This fact, commonplace to
the Germans, was a result of the psychology of the authorities,
of the political situation and of the mentality of the professors
themselves. Anxious to cultivate his popularity by flattering the
vanity of his subjects, each prince did his best to attract to his
university, or universities, eminent masters (the "Seven" of
Göttingen, dismissed by the King of Hanover, received, with
the approval of reactionary rulers, many offers). The professors
drove a hard bargain before accepting. They chose the
university which offered the best working conditions and the
best treatment. The renown of a university was not measured
by the importance of its location. It depended on the reputation
of its staff. The university of Berlin declined after the death of
Hegel (1831). The little towns of Bonn, Jena, Heidelberg and
Kiel had great universities. In Austria the German university
of Prague soon eclipsed that of Vienna. Passing from one
university to another according to circumstances (the simultaneous presence at Kiel of Dahlmann and of Droysen (1808–
84) was directly connected with the Schleswig-Holstein affair)
and according to their interests the professors felt little loyalty
to the princes whose temporary subjects they became. Conscious,
on the other hand, of forming the élite of the *Akademiker*, they
met from 1822 onward in national specialist congresses; the
congress of so-called Germanists, which included linguists,
jurists and historians, was held at Frankfurt in 1846; the
German thesis on the duchies was put forward and approved
there.

"German science" was in fact derived from the "science of
man". In the domain of the experimental sciences, as in that
of techniques, the backwardness of Germany in comparison with
France was still considerable about 1850. The naturalist
Alexander von Humboldt (1769–1859) had published his works
in French. Before gracing the university of Giessen, J. Liebig
(1803–73) had come to Paris to attend the courses given
by Gay-Lussac. The German spirit, inclined to abstractions,

had reached its highest point with Hegel (1770–1831). That a revolutionary current, that of the Hegelian Left, should have emerged from his teachings is a fact not without importance in the history of ideas. Political history on the other hand was closer to the conservative trend whose power increased with the rise of Prussia. The strong State which Hegelian philosophy defied was within its rights to demand absolute sovereignty over individuals, in the name of the reason of which it was the incarnation. The only German State worthy of the name was, in the eyes of the Protestant philosopher, Protestant Prussia. But the extraordinary and immediate influence of Hegel was at first exclusively philosophical. The work of the Wurtemberger P. Pfizer (*Correspondence between two Germans*) which in 1831 recommended a Germany separated from Austria and placed under Prussian hegemony was at that time merely the anticipation of an individual.

Before the Prussian mission, the mission of Germany had been preached by philologists, jurists and above all historians before whom learned Europe had long bowed respectfully. This admiration rested on the very ambiguity of "the German science". Guizot, Mignet, Michelet, all took part openly in party struggles; it was the most fiery period of the times and a glittering style often marked a somewhat fragile documentation. What a contrast with the labours of a Niebuhr collating the "sources" of Roman history, or with the prodigious efforts of the Göttingen team which published from 1826 onward the *Monumenta Germaniae historica*, the foundation of the reputation of Germanic erudition! But this was the bulwark of a partisan conception of law, philology and history. Doubtless the German universities would have rejected this accusation. They sought to serve truth, but it was a truth in accord with the theses of Herder systematized by Goerres, Arndt, and Jahn! The jurist Savigny (1779–1861) rejected in the name of *Deutschtum* the Civil Code of foreign importation. J. Grimm (1785–1863) associated national sentiment with the language spoken. As for propaganda by History, it was affirmed ingenuously after 1840. The national cohesion of Switzerland and also the anxiety not to shackle the efforts of the cantons struggling against the

Catholic *Sonderbund* tempered the annexationist ardours of the professors, for the most part Protestant (in 1846 out of twenty-two universities in the German Confederation only six, three of which were in Austria, were Catholic). As regards Belgium and the Netherlands aspirations were expressed without constraint; the Catholic conservative Buss and the Protestant liberal Welckler were in agreement to discover in the first "pro-Flemish" claims a "Germanic national movement". From the German *Volkstum* of the Flemish provinces they passed gaily on to the German *Volkstum* of the Netherlands. Others saw in anti-Danish Norwegianism a manifestation of a German Scandinavianism. The affair of the duchies was the model illustration of the mobilization of the universities in the service of the national cause.

### The Liberal Inclinations of Prussia and German Opinion

The "refusal" of Frederick William IV to accept the crown of "Emperor of the Germans" in 1849 surprised his most fervent supporters. It was, however, logical to a thinking fed on memories of Prussia's and Germany's pasts. After the international crisis of 1840 the son of the polemist at Jena had not concealed his Francophobe sentiments: N. Becker was granted a pension for his *Rheinlied*. As so many other Germans, he foresaw the danger which lack of a unified command presented in case of war and tried to obtain a reorganization of the defensive system of the *Bund*. Doubtless he dreamed of assuming the supreme military responsibility, but the ambition of the Hohenzollerns excluded any anti-Hapsburg bias. The King bowed before the Austrian veto. Anxious to reinforce the federal institutions, according to the almost unanimous desire of public opinion alerted by the French Rodomontades, he proposed to confide to the *Bund* the commercial policy of the German States. This was an idea alien to a Machiavellian conception of the *Zollverein* which had germinated in a spirit filled with dreams of the Holy Empire!

A Romantic in the manner of most of the German Romantics of the years 1815–40, Frederick William IV admired the Middle

Ages and venerated their institutions. The influence of the Bernese C.-L. de Haller (1768–1854), apostle of a patriarchal monarchy (one God, one king, one father) accentuated his conservative tendencies and his repugnance for the heritage of rationalist thought. He had always preferred Estates representing the "orders" to elected Chambers. He had never freely admitted that relations between a sovereign and his subjects could be regulated by a "scrap of paper". It was, however, from this dreamer, who respected the historical pre-eminence of Austria, this fanatic upholder of medieval absolutism, that intellectuals and bourgeois alike expected some coherent action in order to prepare for German unity under the direction of a liberal Prussia.

At first Frederick William IV enjoyed the reputation for liberalism which public opinion willingly accords to the successor of an authoritarian. Vague promises and a few spectacular gestures confirmed the first impression. An amnesty for political prisoners allowed the return of the popular Arndt. The censorship slackened. The debates of the Estates were published. Political life revived. At first there was criticism of the omnipotent bureaucracy and then a constitution was demanded, the first stage of a reign placed under the aegis of Germanic freedom.

This optimistic interpretation of the intentions of Frederick William IV found particularly enthusiastic supporters in a region long filled with prejudices against Berlin. Profoundly German, but attached to the achievements of the French Revolution, the Catholic Rhinelanders had felt ill at ease after 1815 in an absolutist State based on an aristocratic Protestant society. The defence of Rhenish Law, that is to say French Law, expressed not the wish for secession but a refusal to return to the *ancien régime*. The industrial and merchant bourgeoisie of the more active Prussian provinces did not like the Estates set up by Frederick William III for the benefit of the nobles but it appreciated the advantages to be drawn from the *Zollverein*, even though it judged excessive the concessions accorded British imports. It very soon conceded that economic union would pave the way to political union. It was ready to work for the moral unity of the kingdom and for the hegemony of Prussia in Germany, but on the condition that it should participate in the conduct of affairs in assemblies recruited on the basis of a high property qualification. That was the bargain which Hansemann had offered vainly in 1830 to Frederick William III. Under Frederick William IV, who put an end to the conflict with the Catholic Church about mixed marriages (the Cologne affair), Rhineland particularism became a thing of the past. Links were forged between the moderate bourgeois of Cologne and the advanced intellectuals of Königsberg like Jacoby. Complete freedom of the press was demanded in both the west and the east, as well as a ministry responsible to a National Prussian Assembly. The *Patente* of 3 February 1847, published after countless hesitations, was a derisory concession. The United Landtag, a new assembly which perpetuated feudal traditions, mustered the members of the eight provincial Estates in Berlin. The preponderance of nobles in it was overwhelming. This caricature of a parliament without periodicity was summoned, at the good pleasure of the King, to vote new taxes and to present petitions. In his opening speech in April 1847 the King confirmed his opposition to real political changes. However the Rhineland liberals did not despair of modifying the ideas of a sovereign who was considered susceptible to influence. In the south where, since the cavalier expulsion by the Berlin police of the Baden deputies Hecker and Itzstein, it was proclaimed that "only the circulation of cattle is free in the *Zollverein*" hatred for Prussia was given free rein. A single paper, the *Deutsche Zeitung* by Professor Gervinus (1805–71) of Heidelberg, tried to stem the Prussophobe current. The view began to spread that Berlin was, with Frankfurt, the main obstacle to unity in freedom.

# [ Chapter Six ]

## The Nationalities of Central Europe

### THE PEOPLES OF AUSTRIA AND THE
### GERMANIZATION OF THE ÉLITE

IN THE COURSE of the centuries Austria had checked
and then driven back the Turks from their assault on the West.
Its victory assured the pre-eminence of Viennese Germanism
over the Magyars and Slavs, of Catholicism over Orthodoxy
and Protestantism and of the nobility over the peasants.
Sheltered by the bulwark raised against the Ottoman Empire,
the "Babel of peoples" thus became the "prison of the peoples",
but those oppressed would eventually prepare the dismemberment of the oppressor State. This thesis appears to reflect, with
some exaggeration, the opinion of the leaders of the succession
States. However, it is beyond doubt that the dismemberment
of 1918 was part of an evolution which commenced with the
clash of 1848. Every nationality participated in the "springtide
of the peoples" according to the degree of its national consciousness and the nature of its relations with the other groups,
especially the Germans and Hungarians, imbued with their
national rights and assured of their own cohesion.

Language and religion either bring together or separate,
psychologically, individuals living side by side. The Empire
was composed of approximately one half Slavs (Czechs and
Slovaks, Ruthenes or Ukrainians, Poles, Croats, Serbs,

[ 137

Slovenes), one quarter Germans, one sixth Magyars, one twelfth Rumanians and less than 2 per cent Italians. Other than Catholics (66 per cent), there were Uniates or Greek Catholics (11 per cent), Orthodox (8 per cent), Calvinists and Lutherans (11 per cent) and Jews (4 per cent). Religion drew the Germans, for the most part Catholics, together, but increased tensions among the Slavs. Akin by language, the Serbs were Orthodox, the Croats and Slovenes Catholics. The administrative organization, which in Galicia united the Polish Catholic nobility and the Uniate Ruthene peasants, separated the Slovenes from the bulk of the Croats. A creation of history, the Empire ignored linguistic affinities.

The partition which the Compromise of 1867 was to make an institution was already sketched out: on the one hand the "German lands" incorporated in the Germanic Confederation; on the other the Crown of St Stephen. The former included the "Hereditary states" north of the Alps peopled by Germans, and to the south Slovenes, Croats and Italians, and also the countries (Bohemia, Moravia, Silesia) of the Crown of St Wenceslas or the Crown of Bohemia with a Czech majority (60 per cent) and a large German minority (37 per cent). Directly dependent on Vienna was the kingdom of Galicia, an Austrian fragment of former Poland and the Bukovina, predominantly Rumanian, seized from the Turks. The Crown of St Stephen was not, like the Crown of Bohemia, a mere historical memory. It symbolized both the refusal to accept absorption into German Austria and the desire to colonize the Slovaks, cut off from the Czechs, the Rumanians separated from their brothers who were still in the Ottoman Empire, and the Serbs and Croats who had settled between the Drava and the Sava.

Moreover the national dreams of the Hungarians themselves, who from the time of the conquest in 1526 to the eighteenth century had victoriously resisted all attempts at assimilation, were presented gradually to a government weakened by its divisions (Metternich, a master of diplomacy, was not a master in the conduct of internal affairs), and paralysed by the burden of the administrative apparatus. The delay of the subject peoples in expressing their national aspirations was essentially due to the attitude of the dominant classes. In their backward economies, a few hundred thousand nobles lived off the exploitation of millions of peasants. At the head of the army, of the bureaucracy and of the puny provincial assemblies, they inclined to the defence of order. The illiteracy of the country people guaranteed the continuance of serfdom. To speak their idioms was to lose caste; the Ruthene nobility had become Polonized, the Slovak aristocracy Magyarized. Save for the Magyar and Polish nobility, the upper classes had adopted German, the language of Viennese civilization. Those who remained, the middle classes whose primary role in the European liberal and national movements is well known, had an insignificant place in the Empire. Industrialization of the metallurgical and textile industries had affected only Vienna, the eastern sections of the Alps, northern Bohemia and, above all, Moravia. The manufacturers, satisfied with a customs régime which protected them against the competition of the *Zollverein*, took little interest in politics. At the Diet of Lower Austria, which had its seat in Vienna, a few daring deputies, in liaison with the universities, demanded freedom of the press. The salons of the capital restricted themselves to a war of epigrams against Metternich, but a nationalist liberalism took deep root in the most aristocratic society of the empire.

## RISE OF THE MAGYAR MOVEMENT: ARISTOCRATIC LIBERALISM, SOCIAL AND NATIONAL OPPRESSION

The state of society explains the character of the Magyar movement and its hesitation in tackling the essential problem, that of peasant emancipation. The influence of the industrial proletariat and the bourgeoisie was negligible. Out of a population of twelve million (Hungary and Transylvania) on the eve of 1848 there were no more than 23,000 factory workers and 35,000 miners. In the large agricultural townships there were a million artisans and petty traders deprived of political rights, often Germans or superficially Germanized, such as very many Jews.

Several millions strong, the peasantry was a class of pariahs. The serfs subject to feudal dues and to forced labour for their lords were not the most wretched, for the proportion of landless serfs increased under the effect of the demographic upsurge and the more or less legal encroachments of the nobility. In 1848 in Hungary alone 539,000 serfs had holdings or a fraction of a holding; 826,000 (of whom 98,000 did not even possess a hovel) were reduced to the condition of casual labourers and only worked, according to Kossuth, about fifty days a year. Save for the Slovaks (two million) and the Ruthenes (400,000) they spoke the language of their oppressors; those of the principality of Transylvania and the Banat were for the most part Rumanians and Serbs. In 1848 the nobility tried to create the "holy union" of landlords and serfs throughout the kingdom against the insurrections of the non-Magyar peoples. Its success was only partial as the aristocracy for the most part refused to accord to the mass of the people any place in the society of the State.

The 680,000 nobles represented 5 per cent of the nation. This large class was also much differentiated. The magnates, scarcely 1,500 in number, were very great landlords who lived for a considerable part of the year in their palaces at Vienna. Very many held high State office. Nothing predisposed them to question political institutions or social structures; Count Szechenyi (1792–1860) and Baron Eötvös (1813–71) were striking exceptions. The petty nobility made up three-quarters of the aristocracy. Rooted in the countryside, for the most part deaf to Western ideas, it was reactionary in internal affairs and revolutionary in external ones. For the most part poor, it clung fiercely to its seigniorial privileges, fiscal (exemption from taxation) and political. The right to vote was, moreover, the ultimate prerogative preserved by 30,000 nobles officially enrolled on the list of taxpayers! The assemblies of fifty-five *comitats* (counties) were the parade ground of this "nobility in sandals" which despised the serfs, envied the magnates, and fought against Germanic absolutism. Through fear of this intractable class the Government no longer summoned the Hungarian Diet after 1811, till agitation in the *comitats* forced the Emperor to do so in 1825.

1825 marks the beginning of the resurgence of the Magyar nation. While Vienna once again recognized the existence of the "Hungarian constitution", the Magyars undertook the rehabilitation of their language. Szechenyi founded the Hungarian Academy. The poet Vörösmarty (1800–55) devoted an epic to the glory of Arpad, the legendary Hungarian hero. Magyar Romanticism was essentially national and patriotic in inspiration. In 1837 Vörösmarty published his *Appeal to the Hungarian Nation* and the national theatre was opened. Soon the historical dramas of E. Szigligeti (1814–78), inspired by Dumas and Victor Hugo, replaced the translations of German pieces. Baron N. Josika (1794–1865), at first a disciple of Walter Scott and then of Eugène Sue, created the popular historical novel. Very soon Magyar Romanticism broke with German Romanticism to turn westward, above all to France. There were many magnates who spoke French perfectly; sensitive to the enchantments of Paris and to the emancipating work of the French Revolution, Eötvös wrote novels condemning the ascendancy of the feudal lords. Of Serbian stock, Petöfi (1823–49), the idol of the Pest democrats, became the bard of the serf class and of the Hungarian homeland before giving his life for them on a Transylvanian battlefield.

The example of Petöfi, the plebeian, and of Szechenyi and Eötvös, magnates and persons of considerable political importance, bears witness to the originality of the Hungarian situation. If, in the Europe of enslaved nations, the "awakeners" were often isolated intellectuals, in Hungary men of action were willing to put into force the national ideas of the committed writers. Since the re-establishment of the Diet, these were recruited essentially from the upper ranks of the nobility. The Table of the Magnates was naturally the meeting-place of the great seigneurs. The Table of the Estates, on the other hand, included, over and above the symbolic representation of the towns (2 deputies) and a delegation of the Croatian Diet, 110 deputies, two for each of the 55 *comitats*. By force of circumstances it became the assembly of the middle nobility, the petty nobility being as a rule too poor to solicit unpaid duties in Pressburg (Bratislava). Its absence made easier the penetration of reformist ideas in the Table of the Estates but did not weaken the harshness of the national claims; when it was a question of fighting for the Hungarian language or for Hungarian autonomy, the nobility formed a bloc.

On the proposal of Szechenyi, regularly renewed since 1825, Magyar, from 1833 to 1844, replaced Latin in the deliberations of the Diet, the administration, including that of the *comitats*, and education. But the Croat aristocrats, who were formed into a sketchy kind of State organization, resisted the Magyar aristocrats, even as they in their turn resisted the Austrian bureaucracy. At the Diet of Agram (Zagreb) the debates were always in Latin and it was in Latin that the Croat deputies continued to express themselves at the Diet of Pressburg. This national opposition, which the "Illyrian" movement reinforced, aroused the anger of the Magyar nobility. In 1842 the petty nobility of the *comitats* denounced it to Ferdinand I (a mental defective who became king in 1835) as treason. In 1843 the Croats who refused to make use of Magyar at the Table of the Estates were received with insults. Szechenyi was almost the only one to protest against forced Magyarization. The Austrian Government, displaying its sympathies for a Catholic people, authorized provisionally, alongside Magyar, the use of Latin at the Diet and left Croatia free to make use of it in the administration. Thus encouraged, the anti-Magyars became exasperated. By proclaiming Croatian as the language of its deliberations in 1845 the Diet of Agram threw down a challenge to the Diet of Pressburg. This dualism, which in 1848–9 Austria used against Hungary, caused her no uneasiness. For the Vienna bureaucracy had no suspicion of the revolutionary potential of the national movements, and its attitude towards Magyar linguistic demands proves it.

On the other hand she considered, as in the great days of the Holy Alliance, that the existence of the Empire was linked to absolutism. Faced with unmanageable characters, she had to scheme. In 1825 the Diet obtained the right of periodicity. Little by little, a parliamentary life of western and bourgeois type accommodated itself to the aristocratic society of the eastern frontiers. Animated by Eötvös and then by Deak

(1803–76), who was to be one of the authors of the *Compromise* of 1867, the Liberal Party was the artisan of this evolution. In 1834 it demanded freedom of the press and the transformation of the Diet into a real parliament with a government responsible to it. Won over to the ideas of Szechenyi, a bold economist but a moderate in politics, it wanted to put an end to the exploitation which kept in subjection a nation compelled to sell its raw materials at prices fixed by Vienna without being able to manufacture them (Hungary bought fabrics manufactured from its own wool from Austria!). This great project presupposed the participation of all productive forces in the necessary transformation of a colonial economy. Some nobles were conscious of this, and, grouped around Deak, proposed the abolition of their own privileges; the right of suffrage (which would be extended to the liberal and economic professions), fiscal immunity and seigniorial rights. This programme of innovation, the work of a few members of the "third estate" recruited from the more enlightened members of the middle nobility, clashed with Austrian prejudices and interests, with the prudent conservatism of the magnates and, above all, with the blind egoism of the petty nobility. During the 1839–40 session the Liberal Party succeeded in imposing on the Upper Chamber some measures favourable to the peasants (prohibition of corporal punishments, possibility of emancipation for the serfs). Eötvös and Deak understood that the primary condition for essential reforms was to make the petty nobility toe the line. Their "centralism" advocated a strong Magyar government based on a representative assembly of the nation. It gained ground in the Liberal Party whose influence soon began to extend beyond the narrow framework of the Lower Chamber.

Since the beginning of the eighteen-forties political life had ceased to be the concern of a few initiates only. For having divulged and commented in a lithographed broadsheet on the debates of the Diet, Lajos Kossuth (1802–94) had been thrown into prison (1837–40). The administration thenceforward authorized the publication of speeches in the Diet . . . provided that the names of the orators were not revealed! It had to take

account in the future of public opinion restricted, certainly, to
a small number of intellectuals, but dangerous because of their
attachment to an impassioned and reckless man. With a
martyr's halo, Kossuth founded in 1841 the *Pesti Hirlap* (*Pest
Journal*) which soon had seven thousand subscribers, twice as
many as the French *National*. This prodigious success was above
all that of a great journalist, with an exceptional gift for oratory.
Polemic and intractable, the "Hungarian Demosthenes" loved
to oppose the pacific Szechenyi. However, the views of the
lawyer from the ranks of the petty nobility were markedly less
broadminded than those of the great seigneur. Spokesman of
the Liberal Party, Kossuth essentially supported Szechenyi's
programme of political autonomy. But he paid little heed at
first to the fate of the peasants; contrary to Eötvös and Deak he
fostered the chimera of founding a democratic life according
to the viewpoint of the petty nobility, whose anti-Slav prejudices
he shared, on the tumultuous agitation of the assemblies of the
*comitats*. When Szechenyi advised handling the Croats with
circumspection, the *Pesti Hirlap* flatly accused him of treason!
Almost up to the end of the insurrection of 1849 Kossuth was
to oppose any agreement with the other nationalities. He was,
however, able, whenever Magyar supremacy was not in
question, to profit by the lessons of experience. The readers of
the *Pesti Hirlap* and the influence of the writings of Saint-Just,
Cabet and Louis Blanc in the literary circles of Pest were not
to be mistaken for the real strength of the Liberal Party. An
alliance with the peasantry would assure the political opposition
reasonable chances of extorting concessions from a government
skilful at arousing social hatred against a nationalist nobility.
In this regard the Ruthene peasant risings (the emperor's
"faithful Galicians") against the Polish seigneurs (1846) were a
warning. Kossuth was thenceforward convinced of the urgent
need to abolish serfdom and to suppress forced labour dues;
but he knew also that the petty nobility would never willingly
sacrifice its privileges for the interests of the nation and he
suspected a tendency to compromise with the rights of Hungary
in the prudent attitude of the liberal parliamentarians. This
romantic, enemy of half-measures, breaking with his class and

his political friends, founded the Radical Party, a party pledged to political emancipation for the Magyar people and social emancipation for the peasantry.

His popularity incited the liberals of the Lower Chamber to attack the Austrian administration. Metternich conceived the bold plan of putting an end to parliamentary unrest by dressing up the Liberal programme in his own manner! Like Eötvös and Deak, he wanted to increase bourgeois representation in the Table of the Estates but at the expense of the nationalist middle nobility. Like them also, he aimed to reduce the influence of the petty nobility. However, by placing civil servants at the head of the assemblies of the *comitats*, he dreamed less of regenerating them than of obtaining "good elections". This administrative reform, which gained the support of Szechenyi and another of the magnates, Count Apponyi (1808–91), for whom would be created the post of Hungarian Chancellor, appeared in the circumstances as an enterprise of centralizing and absolutist Germanism. At the elections of 1846 Deak and Kossuth, reconciled against Vienna, defended the bastions of the petty nobility with even more spirit than the conservatives, the traditional supporters of assemblies closed to the very idea of reform. At the opening of the Diet of 1847 the liberal and democratic coalition had a majority at the Table of the Estates. Conceived against the plans of Metternich, the programme of the opposition reflected almost exclusively the national aspirations of the Magyar nobility. It vigorously demanded for the aristocracy the right of administering and governing Hungary within the framework of the Empire (no one at that time envisaged secession). Despite the troubles in Galicia, it postponed any solution of the agrarian problem; despite the Croat resistance, it showed a haughty disdain towards the Slavs and the Rumanians. To the extent that it would inspire the actions of the Magyar government after the fall of Metternich, it mortgaged the destiny of the revolution of 1848–9.

While Slavs and Rumanians were to make it pay dearly for its arrogant incomprehension, Magyar nationalism received the moral support of the Italian republicans and was to benefit by the aid of many Polish patriots. Even before 1848 the movement had given evidence of its sympathies for the Lombardo-Venetian bourgeois and the nobles of Galicia. Proud of its national cohesion, the Magyar nobility felt attracted towards those peoples who, as it was doing, drew the will to resist all attempts at Germanization from the grandeur of their past and the richness of their civilization. On the other hand, it held Slovaks, Serbs and Croats as a rabble of slaves, "a Slav is not a man", subject to aristocrats in favour at Vienna. Efforts to endow with national languages peoples unknown to the west (V. Cousin did not believe in 1840 that Slav was spoken in Bohemia!) appeared to them ridiculous intrigues of anti-Magyar Germanism.

THE SLAV RENAISSANCES

The German democrats, enemies of pan-Slavism, were no less disdainful. No one affirmed with more stinging irony than Engels the artificial character of the "Slav renaissances". On the morrow of the revolution he was to evoke the "lucubrations of a few Slav dilettantes of the science of history", forced to speak in German at the Congress of Prague in June 1848, and was to present the great Palacky, defender of the "moribund Czech nation", as a "German savant unable to speak, even at the present time [1852], Czech correctly and without a foreign accent".

*The School of Herder and of "German Science"*

This prejudiced judgement contained an undeniable grain of truth; the reawakening of the Slav nations was the work of a minority of intellectuals nurtured on German culture. From Germany they had caught the contagion of Romanticism ("Slav Romanticism, deserter of German Romanticism", J. Ancel) which engendered the cult of vanished nations and taught the way to prepare for their resurrection. They wanted to hasten the fulfilment of the prediction of Herder, friend of the Slavs: "Fallen nations, nations formerly free . . . you will

emerge from your long slumbers!" On the model of the
Prussian philosopher, they sought the *Volksgeist* of the nations
in folk-tales and folk-ballads, the foundations of renaissance
in language and history. But unlike the Poles, the other Slav
peoples did not possess a literary language. Some of them, like
the Slovaks, had never formed a State. The language had to be
created, the history to be written. Hence the leading role of a
handful of philologists and historians, disciples of Herder and
the German masters, in movements which belonged more to
literature than to politics.

Attendance at German universities had not only inspired the
works, it had also had a profound influence on the behaviour,
of these "awakeners" of the peoples. Dobrovsky (1753–1829),
a Catholic priest brought up in the atmosphere of the *Aufklärung*
(he was a freemason) wrote in Latin and in German though he
was the author of a *Scientific Grammar of Czech*. The Romantic
generation to some extent merited Engels' sarcasm. Šafarik
(1795–1861) who adopted the Czech language in 1837 at first
published his *History of the Slav Language and Literature in All
Dialects* in German. Palacky (1798–1876) reproached Dubrovsky
for not using Czech; but it was in German that he began to
publish from 1836 onward his great *History of Bohemia*, the first
Czech edition of which was published after 1848. The Slovene
Kopitar (1780–1844), who edited in German a *Grammar of the
Slav Language of Carniola, Carinthia and Styria*, personified these
erudite Slavs who, with the encouragement of the authorities,
were preparing peacefully, without realizing it, the dismemberment of the Empire. The Croat patriot Gaj (1809–72) and
Dobrovsky enjoyed the favour of Francis I. Metternich, his
colleague and rival Kollowrat and the Archduke John
subsidized Czech societies and schools. This tolerance was not
without reservations; by cultivating their little gardens, the
Slav élite were to revive ancient quarrels and to escape the
dreaded seductions of the great Slav power of the east.

These calculations underestimated the moral consequences
of a common intellectual foundation. The students of the
Austrian Empire met at Leipzig, and at Göttingen where the
philosopher Schlözer had created a seminary of Slav studies.

In the university of Jena, made illustrious by the science and liberalism of its masters, the mystical and patriotic spirit of the *Burschenschaft*, founded by the historian Luden, had left its mark above all on the Protestants Šafarik, Palacky and Kollar (1794–1852). It was known from the enthusiastic account which he gave to his students in Czech that Kollar had taken part in the Wartburg manifestation. In *The Daughter of Slava* (1824), which described the misery of the Slavs under German occupation, this disciple of Arndt transposed the national aspirations of German Romanticism.

In the universities of the Empire, where there were no politics, young men hitherto separated by administrative barriers, language and religious prejudices discovered affinities while they were studying eagerly the origins of their nation, under the direction of erudite Germans or Slavs. Despite a Kollar or a Kopitar, the university of Vienna suffered from the proximity of the central police apparatus; that of Prague, on the other hand, enjoyed an incomparable prestige. Two men had founded its reputation: the Czech Dobrovsky and the German Mainert (1773–1844), philologist and poet, an enthusiastic pupil of Herder. From 1833 Šafarik sketched out, in the manner of Herder, the image of a Slav nation decked with idyllic virtues which Romanticism attributed to primitive peoples. Freely preached with energy and enthusiasm in the most ancient of German universities (1348), "Slavism" made, in 1848, the capital of Bohemia "the Mecca of the Slavs of the empire" (R. Portal).

By the end of the eighteen-thirties this was already a state of mind. Dispersed intellectuals pursued parallel studies. From Prague, Dobrovsky exercised a benevolent authority over Slav philologists; after him, his disciple Kopitar liberally placed at the disposal of savants the wealth of the imperial library which he administered. He supported attempts to create a Slovene literary language; he was also the guardian angel of the Serb Vuk Stefan Karadžić (1787–1864) whom he encouraged to publish the first Serbian grammar and whom he introduced to Ranke and the brothers Grimm, thanks to whom the work of this self-taught genius was revealed to Europe. Within the

Empire he induced Gaj to recommend to the Croats the adoption of the dialect of Herzegovina which Karadžić had already proposed to the Serbs. The Serbo-Croat language with two alphabets, Cyrillic for the Serbs, Latin for the Croats, was recognized in 1850 as a common literary language. The idea of a linguistic union of the southern Slavs was inspired by the activities of the leaders of the Czech renaissance in their attempts to bring together the northern Slavs. It was praised by Šafarik, the master of Gaj, and by Kollar, his idol. The works of these disciples of German Romanticism gradually became known to a small élite. Germanized nobles founded in Prague the Museum of Bohemia (1818), a Czech library and a study centre which Palacky directed from 1827. In imitation of the Matica of Neusatz (Novi Sad in Hungarian territory), a provincial academy and the centre of diffusion of Serbian folk-songs created by the young pupils of Karadžić (1826), a Czech Matica was created at Prague under the auspices of influential magnates (1831). A lecture centre and publishing house, it printed works in Czech from 1840 onward.

## Croat Realizations and "Illyrian" Tentatives

The Croat aristocracy which saw in German culture a rampart against Magyarization was at first opposed to Gaj's efforts in favour of Serbo-Croat. It was from the Emperor himself that Gaj obtained authorization to print a newspaper; in 1835 at Agram (Zagreb) the *Croat Gazette*, soon to become the *Illyrian Gazette*, printed the works of poets. "Illyrianism", the precursor of "Yugoslavism", underestimated the backwardness of isolated peoples, the force of religious prejudice, the resistance of the Magyars, the suspicions of certain circles at Vienna, the susceptibilities of the Prince of Serbia, Miloš Obrenović and his Orthodox clergy (from 1830 they were independent of the Metropolitan of Karlowicz [Karlovci], the centre, with Novi Sad, of the Serbian intellectual renaissance in the Hungarian Voivodina and defender against the Herzegovina dialect of Church Slavonic), and the hostility of the Turks, suzerains of the Serb peasants of Bosnia. In 1843 the King-Emperor forbade the use of the word "Illyrian". "Croatism" on the other hand progressed freely; it recruited supporters outside the intellectuals and among the Catholic clergy, who favoured nationalism here as elsewhere. The nobility ceased, little by little, to regard it as a simple rehabilitation of folk-lore. The conflict between the Magyar and Croat aristocrats certainly hastened the evolution of men's minds; in 1845 Croat became the language of the Diet of Agram (Zagreb).

Thus by force of circumstances and under the stimulus of a man of action, the Croat national idea emerged from the world of savants to enter the political arena.

### Strengths and Weaknesses of the Czech Renaissance

In the Czech lands, on the contrary, the national awakening continued to express itself in the works of the learned men and the dreams of the poets until the entry on the scene of the journalist Havliček (1821–56). What a contrast between the delay here and its amazing advance in the domains which might have been thought eminently favourable to the awareness of nationality! On the one hand, a mediocre disciple of the great Czech "awakeners", a modest province (little more than a million inhabitants) subject to the Magyar yoke since the long distant disappearance (eleventh century) of the ephemeral Croat State, a rural economy and a society of serfs and siegneurs. On the other, the leaders of the Slav renaissances, highly populated provinces (6½ million inhabitants in 1846) conquered at the same time as the Hungarian lands (1526) and, like them, having preserved for three centuries the semblance of a national State (the Crown of St Wenceslas evoked the Crown of St Stephen and the Diet of Prague resembled far more closely the Diet of Pressburg than its subordinate at Agram), and an industrialization unknown to other Slav lands, Russia excepted, accompanied by the formation of a powerful capitalism and the birth of an important factory proletariat.

These economic and social transformations in no way modified the behaviour of the Czechs, who were moreover in a majority of 3 to 2. The consequences of the disaster of the White

Mountain (1620) seemed irreversible. Decimated on the field of battle, exiled, persecuted, the Czech Protestant nobility only survived by becoming German and Catholic. The Bohemian Diet, guardian of the memory of the State absorbed by the Empire, did not belong, as did the Hungarian Diet, to a national aristocracy. Its members were seigneurs or powerful German bourgeois who were mineowners or steelmasters. The use of German being the condition for social climbing, the middle classes had become denationalized; in the Palacky family the usual language was German. On the eve of 1848 the Czech bourgeois who was conscious of his nationality was an exception. In the heart of the Czech lands the towns and especially the capital were natural centres of Germanization. The Czech ball of 1840 where it was the correct thing to speak Czech and to dance Czech dances was generally considered as a sign of bad taste.

Czech was almost always, except in the German districts bordering Austria, Bavaria, Saxony and Prussia, the language of the country people but it was no longer, since the Catholic reconquest, that of the Hussite or Lutheran heresies. The dissolution of the two elements which were formerly the bases of national feeling explains the moral authority of the Hapsburgs. The peasants relied on the dynasty to complete the emancipating work of Joseph II. Their aspirations were entirely social. The same could not be said of the Czech industrial worker. The development of the factories had caused an exodus from the countryside, the main effect of which was to increase in the towns the proportion of Czechs without national consciousness and workers without class consciousness. In 1848 the majority of the Prague proletariat was Czech. Nonetheless it was the Germans who, as in Liberec, were to become involved in the social struggle and were to express in their own language the workers' demands of the time. In the 1844 strike, "the first great manifestation of the class struggle in Central Europe", the German cotton-printers took over the control of a movement which four years later was to arouse "a great fear" among the bourgeois. In the factories of Mulhouse and the workshops of Paris or Lyons a few members of this professional élite had become imbued with the embryonic communism of the secret societies. Faced with technical advances they experienced the classic reactions of the former craftsmen; they destroyed the power-looms and demanded control of the hiring, that is to say a halt to the influx of labourers from the country-side. This egoistic intervention was not the result of an anti-Czech feeling but a simple defensive measure by qualified workers against an unorganized labour force of exceptional docility.

The submissive spirit of all classes of Czech society was the dominant feature of a tragic history which is still incomplete today. It contrasts with the warlike mystique of the Polish "pilgrims". Whether it was or was not an exact appreciation of realities, it throws light on the indifference, even the sympathies, of the Germans of Austria towards the Czech intellectual renaissance and Palacky's attitude, at first sight disconcerting, at the close of the eighteen-forties. The behaviour of the historian is inseparable from ambiguous nationalist concepts directly derived from the German universities. Sometimes Palacky starts from linguistic considerations to paint, not without exaggeration, the centuries-old struggle of the German and Czech peoples; sometimes he refers to history to defend the rights of a Bohemia which if not independent was at least autonomous within the framework of the Empire. In the former instance, he exalts the mission of the Czech people; in the latter, he provides weapons for the classes least attached to the national ideal. At the close of a long life, having witnessed so many uprisings fomented in the name of a principle (the right of the self-determination of peoples) unknown to the Czechs he gave up with proud resignation his hopes of national resurrection: "Every time we have been victorious it was more by the supremacy of the spirit than by physical force and every time we have been vanquished it was by lack of intellectual activity, of moral courage and of audacity." While awaiting the moral awakening of compatriots whom he judged in-constant, feeble and unenterprising, this alliance with the aristocracy does not have the scandalous character later attributed to it. Did not the nobility invoke against Viennese centralism the "rights" of this historic nation which Palacky stressed in his *History of Bohemia?* Was not Rieger (1818–1903), Palacky's son-in-law and reputedly a man of action, in his *Ancient Czechs* a champion of the "rights of the State", that is to say an upholder of a reconstitution of the Kingdom of St Wenceslas? The Diet, which failed to recognize the existence of the Czech plebeians of the countryside and the towns, based its pretensions to transform itself into a real legislative assembly on the "fundamental contract" so dear to "the awakener of Czech national consciousness" (J. Ancel). Such was the meaning of the petition of 1845. The same year the Count of Thun demanded vainly of the nobility respect for the Czech language and Czech culture.

1845 also marks, with the foundation of the *Prague Gazette* and the *Slovak Gazette*, the beginnings both of the Czech democratic movement and of Slovak linguistic autonomy. The activity of the *Prague Gazette* and of its prime mover, the ardent Havlíček, took place in a liberal and nationalist atmosphere of Western inspiration which, since the advent of Ferdinand I, was favoured by a relaxation of police control. Leipzig, university centre and metropolitan of the publishing and book trade, poured out over neighbouring Bohemia, despite the censorship, brochures and translations fit to seduce young spirits surfeited by chilly demonstrations of "historical science". The *Words of a Believer, the Book of the People* by Lamennais, the *People* by Michelet, did not dissociate dream from action. An admirer of Lamennais, Havlíček denounced the extraordinary lack of proportion between the grandiose visions of Czech intellectual pan-Slavism and national exaltation of the sufferings of Huss, and the disaster of the White Mountain and the *de facto* collaboration with the Germanic Catholic nobility. Because it would be better to act for the people than merely "to talk about it", Havlíček prepared for the advent of a democratic State by undertaking the political and national education of a numbed people. Hindered by the censorship from publishing a programme necessarily abstract, the wily journalist gave much space to Irish affairs; the courage of a small nation resisting the oppression of a powerful State had in the eyes of the readers of the *Prague Gazette* the value of an example. The students and a few bourgeois of Prague were won over. They bore witness to their newly aroused democratic and patriotic feelings in the "flash in the pan" of 1848.

## The Beginnings of Slovak Particularism

In Slovakia Havliček's propaganda clashed with the first stirrings of linguistic particularism. Unlike the champions of "historic rights", Havliček looked forward, long before President Masaryk (1850–1937), to the attachment to Bohemia, Moravia and Silesia of a Slovakia freed from the Magyar yoke. This former seminarist, who rejected "the black robe which the Roman assassins of Jan Huss used to wear", had for the language of the Slovak mountaineers, for the most part Catholics, the same disdain as the great intellectuals whom he had reproached for their lack of realism! Nourished on anti-Catholic prejudices, the Slovaks Kollar and Šafarik (the former a pastor, the latter the son of a pastor) and the Moravian Palacky from the Slovak borders identified the Slovak people with the Lutheran minority which had escaped the persecutions. The pre-eminence of the language of Hussism over the Slovak dialects was for them self-evident. Already contested by the abbé-philologist Bernolak (1762–1813), it was ardently disputed by the Catholic clergy who saw in Czech the language of Germanic heretic writers. Against Czech assimilation, against the cultural influence of active German centres and above all against Magyarization, spontaneous or forced (in 1847 Magyar was to replace Latin as the language of administration), Stur (1815–56), a Protestant Romantic moulded in the German universities, took the lead in a movement which aimed at uniting all Slovaks, regardless of confession. A shy and touchy patriot, Stur chose as a literary language the dialect of central Slovakia, the most unlike Czech, which was considered to have been contaminated by German! This programme was made known in the *Slovak Gazette* and aroused a blossoming of poetry inspired by popular tradition. This linguistic schism, born in a region which had never formed a State, separated for the time being the élite of two peoples closely confounded in the works of the Czech "awakeners". This did not prevent Stur from moving closer to the Czechs in 1848 or from preaching a "Czechoslovak" state in 1850. The development of education was to accentuate misunderstandings between neighbouring peoples which were to survive the euphoria of 1918.

### TRANSYLVANIA, CRADLE OF THE RUMANIAN RENAISSANCE IN THE OTTOMAN PRINCIPALITIES

The role of the Rumanians of Transylvania in the formation of Rumania is similar to that of the Serbs of the Voivodina, or the Croats, in the creation of Yugoslavia; the intellectual centre of the nation was in the Austrian Empire, its material base in a State resulting from the disintegration of the Ottoman Empire. The union of Moldavia and Valachia under a hereditary prince (1859) was more delayed than Serbian autonomy (1829). For the Tsar, who was doing his best to denationalize the Rumanians of Bessarabia annexed in 1812, intended to substitute his protectorate over Moldavia and Valachia for the declining suzerainty of the Sultan. By breaking down Russian opposition, Napoleon III responded to the expectations of the intellectuals who in 1848 pushed their admiration for France so far as to want to imitate her revolutionary example while their compatriots in Transylvania were rising against Magyar imperialism.

Transylvania was not to become a part of Rumania until 1918. It was, however, in this province, one of the most backward in the Austrian Empire, that the idea of uniting the peoples of Latin speech separated by the imposing barrier of the Carpathians was born. Conquered by the Hapsburgs in 1699, it was a dependency of the Crown of St Stephen. The Rumanians (about two million) were serfs. Holders of insignificant properties (on average about three hectares), their subjection was not only social but economic; they formed for the great Hungarian nobles (less than 10,000) a labour pool to be exploited at will. They were aliens in their own country. When the Diet, which had not been convoked since 1809, once more met in 1834 at Kolozsvar (Cluj) it was composed of the representatives of the three "nations": Magyars, Saxons (colonists of German stock) and Szeklers (free peasants of Magyar or Magyarized origin). The debates brought into opposition two minority aristocracies; the Germans wanted Transylvania to be dependent on Vienna, the Magyars, more numerous, wanted its incorporation into the kingdom of Hungary.

By this time the Rumanian national movement was a reality. The "awakeners" of the nation were, as in Bohemia, grammarians and historians. These intellectuals were not cut off from the illiterate and pious peasants. The Rumanian spirit was developed "in the shadow of the churches and above all of the Uniate church" (J. Ancel). A section of the Orthodox had in 1700 broken with a Church whose leader lived next to the Sultan, and had adhered to the religion of the Emperor. Thus isolated, the Orthodox Church dozed. Once in touch with Catholicism, the Uniate clergy revived intellectually and became conscious of their national mission. Priests trained at Rome discovered Latin antiquity there and their ancestors, the Dacians. Blaj, the seat of a bishop since 1768, became with its seminary the centre of Romanism and Rumanianism, the cradle of the Transylvanian school. Three men from this clerical milieu personified the spiritual renaissance: Klein (1745–1806), author of the first "Daco-Rumanian" grammar, Sincai (1745–1816), who wrote a *Chronicle of the Rumanians*, and finally, Maior (1755–1821), author of a *History of Rumanian origins in Dacia*. The Dacian myth was to be, together with the exaltation of the national language written no longer in Cyrillic but in Latin characters, the essential element of the Rumanian movement. The Uniate clergy was the propagator of these themes among the peasants of Transylvania.

Dependencies of Turkey placed under a Russian protectorate regulated by the treaty of Adrianople (1829), the principalities of Moldavia and Valachia (3,300,000 inhabitants in 1852) were peopled by wretched peasants and great landlords living in the utmost luxury, the boyars, who had often adopted Greek speech and customs. The Orthodox clergy, the governors (*hospodars*) and their hangers-on were agents of the Hellenization of the upper classes. The prelates and the superiors of the monasteries, "dedicated to the Holy Places", were Constantinople Greeks. The same was true until 1822 of the *hospodars* who were nominated by the sultan. In 1821 Ypsilanti, son of a *hospodar* and aide-de-camp of the Tsar, thought himself able to prepare an insurrection in Greece by stirring up the Hellenized boyars of Valachia! Against this movement a boyar, Vladimirescu, appealed vainly to the peasants, to whom the clergy preached resignation and not love of country. His proclamations ("What can Dacians and Hellenes have in common?") bore witness to the penetration of the ideas from the farther side of the Carpathians. In the course of the eighteen-twenties the nobility of the principalities had begun to renew their links with the past. At the invitation of the boyars a professor of Hermannstadt (Sibiu), G. Lazar (1779–1823), founded in 1816 a Rumanian school in Bucharest. Recourse to Transylvanian professors became the mode and put the seal on the rupture of the boyars with Hellenic culture.

In an endeavour to extend their influence, Turkey and Russia both took measures which reinforced the national feeling of the upper classes. Since the revolt of Ypsilanti the Greeks had lost the confidence of Constantinople; the sultans henceforward chose their *hospodars* from the local nobility. After the Russo-Turkish wars General Kisselef commanding the Russian occupation forces endowed Moldavia and Valachia with identical constitutions (1831–2). Two legislative divans (assemblies) made up of boyars, prelates and a few representatives of the towns (no one even dreamed of including delegates from the peasantry) elected the princes for life. Thus considerations of external policy led autocratic Russia to create on its frontiers two embryonic constitutional States, aristocratic certainly, but Rumanian. Contrary to the hopes of St Petersburg the principalities sought to unite and, what was worse, were inspired by ideologies that were abhorrent to Tsarism.

By the beginning of the eighteen-thirties national sentiment was no longer a Transylvanian import. A pupil of Lazar, the

Valach Eliade known as Radulescu (1802–70), grammarian and journalist, founded the first Rumanian paper, the *Rumanian Courier*. The Moldavian Asachi (1788–1869) published the *Rumanian Bee* in Jassy. This press diffused the works of authors influenced by the West. In Transylvania Latinity was expressed, under the stimulus of the Uniate church, with Rumanian and Catholic fervour. In Moldavia and Valachia it took the form of a delirious enthusiasm for French literature; Boileau, Voltaire, Bernadin de Saint-Pierre, Lamartine, Hugo, were either translated or imitated with equal enthusiasm. Mediocre production, which bore witness to a feverish will to provide as soon as possible a national literature, drove young nobles, the sons of bourgeois or recently enriched peasants to pursue their studies in the new Athens. At Paris the Moldo-Valachians learnt that nationality and democracy were inseparable.

By the end of the eighteen-forties the feeling of a Rumanian community had progressed in Austria and the Danubian lands. In Transylvania the national idea was nourished by resistance to Magyarization which weighed equally on the Rumanians and the Slavs. Barnut (1808–64), the son of a serf and a former seminarist of Blaj, was not content to celebrate Trajan. He defended the rights of the Rumanian language and demanded recognition of the "fourth nation". Even the Orthodox Church emerged from its torpor. With the elevation of Saguna to the episcopate (1847) it was, like its Uniate rival, directed by a patriot. In Moldavia and Valachia propaganda in favour of the union of the principalities was a favourite theme. Professor of history at Jassy, Kogälniceanu (1817–91), the son of a boyar, demanded the reunion of all Rumanians and thus posed the question of a "greater Rumania" (1843). The Russian consul suspended his courses.

### The Pan-Slav Myth

The principalities were only a trump in a game of which the stake was access to the open sea. Nicholas I, enemy of all revolutionary agitation, could not, moreover, stand for a Latin

people permeable by the subversive doctrines of the West. A
number of contemporaries, especially Germans, suspected him
of wanting to annex all the Slav peoples to his empire. The
vague and sentimental Slavism of a Kollar or a Šafarik left
the Tsar indifferent; even more, he joined in the concert urging
the Emperor to forbid "Illyrian" propaganda! Political
pan-Slavism would only cease to be a spectre in the reign of
his son, Alexander II (1855–81).

### The Loyalism of the Nationalities

The awakening of Slav and Rumanian national feeling was
one of the most important facts of the late eighteen-forties.
Seen from afar, it questioned the labours of many centuries.
Links had been forged between the Austrian provinces and
the lands of the Crowns of St Stephen, between the Hapsburg
Empire and the Ottoman Empire. In fact, many nationalist
movements were merely the dreams of intellectuals, but the
mediating activities of the clergy (in Croatia and in Transylvania) among the rural masses could not be gainsaid. Without
doubt the aspirations of serfs were firstly and everywhere
social, but they could not avoid becoming tinged by nationalist
passions when confronted by seigneurs of another linguistic
group.

The harmony which reigned among the theoreticians of the
nationalities (the Slovak linguistic schism was only at its
beginnings) was reinforced by an almost universal hatred of
the Magyars (with the exception of the Polish nobility of
Galicia whose anti-Germanic feeling drove them to a sympathy
with the Hungarian aristocrats). The desire to escape from
their oppression never led to the thought of seceding from the
Empire.

If the Magyars, the most ardent in demanding wider competence for their machinery for crushing the linguistic minorities,
pretended that they were also faithful and loyal subjects of
the Hapsburg "King of Hungary", the Imperial Government was nonetheless sensitive to the tone of the debates in
the Diet and to the verbal violence of Kossuth. In 1846

Metternich affirmed that Hungary was "in the antechamber of revolution".

The liberal, national, anti-German revolution was to break out outside the Empire, in that Italy which had been the reserved domain of Austria ever since the Hapsburgs had added to their crowns that of Lombardy-Venetia.

# [ Chapter Seven ]

# Italy: from a Geographical Expression to the Birth of National Consciousness

By ITS PRESENCE in the peninsula and its influence on Germanic affairs Austria established links between the history of Italy and that of Germany. The revolutionary movements of 1831 which concentrated the Austrian armies and Austrian diplomacy on Italy favoured the German liberal agitation; their setbacks caused the return of reaction in the States of the Confederation. The Italian revolutions and the war with Sardinia, up to the summer of 1848, helped to paralyse the restoration in the Empire and the action against the movement for unification in Germany. The defeat of Austria at Sadowa (1866) led eventually to her expulsion from Germany and from Italy. Other parallels are classic; a high degree of civilization, liberal and national aspirations, a standard-bearer of the ideal of unity (Prussia, Sardinia), a romantic sovereign (Frederick William IV, Charles Albert) and a realist successor (William I, Victor Emmanuel II) well served by a Machiavellian statesman (Bismarck, Cavour). . . . But over and above these apparent similarities what political, moral, economic and social contrasts!

## THE RESTORATION OF THE ANCIEN RÉGIME AND ITS CONSEQUENCES

Italy, like Germany, had under French pressure passed through profound social and political transformations. The first were durable, the second ephemeral. The clergy finally lost their tithes, the nobility their feudal dues. In restoring these powers the States meeting at Vienna appeared to act in accord with an anti-French public opinion.

### The Triumph of Absolutism and Particularism under Austrian Patronage

The term "restoration" showed its full significance in Italy. Whereas in Germany the work of territorial concentration carried out by Napoleon survived, all the former Italian States, except Genoa and Venice, were re-established.

On both sides of the Straits of Messina, the kingdom of the Two Sicilies, the most extensive and the most populous of the Italian States (7,500,000 inhabitants) presented a similar backcloth: huge seigniorial and ecclesiastical properties, a miserable peasantry, brigandage, corrupt officials, and the arbitrary rule of a despotic Bourbon (Ferdinand II, 1830–59). But turbulent Sicily dreamed of an autonomy which the return of the parliamentary constitution of 1812, a British gift ill-adapted to the Mediterranean climate, would guarantee.

The Papal States (2,500,000 inhabitants) formed, on the contrary, a disparate conglomeration: Rome was economically dependent on the Papal Court, the peasants of Latium and Umbria indolently cultivated the vast estates of a few potentates. In the Marches (Ancona) and above all in the Legations (Bologna with its liberal university, Ferrara, Ravenna) liberal petty bourgeois and irreverent artisans execrated the dignitaries of the Church (the Legations were administered, hence their name, by cardinal-legates, the other provinces by bishops) who in the name of the Pope exercised a discretionary authority, relying upon a vigilant police. On the first occasion, the revolutionary spark flashed out and set ablaze the little States of central Italy, which had been entrusted, after various Viennese intrigues, to princes related to the Hapsburgs. The Grand duchy of Tuscany (1,500,000 inhabitants) increased in 1829 by the principality of Massa-Carrara was regarded, under the paternalistic government of Leopold II (1824–59), as a liberal oasis where the masters of the university of Pisa and the writers of Florence were not subjected to any vexatious control. The duchy of Parma, Piacenza and Guastalla had been granted for life to the ex-Empress Marie-Louise. The Austrian General Neipperg, her favourite and later her husband, did his best to rule as an enlightened despot over essentially rural populations. The duchy of Modena, also agricultural, cowered under the rod of iron of Francis IV d'Este (1814–46).

The north of the peninsula was shared between the two powers who were called upon in 1848–9 to confront one another in unequal contest. Lombardy-Venetia (4,500,000 inhabitants) was the result of the annexation of the continental possessions of Venice to the Austrian duchies of Milan and Mantua. An archduke, acting as viceroy, kept himself busy squeezing these rich provinces for the benefit of the imperial treasury. Thanks to administrative procedures and efficient police work, the discontented inhabitants were kept quiet. If the peasants were inert, the commercial and industrial bourgeois resented, above all in times of economic difficulties, the weight of fiscal exactions; the many nobles reproached Austria for not having re-established the feudal dues and for reserving all senior posts for the Tedeschi. The Austrian presence was regarded more and more as a German occupation.

Compared with Lombardy-Venetia, flanked by a powerful empire (by Trentino, Trieste, Istria and the Italian part of Dalmatia), the Kingdom of Sardinia, with its 4,500,000 inhabitants, seemed insignificant. It was not a Prussia, scarcely a Bavaria. As well as its former possessions, Sardinia and Piedmont (Savoy and Nice had been restored to France), it had acquired the former republic of Genoa. Only the active and turbulent bourgeoisie of the great port caused the monarchy, paternalist under Charles Félix (1821–31) and for a long time absolutist under Charles Albert (1831–49), a few headaches. The king relied on the submission of the peasantry, the docility of the clergy and the loyalty of the nobility and the army.

Thus, in an Italy abandoned to the influence of Austria, only insignificant nuances divided the political régimes.

Individual liberties depended on the caprices of princes whose will was uncontrolled. There were no elected assemblies. By contrast to the German liberalism of the south, Italian liberalism was deprived of the parliamentary rostrum, the means of development and of propaganda. Forced to exist in secret, the movement appeared only to follow the paths of violence. As a consequence of long centuries of foreign domination and political dismemberment the vision of universal interest was blurred among men conscious of belonging to the same civilization, of speaking the same language and of professing the same religion. Participation in the "wars of liberation" was half-hearted; timid demands were never raised above the provincial, or municipal level. The caricature of united institutions that national and liberal Germany rejected with indignation would have been immense progress for Italy. The opposition of the Papacy and of the Sardinian monarchy, later to become symbols of the idea of unity, prevented Metternich, who wanted to create an Italian confederation, from being considered by history as the immediate predecessor of Cavour! Italy had again become, in the famous expression of the chancellor: "A group of independent States linked only by a common geographical expression."

### Backward and Divided Economies

The incoherence and lack of co-ordination of the Italian political scene was reinforced by backward and divided economies and by separated and diversified societies. Economic life, which was subjected to slow transformations in the eighteen-thirties, could be summed up as a poverty-stricken agriculture. Fiscal considerations superimposed customs barriers on political frontiers. In Lombardy-Venetia protectionism took the form of a colonial exploitation which tended, as in Hungary, to compensate for the loss of the markets of the *Zollverein*. The Two Sicilies and the Papal Estates were the bastions of reaction and protectionism. The blind Piedmontese protectionism was to last till the end of the eighteen-forties. Tuscany alone was a tiny free trade zone in the heart of Italy.

*The Social Power of the Nobility and Clergy. Insignificance of the Middle Classes*

The crushing majority of the population continued to live in its restricted universe. The peasants who formed the mass of it suffered in a state of "under-development" of the Iberian type. Despite a high birth-rate, and an insignificant emigration (departures for the New World began after 1870), Italy had, within its 1914 boundaries, twenty-five million inhabitants in 1850 as against eighteen and a half million in 1800, that is to say an increase of 35 per cent, one of the lowest in Europe, between those of Portugal (25) and Spain (43). The innovations introduced at the beginning of the thirties were limited to the Po valley (Piedmont, Lombardy) and to a few areas in the centre. Most of the landowners, hidebound and poor, took no part in them. Whereas under a cloudless sky the fate of those who, by dint of saving, had added to the exploitation of their meagre plots that of lands leased from the nobility and the city bourgeoisie would have been acceptable, an inconceivable misery reigned in the States of the Church and in the Two Sicilies. In those roadless districts, an over-abundant and ignorant proletariat inefficiently cultivated the latifundia of the great seigneurs. Lacking more honourable activities, smuggling and brigandage were, in southern Italy, complementary resources. The Calabrian brigand was not a character of fiction.

The ranks of the artisans were unable to absorb the overspill of the countryside. The number of home-workers and those who worked in tiny workshops rose, it seems, to a quarter of the peasant population. Some artisans worked for a time in France and in England, but they were less liable to become imbued with alien ideologies than the Germans, as Mazzini noted bitterly. The industrial advance in the north, in Tuscany and even in Naples between 1830 and 1840 should not lead us astray. The first railways, opened in 1839 and 1840 from Naples to Portici, from Milan to Monza, were for the service of the Courts. The Piedmontese network of economic interest was not laid down until 1845; in 1859 Italy had less than two thousand kilometres of track to exploit. There were few factories, save for cotton (Novara, Monza, Florence, Naples) and metallurgy (Turin, Livorno, Naples). On the whole, they produced poor results. Per inhabitant Italy consumed three times as little cotton (0·1 kg.) and produced twice as little cast iron (2 kg.) as Spain. The new bourgeoisie and the new proletariat scarcely counted.

Faithful to the Popes who relied on Austria to oppress their subjects and to the princes who abandoned to them the responsibility of censorship, the omnipresent clergy (about 150,000 priests) tried to protect the masses from liberal and national influences. Hence the religious indifference and the anti-clericalism of most of the first champions of liberty and unity; thence also their long series of setbacks. No enterprise could succeed without the co-operation of the clergy.

Similarly the nobility was not to be ignored. The feudal and warrior class, rough and uncultured, living on its lands in the manner of the Junkers and the Hungarian petty nobility, was only to be met with in Piedmont. The great landowners of the Papal States, of Calabria and of Sicily lived in their palaces, close to the Court and its sinecures. On the whole, the nobles led a difficult town life, since the French domination had abolished their seigniorial privileges, consequently, they did everything possible to preserve their monopoly of high rank and exalted offices. In Germany the bourgeois who had made his way dreamed of being granted the privilege of adding the particle to his name; in Italy the winning of a title was the measure of social advancement. The sovereigns had responded generously to the appeals of ambition and vanity; counts, marquises, dukes and princes abounded. The nobility of recent date was not the least of those eager to confine the middle classes to the exercise of the liberal professions.

On the other hand, the sons of the nobility and of the urban bourgeoisie met in the universities, and paid no heed to social barriers. Certainly the Italian universities had not played the exclusive role of the German universities in the formation of national feeling, and the mission of Italy had not been preached by professors of international reputation. Nonetheless, as in

Germany and for the same reasons, the twenty-four universities (an enormous number!) had become, in the epoch of particularism and reaction, the centres of the national ideal and of relatively free thinking. Bologna was the centre of the insurrection of 1831; in 1848 masters and students of the universities of Pavia, Genoa and Pisa rose without distinguishing between origins against the Austrian domination.

FROM THE LIBERALISM OF THE CARBONARI TO THE UNIFYING DEMOCRACY OF YOUNG ITALY. THE MYSTIQUE OF THE CONSPIRACY

The mystique of the bold political coup hatched by a small number of conspirators is romantic and, by tradition, Mediterranean. The continuity is evident between the conspiracies of the Carbonari and several of the Italian exploits of 1848. Temperaments quick to act without thinking became discouraged when they discovered the inertia of the masses, the regional resistance and the strength of Austria. In 1820–1 both northern Italy and southern Italy separately tried to put an end to the Spanish domination. Officer members of the Carbonari rose at the example of their Iberian colleagues. General Pepe (1783–1855) who was to defend insurgent Venice in 1848–9 imposed in July 1820 the Spanish constitution of 1812 on the King of the Two Sicilies. This enterprise, the manifestation of a particularist liberalism, provoked violent separatist unrest in Sicily. The bourgeois of the eastern coast demanded autonomy. The nobility, supported by the clergy and the populace, demanded independence together with the enforcement of the Sicilian constitution of 1812. While the liberals of Naples and the insurgents of Palermo argued, Austria, the mandatory of the Holy Alliance, sent an army which crushed Pepe and occupied Naples on 24 March 1821. A month later order was restored in the north. Hatred of the Tedeschi animated not only the Piedmontese but also all educated youth. It sent its agents to prepare a national uprising in concert with the Carbonari of Milan and the Papal States. For long months the conspirators beat about the bush and decided to act only when the Austrian troops had made a move against the Neapolitan revolution. Their leader, Count Santarosa (1783–1825), a romantic champion of oppressed nationalities (he was to die for the Greek cause) thought, somewhat lightly, that he had won over Charles Albert, Prince of Carignano. The insurrection broke out at Alessandria on 10 March; a provisional Government proclaimed the King of Piedmont as King of Italy and tried to impose on him also the Spanish constitution of 1812! The very reactionary Victor Emanuel I abdicated in favour of his brother Charles Félix, at that time absent from the country. Charles Albert had not participated in the *pronunciamento* but, as revolutionary regent, conceded the liberal constitution which Charles Félix had rejected! That reputation for inconstancy and double-dealing which was to weigh heavily during the dramas of 1848–9 on the policies of the "Italian Hamlet" dated from March 1821. On 8 April the Austrians routed the discouraged troops of Santarosa at Novara. Neither the national idea nor the liberal idea had roused the people of the north from their passivity. In Sicily, had the lower classes appeared on the scene, they would have been filled with hatred of the Neapolitan régime, whatever it might have been. Subjected more drastically than ever to the tutelage of Austria which for several years occupied Naples, Ancona and Ferrara, Italy lapsed into its torpor. The revolutionaries sought refuge in Geneva, Paris and London.

After July, Paris openly became the centre of agitation with the formation of the Committee of Italian Emancipation. The insurrection in Russian Poland, which kept the attention of Austria fixed on Galicia, stimulated its enthusiasm. By drawing into an ambush the ingenuous liberal leaders (3 February) the Duke of Modena provoked the explosion. The revolution overthrew him, drove Marie-Louise out of Parma, and triumphed in a few days in most of the Papal cities. It did not extend to central Italy where, moreover, the peasants remained indifferent or hostile to movements led by lawyers, merchants or artisans, often anticlerical. The adherence of the petty bourgeoisie to political life, by comparison with the revolts of 1820–1, was something new. The revolutionaries of Modena,

Parma, Bologna, knew nothing of one another. At Bologna, the friends of Buonarotti, especially the Baron Zucchi (1776–1864), formed a government which proclaimed the downfall of Papal power and summoned an Assembly of the Free Provinces of Italy; on 23 February the State (so-called!) of the United Provinces of Central Italy was constituted. This pompous phraseology masked an incurable particularism. The action of the Bolognesi forestalled a similar attempt on Rome; even more, under pretext of having their neutrality respected, they disarmed the liberals of Parma and Modena in flight from the Austrians! Zucchi, vanquished, was sentenced to twenty years' imprisonment (the 1848 revolution was to free him). Austria restored Papal power.

But thenceforward there was no longer a free-for-all in Italy. In the eyes of a section of the French parliamentary Left, of the members of the secret societies, and of the Bonapartists (the future Napoleon III and his brother Charles Napoleon had taken part in the move against Rome) Italian affairs had become, almost as much as Polish, French affairs. The pacific Louis Philippe was forced to take note of the interventionist tendencies of the Parisian populace. Casimir Périer demanded that Austria evacuate the Papal States. At the beginning of 1832 the Austrians reoccupied Bologna and Ravenna at the request of the Pope, now at his wits' end. But the French occupied, on their own authority, Ancona which they were only to leave on the departure of the Austrians in 1838. Under the pressure of French opinion international policy was monopolized by the Italian question.

The liberals who had hoped for French aid regarded the intervention of 1832 as derisory. The mistrust which had become lulled after the downfall of Napoleon awoke once more. The repeated setbacks of Carbonarism, incapable of stirring up the masses, despite recent popular support, discredited it. With his Young Italy Mazzini (1805–72) did his utmost to win over the anti-Carbonari and anti-French currents; the moral and spiritual education of the people was the condition of a liberation which would owe nothing to France. Its ideal was the nation. He did not picture it, in the German manner, as a living organism driven by a mysterious force. Language was only one element of a conscious sentiment: "The country is above all the consciousness of the country." This conception was very close to that of the French democrats. Like them, and contrary to the views of most of the Italian patriots, Mazzini was the champion of a united, democratic and social republic. This grandiose programme presupposed the abolition of the princely sovereignties, of the temporal power of the Pope to which very many Catholics both within Italy and outside it were attached, and the expulsion of the Austrians. With the help of God, a God alien to Christianity, and of humanity the people would accomplish its national and international mission. This Messianism, hostile to French Messianism, dreamed of an Italian revolution arising out of European movements fomented simultaneously by the Italians. If the foundation of Young Europe was the expression of an original thought, the means employed recalled the past. Mazzini had condemned the improvisation of the Carbonari; however, from 1833 to 1845 countless conspiracies were exposed and insurrections, always badly prepared, continually broke out. The participation of the Poles in the expedition against Savoy gave, for a time, a European tinge to mad enterprises which were purely Italian. In 1844 two Venetian nobles, officers of the Austrian fleet, the brothers Bandiera, deserted and landed in Calabria with a handful of fellow-conspirators; taken in ambush, they were shot together with seven of their companions. The sacrifice of these young men of high rank, imbued with the purest patriotic motives, had an enormous moral repercussion. In practice, it meant the death-blow to a movement of which the leader organized operations which had no hope of success, from London, without ever placing himself at their head.

### THE RISORGIMENTO: WRITERS AT THE SERVICE OF THE NATIONAL IDEA: ALBERTISM OR NEO-GUELPHISM?

Anti-Carbonari and anti-Mazzini, the Risorgimento (Resurrection), which owed its name to Cavour's paper, was also heir to Romanticism. Contrary to French Romanticism, Italian

Romanticism had always been liberal and national. After 1830 literature was almost identified with politics. The great poets Manzoni (1785–1873), a prudent patriot (his ode *March 1821* to the Piedmontese revolution was not to be published until 1848!), and Leopardi (1798–1837), very critical of the liberal politicians, pledged themselves feebly. Writers of the second order exalted with success country and liberty: Niccolini (1782–1861), professor at Florence, who composed tragedies with evocative titles (*Arnold of Brescia*), Guerazzi (1804–73) of Livorno, author of historical novels (*The Siege of Florence of 1530*) without the qualities of Manzoni's *The Betrothed* but which inflamed the young and made him in 1848 a member of the Tuscan Government. At the German School (Niebuhr represented Prussia at the Holy See) philology and history were placed at the service of the country.

The feeling of an economic solidarity seemed to have supported the idea of union somewhat indifferently. Without a doubt a section of the bourgeoisie, then in formation in Piedmont, in Lombardy and in Tuscany, would have welcomed the destruction of customs barriers. But "a Zollverein is not a country" (Renan). Doubtless the congresses, in imitation of those of Germany, held each year from 1839 onward in a different town, accustomed several hundred delegates to envisage economic problems in a national setting. But they had no effect on any political programme.

The Risorgimento was the work of writers, aware of the uselessness of conspiracies animated by hatred of Catholicism and its head. At the time when Gregory XVI (1831–46), with the help of Swiss mercenaries and foreign volunteers, fought his intractable subjects, the idea of a Church become liberal was a bold one, even though familiar to some Catholics: those of Ireland, of Belgium and the supporters of Lamennais. Let us, however, beware of imagining external influences, since Italian historiography asserts the absolute Italianism of the Risorgimento! It was in France, however, that in 1836 Tommaseo (1802–74) wished (*New Hopes for Italy*) for a reformist Pope federating the Italian States. In 1834 the thesis was taken up again with incomparable brilliance in a book

published at Brussels by the Abbé Gioberti (1801–52) with
the deliberately provocative title of *The Moral and Civic Primacy
of the Italians*. There are to be found in this Piedmont theologian,
who was for a time the companion of Mazzini, the traits of the
founder of Young Italy, in particular the exaltation of a people
which had done everything in the world which was worth
while (was not Napoleon an Italian?). Gallophobia was
nourished by the memory of the "scoundrels" who had seized
the Pope and occupied Rome. Nonetheless, the nationalism of
Gioberti, less exigent than that of Mazzini, appealed not to the
spirit of sacrifice but to a sudden realization of the grandeur of
Italy. Finally, it was in accord with the religious traditions of
the nation and the liberal tendencies which began, under the
influence of the philosopher Abbé Rosmini (1797–1855), to
win over a section of the clergy. Save for the Jesuits and a handful of democrats who were enemies of the temporal power, only
a few far-seeing spirits saw the weaknesses of a programme
whose realization depended on three gambles: liberalization
of an ultra-reactionary régime, the end of princely particularism
and above all the passivity of Austria. The following year Count
Balbo (1789–1853), a Piedmontese for long a refugee in France,
published in Paris the strongest refutation of neo-Guelphism.
In his *Hopes for Italy*, a title inspired by the *Hopes* of Santarosa,
who had been his leader, Balbo denounced the egotism of anti-
French rodomontades (Gioberti, like Mazzini, annexed
Corsica!) and the pretension of building Italy while ignoring
Austria. The irremediable weakness of the Italians imposed a
recourse to patient diplomacy which would eliminate an Austria
expanding in the Balkans from Lombardy-Venetia. The house
of Savoy would head the confederation envisaged by Gioberti.
In 1845 Gioberti seems to have been influenced by Balbo's
criticism; in his *Prolegomeni del Primato* he vigorously attacked the
Jesuits and omitted to assign any directive role to the Papacy.

   On the occasion of a last attempt at an insurrection of
Mazzinian origin at Rimini (1845) there appeared in 1846 a
violent pamphlet (*About Recent Events in Romagna*) against the
internal administration of the Holy See and its complacent
attitude towards Austria. This slim paper by d'Azeglio (1798–

1866), a Piedmontese noble, son-in-law of Manzoni and friend
of Balbo, helped at least as much as the more elaborate work of
Balbo himself, to increase the number of those who, rejecting
the mystique of conspiracies, counted on the King of Sardinia
to found the liberty of Italy. It might be said that it created a
new party, the Albertist party.

At least up until 1843 nothing seemed to forecast that Charles
Albert would embody the national and liberal idea. The
patriots recalled the recantations of the Prince of Carignano in
1821. Charles Albert rejected, as did Frederick William IV,
the very principle of a conceded constitution. After the troubles
in central Italy and the threat of intervention by the July
Monarchy, his reactionary policy and his anti-French feelings
brought him closer to Austria, with which he secretly concluded
an alliance.

However, the equivocal regent of 1821 had not forgotten the
intrigues of Metternich to keep him from the throne; for a long
time his resentment stemmed from "the king's secret". It began
to betray itself in actions influenced by the campaigns undertaken by the Piedmontese in favour of a monarch who was
supposed to be a liberal. It is admitted today that the Sardinian
reforms were more timid than those introduced at the same
period in Tuscany, or even in the Two Sicilies. Charles Albert
was acting on the principle of enlightened despotism, abolition
in the island of Sardinia of the last traces of the seigniorial
régime, promulgation of codes by France. . . . A few cultured
nobles praised this prudent reformism and cited as an example
the king who, on their appeal, had encouraged agriculture,
industry and the construction of a railway network and had
toned down protectionism. In fact, from 1843 the defence of
Piedmontese economic interests was both the origin of incessant
conflicts with Austria and the occasion for showing the
attachment of the House of Savoy to the cause of Italian
independence. To his counsellors, who dreaded the consequences of a tariff war, Charles Albert replied proudly:
"If Piedmont loses Austria, it will gain Italy!"

In a tense atmosphere the conservative and particularist
Piedmontese nobles found in the books of their contemporaries

the problems of national unity. Though made uneasy by neo-Guelphism, with its democratic abbés who awaited the regeneration of the state from a Papacy friendly to Austria, Albertism won them over; the accession of their king to the control of a confederation would doubtless be for them, already masters of the Sardinian administration, a promise of advancement. Finally, the leaders of the movement were reassuring. Of aristocratic origin, like Balbo, d'Azeglio or Benzo, Count of Cavour (1810–61), they had no contact with the agitators. They thought more of the liberation of Italy than of the liberty of the Italians. D'Azeglio was an aesthete, fundamentally conservative, Balbo dreamt only on unity, Cavour, the most progressive, was known above all for his economic liberalism of the Manchester type. In his *Risorgimento*, founded in Turin in December 1847, he was to try to win over the middle classes by demanding a constitutional régime with an assembly recruited on a widely based property qualification. The action of this Albertist organ had been prepared for by a fanfare of writings which, openly or clandestinely, had penetrated everywhere. Criticism of the administration of the Holy See was an indirect means of serving the cause of Charles Albert; Durando (1804–69), a Piedmontese officer (who was to command the pontifical troops in 1848!) made a name for himself by preaching the suppression of the temporal power. Hatred of the domination of the Tedeschi was the essential factor of moral support for the Sardinian dynasty by a section of the upper classes, of the bourgeoisie and of the ordinary townspeople. In a country where socialist and communist ideologies imported from France had only affected a few secret societies, social emancipation was confounded with national emancipation.

This point of view was also that of the democrats, whose divergencies affected their institutions. Mazzini had clearly proclaimed in 1840 that improvement of the lot of the workers was a condition of the liberation of Italy; moreover, on the eve of 1848 he devoted his greatest efforts to defending intransigently his unitary republic. More aware of realities, the Lombard historian Cattaneo (1801–69) preached a federation of Italian republics.

The federal idea brought together the partisans of the king of Sardinia; the liberal idea kept them apart. Charles Albert had abandoned none of his prejudices against a constitutional régime. His attitude enhanced the confusion which reigned in men's minds at the beginning of 1846. The proud conception of independence (*Italia farà da se*) which Mazzini shared with the greater number of Italians until the disasters of 1848–9, allied to a hesitant character, postponed the dreams of unity to a distant future. Watchful of the formation of a public opinion more and more hostile, the Austrians noted the pernicious effects of the "venom of literary propaganda". But Metternich did not take the vacillations of Charles Albert seriously. The unforeseen took place at Rome. The election of Pius IX (17 June 1846) overturned Italian political life and unleashed, from the south to the north of the peninsula, troubles to which the dearness of commodities and the rise in unemployment imparted social overtones.

*PART TWO*


THE EUROPEAN REVOLUTIONS

[ Chapter Eight ]

# Economic, Social and Political Crises (1846– January 1848)

EVEN IF the Parisian explosion of February meant that the European revolutionary movements of spring 1848 were on a scale hitherto unforeseen it did not create them. Whereas France, which modern historians describe as ready to overthrow a rotten-ripe régime, seemed so strong that as early as February the mistrustful Palmerston proposed an increase in military expenditure to parliament, Europe too, from 1846 onward, had been subjected to tremors which demanded the skill and wisdom of diplomats and aroused the fears of the authorities.

## THE SOCIAL AND ECONOMIC DIFFICULTIES OF EUROPE

According to Marx (*Class Struggles in France, 1848–50*) the economic crisis of 1845–7 provoked a social crisis which in turn engendered the political crisis of February. This schema, calculated to fascinate logical minds, explains, to borrow a phrase of the English historian Cobban, "the revolutions which took place" but did not always take account of "the revolutions which did not take place".

The crisis of 1845–7, as those which preceded it in 1816–18, 1825–32, and 1836–9, belonged to the decennial troubles of European economy. But "though there were decennial economic crises, there were not decennial revolutions" (E. Labrousse). Undoubtedly the United Kingdom provided obvious correlations between periods of economic depression and the upsurge of political fever. Nonetheless, the great British movements of 1816–19, 1831–2 and 1838 ended abruptly. Undoubtedly the July Revolution and its prolongations (the insurrections in Lyons and in Paris in 1832) burst out in times of economic depression. However, neither the crisis of 1816–18 nor that of 1836–9 (if one excepts the Blanquist outbreak of 12 May 1839 in which German workers took part) coincided with periods of political unrest. The economic manifestations and the social consequences which can be observed in the 1845–7 crisis having been the subject of numerous studies, it will be enough to evoke them in their geographic framework to appreciate their political import.

### The Foodstuffs Crisis of 1845–6 and the Economic Crisis of 1847

The crisis of 1845–6 at first took the form of a shortage of foodstuffs. The last crisis of this nature, it was caused firstly by an agricultural crisis, due not to glut as in our own days but to shortage. In 1845 the potato blight (phytophtora) began to attack potatoes and bad weather affected the cereal harvests. The harvest of 1846 failed completely. The importance of bread and potatoes in the diet of the poorer classes is well known! Great Britain survived the beginnings of the crisis well enough, continuing, without qualms of conscience, to import grain from an already destitute Ireland; the prospect of the imminent repeal of the Corn Laws drove producers and merchants to get rid of their stocks. A quarter of wheat fell from sixty-four shillings in October 1845 to forty-seven shillings in August 1846. As the governments of the traditional suppliers of the United Kingdom forbade the export of cereals, the price again rose to sixty-five shillings in November, to seventy-eight shillings in March 1847 and to a hundred and two shillings in May! From July onward the influx of Russian and American cereals and the prospect of rich harvests to come finally reversed this trend; the price fell to forty-nine shillings in September. After

the catastrophic harvests of 1846 the price of potatoes quadrupled in some French districts and the average nationwide
price of a hectolitre of wheat doubled in a year. Doubtless the
Midi was somewhat favoured by the proximity of Marseilles
where cereals arrived from Odessa. In May 1847 a kilo of bread
cost seventy centimes in Paris, fifty-five in Lille, that is to say
double the price regarded as tolerable by the masses. In the
autumn a decline of prices began which continued under the
Second Republic; from thirty-eight francs in May the price of
wheat fell once more to twenty-two francs in September. In
Belgium hundreds of thousands of Flemings, whose living
conditions were normally very hard, experienced a famine on
the Irish scale. The increase in the death-rate in comparison
with the Walloon provinces of Hainaut and Liège became
greater, due to undernourishment, the "Flanders malady" of
famine fever; typhus also contributed. Typhus spread also
among other weaver-farmers; in 1847 it claimed 16,000 victims
in Silesia. In the Germanic Confederation Kuczynski says that
from 1844 to 1847 there was a rise in wholesale prices (135 per
cent for potatoes, 88 per cent for rye)—far less than in retail
prices. On the Durlach market, one of the best supplied in
Baden, the price of wheat quadrupled between January 1845
and May 1847; the cost of a three pound loaf of "black bread",
taxed as everywhere, almost doubled from August 1845 to
March 1847. On the eve of the revolution it was to fall, due to
the combined effects of the general fall in prices and of government intervention, to the level of January 1845.

When the agricultural crisis ended, an economic crisis

"foreshadowed in the autumn of 1845 by massive speculative
unloading of railway stocks, but checked in the summer of 1846
by . . . the imminent abolition of customs duties on cereals . . .
finally broke out in the autumn of 1847 with the bankruptcy of
the great colonial mercantile companies of London. . . . The
repercussions of this crisis had not yet ended on the continent
when the February revolution broke out" (Marx).

Let us add that speculators had extensively anticipated the
profits of the railways in France and also in Germany, that the

"railway fever" had led to excessive investments in metallurgy and that the export of currency against large cereal imports had contributed not a little to a shortage of liquid cash. Diminution of the gold reserves forced the Bank of England and the Bank of France to raise the bank-rate. The price of loans increased universally. The difficulties of the banks affected the enterprises which they supported. The Rothschilds of Frankfurt were openly suspected of planning the destruction of German industry by organizing the bankruptcy of their associates.

The slump in industry and commerce of 1847 was to a great extent a consequence of the agricultural crisis. The rises in the price of foodstuffs, far from profiting the immense army of agricultural wage-earners or the small cultivators, so numerous in Ireland, Flanders and southern Germany (since they had nothing to sell), crippled their purchasing power, and still more that of the miners, the factory workers and the artisans. Stocks accumulated, unemployment increased and wages went down. From August to October 1847 England was in the grip of a crisis that Halévy judges was more serious than that of 1825. In January Manchester had more than three thousand unemployed. In the second half of 1847 the metallurgical industry was, for the first time in France, a sign of its growing importance, hit by the recession. The textile industry was, however, the most vulnerable, the home-weavers only surviving by accepting famine wages. In Germany unemployment affected a quarter of the home-weavers at Chemnitz and the manufacturers in southern Baden ceased work. The crisis was the occasion of a fresh campaign against the *Zollverein*. Belgium afforded the striking example of workers' difficulties in a declining as well as in an expanding economy. For the most part the Flemish country people, half-peasants, half-workers, were unable to buy the products which their tiny fields usually yielded; the ancient linen industry, for long in decline, died out. What a contrast to the vigour of the Walloon provinces, reliant upon coal and metallurgy! "The men of Hainaut and Liége were to hear the news of the 1848 revolution at a time of increasing industrial prosperity" (Demoulin). This brilliant façade marked two arduous years; from 1845 to 1847 wages increased only 7 per cent in the coal industry, whereas rye and potatoes doubled in price.

To what extent did these crises—that of foodstuffs in 1845–6 and that of the economy in 1847—pave the way to the great changes of March 1848?

## Consequences of the Foodstuffs Crisis

*The Subsistence Troubles.* The first of these crises, that of foodstuffs, roused the anger of the masses against their governments and predisposed them to rebellion. At a time when many still baked their own bread, grain was moving unceasingly to the markets and the mills. The famine-stricken, giving way to the temptation of intercepting it, organized forced sales at fixed prices, or resorted to pure and simple robbery. Their tumultuous assemblies created insecurity in the French countryside. The town bakeries were taken by assault. These "subsistence troubles" recalled those of 1789 and of 1830 but they assumed dimensions which were no doubt explicable by the more rapid diffusion of news through the press. Despite severe repression, order was not restored by its professional defenders but by the return of good harvests. The map of the troubles which Gossez has drawn up from the police reports is also that of the areas of penury; the north, the west and the centre, politically calm, were the most turbulent. In the spring of 1847 the disorders in Scotland, in south-west England, in Brussels, Berlin, Ulm, Vienna, Genoa, the Romagna, Lombardy and Tuscany, also had a purely economic origin. Doubtless the secret societies tinged with communism as in Tuscany, or republican agitators as in Baden, did their best to exploit the hatreds born of misery. In the Odenwald, where the smallholders, already subjected to the exploitation of the *Standesherren* and the *Grundherren,* and burdened with debts at usurious rates of interest were reduced to hunger an anonymous tract boldly fixed for 12 April 1847 a revolution whose final aim was the setting up of a free state (*Friestaat*) on the model of the United States. Its immediate objectives were: destruction of the nobility, expulsion of the Jews, assassination of the tax officials and the seigneurs!

Though military precautions kept the peace, the social part of this programme was to be realized in March 1848 when anti-noble and anti-Semitic jacqueries were to break out under cover of the political changes taking place at Karlsruhe.

*The Galician Jacqueries.* In Galicia the foodstuffs crisis led to an explosion not only social but religious, national and even political. The Ruthene serfs and Uniates of Galicia had paid no heed to the efforts of a few priests of the university of Lemberg (Lwow) in favour of the Ukrainian language. They had reasons enough to detest the great Polish landlords who, with the Catholic clergy, were chosen to represent their interests in the Diet. The bad harvest of 1845 made them receptive to the social aspects of the clandestine propaganda of the Reds of the Polish Democratic Society of Paris who were preparing an uprising of the three Polands, under the direction of Mieroslawski. At the beginning of 1846 they massacred about two hundred of the great Polish landowners . . . invoking the agrarian programme of a Polish insurgent government set up in Cracow! This jacquerie was to provide Vienna (which did not discourage it at first, to say the least!) with an opportunity to annex the republic of Cracow.

*Agrarian Crimes, Prelude to the Revolution in Ireland?* The relative calm of Flanders was in contrast to the Galician civil war and the Irish agrarian crimes. It was not explicable either by better material conditions or by a lower cultural standard. The confessional unity of the French-Belgian state had, perhaps, deprived the Flemish peasants of the weapon of religious passion. At the beginning of 1847 Ireland, after a series of disastrous potato harvests, fell prey to the "great famine". The situation of a rapidly growing population living from the exploitation of smaller and smaller holdings (according to an enquiry in 1835 more than two million persons were un-employed for half the year) seemed without solution. The philanthropic spirit inspired Peel and his Whig successor Russell to purchase maize from the United States and to open charity workshops at great expense. The Irish famine had served as a pretext for Cobden's League to begin its propaganda once more and justified the introduction of free trade which, before finally ruining the small farmers, brought no immediate improvement. The action of the masses, even more spontaneous than in Galicia, aroused the admiration of Marx who regarded it as a manifestation of the class struggle. But this was coloured, as always in Ireland, by inexpiable religious hatred and more or less conscious national resentments. Henceforward unable to pay his rent regularly, the Irish Catholic peasant was haunted by fear of being evicted. However, the English Protestant landlord and the farmer who replaced the evicted man knew that their days were numbered for, in the vicious circle of evictions and agrarian crime, the guilty profited by the active complicity of the local people and, if they were captured, they were acquitted by juries who deliberated under duress. The modification of a penal legislation unsuited to endemic unrest was hampered by the intrigues of Westminster; where Peel had failed Russell succeeded in November 1847, at a time when members of Young Ireland were trying to give definite direction to a hitherto anarchic movement. In January 1847 Smith O'Brien (1803–64) founded in Dublin the Irish Confederation which called on "physical force" to win independence. Ten days before the February revolution, Mitchell (1815–75), the most impetuous of its members, launched a call to insurrection in his *United Irishman*.

### The Social Consequences of the Economic Crisis

*A New Chartism Directed Towards Europe?* In the Europe of 1846–7, undernourished, in the grip of a recession and bristling with customs barriers, Great Britain, despite free trade, remained an island. At the time of record prices of cereals and of the great depression which lasted from August to October, the workers recalled that the Chartists had denounced the propaganda of the League as an industrialists' plot. The unemployment in the cotton-spinning areas also seemed to justify the sinister prophecies of the protectionist Tories who, as much by principle as out of hatred for the manufacturers, had

contributed to give the United Kingdom the most progressive
workers' legislation in Europe. While the free-traders condemned in the name of liberty the "system of charitable
government" (Stuart Mill), Lord Ashley, promoter of the laws
of 1833 and 1844, had the Factory Act of 1847 passed, which
from 1 May 1848 limited the working day for women and
"young persons" (from thirteen to eighteen years old) in
industry to ten hours. This law was also to be of benefit to men
because of the need for shift work. It was more liberal than the
ephemeral decree of the French provisional government (March
1848) which was hailed as the major achievement of the
proletarian revolution. It justified the action of the National
Association of United Trades for the Protection of Labour,
which was hostile to Chartist violence. A semblance of the
strong popular movement of 1842 still persisted under the
control of O'Connor. James Bronterre O'Brien, a revolutionary
of the Babeuf type, had broken away from an organization
dominated by his reformist rival. In 1843 Chartism had adopted
the Land Scheme; the division of the great estates into small
individual lots (in no way comparable with the Owenist or
Fourierist colonies) would turn unemployed workers into
opulent farmers. The crisis of 1847 relegated this visionary
project to the kingdom of Utopia. The elections marked by
the Whig triumph expressed the satisfaction of the free-trade
bourgeois businessman and disregarded the sufferings of the
workers. In most constituencies, lack of means reduced Chartist
candidatures to a minimum. Thus the election of O'Connor
at Nottingham seemed a divine intervention. If, a few days
before Parliament met, the executive committee of the Chartists
issued an appeal asking for a "national petition" (20 November
1847), resorting by instinct to a typically British procedure of
exerting popular pressure on parliament, it also became
involved, under the influence of its Left wing, in "democratic
and socialist internationalism". Doubly insular, O'Connor
wanted to ignore Europe and, even when he had taken refuge
in London, its revolutionaries. But he had to resign himself to
letting his fiery collaborator Harney (1817–97), editor of the
*Northern Star*, publish information about opposition movements

on the continent. Harney met Engels in 1843 and took an interest in the activities of the Federation of the Just of Schapper and Bauer, which in the summer of 1847 became the Federation of Communists, to which Engels and Marx, then at Brussels, adhered. Under his direction the Fraternal Democrats, London Chartists European in Spirit, began a sustained correspondence with the International Democratic Association of Brussels, made up of a few Belgian radicals, some proscribed Italians, Poles (Lelewel) and Germans, with Marx as vice-president. It was not, therefore, by chance that a few days after the beginnings of the new Chartist campaign two meetings were held almost simultaneously in London which, because of the participation of Marx, were to become red-letter days in the history of European socialism. The congress of the Federation of Communists, which rallied a handful of Germans, was preparing the social revolution and entrusted Marx and Engels with drawing up a programme of action applicable to all countries; this was to be the *Communist Manifesto*. The congress passed unremarked; the *Manifesto*, published after the outbreak of the revolution, was to be without effect on the movements inspired by nationalism. Harney was to adopt it with the intention of regenerating Chartism. The Fraternal Democrats, commemorating the Polish insurrection in the presence of Marx (enemy of the "degenerate" Slavs, he shared the sympathies of the democrats of his time for a people unshakably hostile to the Russians), proclaimed their attachment to the sacred cause of the emancipation of peoples. This effort, which clashed with the apathy of the older form of Chartism which was indifferent to everything which took place across the Channel, showed the desire felt by a revolutionary minority for something new. In January and February 1848 meetings tried, as in the great days of Chartism, to mobilize the hundreds of thousands of unemployed created by the economic crisis, this time in the service of a movement aware of Europe.

*Weakness of the Workers' Movement in Germany and France.* There was nothing comparable on the continent. Always the same spectacle; the number of the destitute, beggars, thieves, criminals, increased; even as the attacks on machines increased. The organization of the working classes remained embryonic. The Associations of Workers (*Arbeiterbildungsvereine*) which pullulated in Germany only continued the work of the associations for "the encouragement of the well-being of the labouring classes". Their aims were philanthropic only. In Berlin and Hamburg associations of guild-workers (*Handwerkervereine*), animated by former adherents of the Federation of the Just, broadcast the Communist and republican ideal of Weitling, whose influence remained predominant despite his break with Marx who rejected the conception, borrowed from Blanqui and the Parisian secret societies, of a revolution arising from the activities of a few resolute leaders. Marx's name was not unknown, contrary to a statement many times repeated, for, in the States where the censorship was relatively mild, the democratic press contained frequent paragraphs on his literary activity in Paris and Brussels. Very favourable to Louis Blanc and to his "organization of labour" this press was far from welcoming to Marx and Proudhon whom it depicted as nebulous philosophers, proud and irascible. When Marx published his *Misery of Philosophy*, a reply to Proudhon's *Philosophy of Misery* in June 1847, ironic commentaries saluted the squabble between these two personages avid of publicity. On the eve of 1848 the only "Marxist" group in Germany (according to a recent historian it had less than a hundred adherents) was at Cologne where Marx edited the *Rhineland Gazette* from 1842 to 1843. In December 1847 the physician Gottschalk (1815–49) founded a section of the Federation of Communists, but this admirer of Marx still remained receptive to the type of communism imported from France by the heretic Weitling.

In France the Icarian groups (those who were followers of Cabet) peaceably continued their task of educating the workers. Their master did not admit that "the social question can be solved by firearms" (G. Duveau). The communists of the Parisian secret societies, even though permeated by agitators, did not believe that the distress of the lower classes would provide the occasion, awaited for the past fifteen years, for imposing a social republic on France. As in Germany the revolution was not to break out in a prosperous economy and a cloudless social atmosphere but at the moment when, after the ending of the foodstuffs difficulties, the crisis of 1847 would seem to have passed its peak. It was to arise from political causes which were to range, temporarily, in the same camp a handful of partisans of profound social transformations and a large section of the resolutely conservative middle classes.

### THE AFFAIRS OF SCHLESWIG-HOLSTEIN, OF CRACOW AND OF SWITZERLAND: INTERNATIONAL ASPECTS AND INTERNAL REPERCUSSIONS

Movements which, contrary to those of 1830, owed nothing to the Parisian unrest, never ceased to threaten the order established in 1815, from 1846 to February 1848. The affair of Schleswig-Holstein, the suppression of the republic of Cracow and the civil war in Switzerland forced the powers to make choices in which public opinion played its part: the essential causes of the growing unpopularity of Guizot, of Metternich and of the Diet in Frankfurt were diplomatic policies in contradiction to the wishes of the peoples. The matter of the Franco-Spanish marriages modified the conditions of international life from autumn 1846. The rupture of this *entente cordiale* brought the July Monarchy closer to Austria and to Russia, the symbols of absolutism! The role which the liberals and the Anglophobe democrats dreamed of for France was gaily assumed by Palmerston, that new Pitt, who encouraged subversion in Switzerland and Italy. By the end of 1847, stimulated by Swiss radicalism, liberal and national aspirations forcibly expressed in southern Germany. In January 1848 the particularist and liberal insurrection in Sicily and the anti-Austrian riots in Milan forced Italy into the era of revolutions.

### *The Vigil of Arms in Schleswig-Holstein*

Since the *Open Letter* of Christian VIII (July 1846) Germanic nationalism and Danish nationalism clashed even more vigorously over Schleswig-Holstein. At the congress of Germanists, philologians and historians, held in 1847 at Lubeck on the borders of Holstein, Dahlmann and the brothers Grimm once more recalled that German science was at the service of German *Volkstum*. Until his death (20 January 1848) Christian VIII harshly repressed all acts of insubordination. Frederick VII on his accession to the throne tried to reinforce the spirit of resistance to German pretensions by granting in his Royal Rescript of 28 January a common constitution for all his States. The bourgeois and the university of Copenhagen criticized the conservative nature of the new institutions and protested that the Germans would have a representation at the Diet roughly equal to that of the Danes. The German opposition protested against the incorporation of the duchies in the kingdom with the unanimous support of Germany itself, where subscriptions were opened to arm "our separated brothers". European opinion was to discover with astonishment the persistency of the German desire to annex Schleswig and also the terrifying complexity of an affair which at first had concerned only the governments of London and St Petersburg, which were directly interested in the integrity of the Danish State.

### The Annexation of Cracow, Last Defeat of the Peoples

On the other hand, the incorporation of the republic of Cracow into Galicia was one of those minor events which stirred up popular passions and agitated the chancelleries. Since 1815 Cracow had been the sole remaining fragment, continually menaced, of independent Poland. Its annexations (November 1846), effected with the complicity of Russia as Prussia had fallen into line with Metternich, seemed a fresh challenge by the "Holy Alliance of the kings" to the "Holy Alliance of the peoples". Democrats and moderate liberals increased their pressure on governments to make Austria disgorge its prey. British reactions were the weakest; only the Chartist Left-wing was Polonophile. In Germany love for Poland was merged with hate for tsarism. Arrested a few days before the insurrection which he was preparing in Poznan, Mieroslawski was sentenced to death with ten of his companions. Prussian public opinion won him grace. Investigation of the secret records of the Diet reveal that in June 1847 Bavaria and Baden, sitting under the presidency of Austria, had not been afraid to stigmatize the rape of Cracow. In France, where the Polish cause was the origin of the "great republican battle" of June 1832, the events in Cracow and Poznan aroused great emotion. For the Polish émigrés Mieroslawski was a French hero. In February 1846 the occupation of Cracow by the Austrian, Russian and Prussian troops stirred up a lively concern which far surpassed traditional political cleavages. At the news of the annexation, the government paper *Journal des Débats* waxed indignant. The estrangement from London prevented any action in common. The English alibi, which French diplomacy was later to invoke interminably to justify climbing down in matters of quite different import, could not satisfy an over-excited and Anglophobe public opinion, to appease which Guizot sent a note of protest to Vienna. In vain! The impression that the July Monarchy had finally broken with its origins was reinforced when France seemed, in Swiss affairs, to take the side of the Holy Alliance.

*The Triumph of Swiss Radicalism, First Victory of the Peoples*

The *Sonderbund* crisis, that dramatic episode of Swiss history, because of the unrest in neighbouring countries and the European liaisons of Swiss radicalism, acquired international importance. The governments of the southern States of the Germanic Confederation and their oppositions were equally convinced that the victory of the adversaries of the *Sonderbund* would be contagious. Anxious for peace in Germany and Italy, Metternich wanted to seize the chance awaited since 1830 of destroying a centre of permanent turbulence by driving out the political refugees (in Switzerland Mazzini had founded Young Europe and Weitling had introduced his Federation of the Just), especially the Germans of Zurich where the *Comptoire littéraire* of Fröbel published Herwegh, Ruge, Marx, etc. Guizot was unwilling to get involved. The question which disturbed him was that of the freedom of secondary education which the legitimists openly and the Jesuits secretly supported. Prepared to reach a compromise with the French Church, he could not encourage a movement abroad which enjoyed the sympathies of Right-wing extremists without arousing the protests of Left-wing extremists. For the defenders of the University of Paris were allies of the Swiss radicals. Co-authors of the pamphlet *The Jesuits* (1843) Michelet and Quinet vituperated against the *Sonderbund*, the instrument of international clerical reaction, and the schemings of the accursed Company of Jesus. In the Chamber, O. Barrot calmly proclaimed that the only intervention worthy of a government faithful to the mission of France would be to help Swiss radicalism to destroy the *Sonderbund*, which owed its allegiance to Austria! The republicans applauded, as also the Orléanists (Thiers). Their desire to oust Guizot had turned them into defenders of ideas which they would vociferously disapprove in 1848. But the eminently confessional character of the Swiss quarrels weakened the camp of the partisans of the nationalities; ready to denounce, alongside the anti-clerical democrats, the oppression of the Poles, Montalembert warmly took sides for the *Sonderbund*. The Protestant Guizot sent arms secretly to the Swiss Catholics while officially preaching, for fear of being dragged into open conflict, first non-intervention and then collective mediation, to which Metternich was favourable and which Palmerston, friend of the radicals, opposed behind the scenes. The crushing offensive of General Dufour, who in twenty-six days occupied the Catholic cantons (30 November), discredited Guizot, Metternich's uncomplaining associate, even more; in Switzerland and throughout Europe it encouraged the party of revolution.

Drunk with victory, the Swiss radicals embarrassed even their closest friends; the conservative government of Neuchâtel, with the agreement of its suzerain, the King of Prussia, had taken up a neutral attitude in the conflict with the *Sonderbund*, and the Diet made preparations for the military occupation of the canton. Palmerston called it sharply to order. Everywhere the radicals treated the vanquished without leniency. When, at the reformist banquets, easy-going bourgeois proposed toasts to the victors over the *Sonderbund* they were answered by Michelet and Quinet with a moving appeal for moderation: "Terror appears to us like a steep staircase, where if one descends the first step one will descend all. . . . In the name of Brotherhood do not descend the first step!" The anxiety of tactfully handling London, which was doing its best to forestall excesses, and also that of not over-irritating Vienna, Paris, Berlin and St Petersburg, hostile to any modification of the Federal Pact of 1815, drove the Diet to moderate the ardour of its hotheads.

The national revolution of 1848 having taken place in 1847, there is a strong temptation to regard the great European upheavals as marginal. This point of view does not accord with the feelings of contemporaries which Marx expressed on 30 December 1847 in the *Deutsche Brüsseller Zeitung*, where he hailed a victory which "profited the popular parties of all the countries of Europe". This triumph, after so many reverses, of the principle of the sovereignty of peoples and the independence of nations, taught a lesson: abandoned to her own resources powerful Austria had had to withdraw when faced by a handful of resolute adversaries.

### THE LESSONS OF SWISS RADICALISM: SOUTHERN GERMANY, CENTRE OF THE DEMOCRATIC AND UNITARY MOVEMENT

When Halévy asserted that the revolution of 1848 did not arise from the Parisian barricades but from the Swiss civil war, he was doubtless thinking of the German revolutions. No perceptible sign was evident in Prussia. Opened in April, the *United Landtag* came to an end in June after vain and interminable palavers which showed that the idea of a liberal Prussia dragging Germany towards unity was a dream. The Rhineland liberals delivered fiery speeches on the advantages which a constitutional régime, struggling against the abuses of bureaucracy, would bring to the monarchy. Attentive to the counsels of the Junkers, one of the most eloquent of whom was a young deputy called Bismarck, the king conceded nothing and promised nothing. Why should the complaints of liberals hostile to adventure, or the attacks of a few democrats whose divergencies were harshly penalized, make him uneasy?

In the southern States, on the other hand, an agitation reigned which was to mount to a paroxysm at the victory of the Swiss radicals, whose cause was almost as popular as that of the Germans of Schleswig-Holstein. These sympathies, made easier by linguistic kinship, were inspired by the feeling of close ideological similarity.

The religious situation favoured an understanding with the enemies of the Jesuits. In the heart of Protestantism the sect of the Friends of Light (*Lichtfreunde*) held, like the conservative majority, that the struggle against the partisans of the Holy See was an expression of loyalty to the spirit of the nation. Subjected to a mediocre clergy of functionaries who willingly relied on the Protestant State to shake off the tutelage of the bishops and who paid little heed to the Pope, nothing prompted the Catholics of the south to break a lance in favour of the Jesuits. The efforts of a few prelates who sought, with the aid of the Papacy, to raise the moral level of the priests and to fight against this tendency to insubordination did not produce fruit until the second half of the nineteenth century. The double check of German Catholicism (*Deutsch-Katholizismus*) and the Ultramontane response in Baden was an irrefutable proof of this. In 1845 Ronge preached the new religion of Heidelberg at Konstanz without success; in a district where for decades a considerable section of the clergy had demanded the abolition of ecclesiastical celibacy and the inauguration of a synodal parliamentarianism he achieved nothing except the troublesome perspective of replacing a distant and Italian pope by a nearby German one. Professor Buss (1803–78) who was to be the most outstanding Catholic in Germany from 1846 to 1850, tried to mobilize the peasants of the Black Forest against the enemies of religion. On the model of O'Connor he launched petitions and founded Catholic associations. This "German Veuillot" made the *Süddeutsche Zeitung* of Freiburg into an Ultramontane organ. Historians stress with reason the novelty of an action which cleared the way to the formation of a Catholic party, but have neglected to mention that in the constituencies called upon to become the fortresses of the *Zentrum* all the Catholic candidates, Buss excepted, were wiped out in the elections of April 1846. Since the suffrage was a very wide one, this rout was attributable to the indifference of the Catholic masses of Baden. In 1848 Buss was to resign under popular pressure and to solicit elsewhere a seat in the Frankfurt parliament. In Wurtemberg the bishop Keller led a campaign similar to that of Buss and met with the same lack of understanding.

The nature of the support to be given to the Berne radicals accentuated the differences between the parties. The liberals, who never ceased to make progress (in Baden they had just won the elections), no longer practised systematic opposition to ministers ready to make concessions. They maintained that a diplomatic approach would be enough to divert Austria and her allies from an intervention in favour of the *Sonderbund*. Several parliamentarians rejected every compromise with monarchical particularism and demanded support for the Swiss radicals, to whom they began, moreover, to lend their name. Funds were collected and volunteers enrolled in Baden and Wurtemberg. The governments solicited Frankfurt to despatch federal contingents which would maintain a sort of *cordon sanitaire* around the Swiss source of infection. At the end of 1847 even the word revolution was made use of by ministers famous for their self-control. At the root of this psychosis were typically German associations, apolitical in principle and therefore authorized, where young people of all social classes met, in Wurtemberg and Baden at choral groups, gymnastic associations dear to the *Turnvater* Jahn and, naturally, shooting clubs. They participated enthusiastically in the propaganda in favour of the Swiss republicans. With a kernel of extreme left militants, they became centres of diffusion for revolutionary doctrines. Following a movement recently started, they inclined at their annual feasts to federate into large regional groups. The governments were above all afraid that this might result in that association of all German gymnasts of which the most ardent of the young people dreamed, for they might well have reason to fear a large party inspired by Berne radicalism.

Baden radicalism advanced in public opinion as the tensions within the Swiss Confederation increased. Its programme was a synthesis of the claims of liberalism in the twenties and thirties conceived within the framework of a small estate, and of social and political demands which foreshadowed a transformation of society and the destruction of the Germanic Confederation. Two men personified these tendencies and made Mannheim the great opposition centre: Hecker (1811–81) was a Romantic without a doctrine until his meeting with Struve (1805–69). A déclassé aristocrat (it was only in 1848 that he renounced the particle), Struve had known a long series of setbacks; first as magistrate, then as lawyer, he had made no impression. The electors had refused to send him to the Chamber. It was in journalism that he at last found his place, from 1845 onward. His conflicts with the censorship ended by transforming this embittered man into a theoretician of revolution. Admirer of the men of '93, reader of Saint-Simon, Fourier and Louis Blanc, he dreamed of a democratic and social Germany set up by force. Enchanted, like so many of his political co-religionists, German and Swiss, by the American myth, he rejected the myth of Jacobin centralization; a federal republic would replace the confederation of dynasts. These views, which a year later shocked the majority of the *Vorparlament*, were put forward on 12 September 1847 in the little town of Offenburg to two hundred members of the Association of Friends of the Constitution. The text approved and published envisaged reforms of extreme boldness. Certain political demands stemmed from classic liberalism (freedom of the press, and of assembly), whereas others were inspired by hatred of professional armies and bureaucracy (creation of a militia analogous to the French National Guard), yet others (election of civil servants) went beyond the normal demands of 1848. Social reforms capable of frightening the propertied classes and inflaming the poor by reason of their very imprecision (diminution of the disproportion existing between capital and labour, and the well-being, education and training of all) gave rise to fresh preoccupations.

The German question was touched on indirectly (the Diet must abolish the repressive legislation of 1819–20 and 1832–4) and directly: "A representation of the German people of the *Bund*" must be immediately appointed. Without doubt the liberal monarchist Welcker had in 1831 launched the idea of an elected parliament from the rostrum of the Chamber; but at Offenburg these were men without a mandate who took it upon themselves to work for the setting up of a German republic based on the sovereignty of the people. The Offenburg meeting of 12 September 1847 was, on the German and even the European scale, a manifestation of revolutionary character, compared with which the French reformist banquets seemed tame. The Radical party aimed at becoming a mass party; its supporters were young and in close touch with the people. It included none of those professors, the obligatory ornaments of the parties which had their roots in parliament, but alongside physicians and lawyers from the former *Burschenschaft* there were innkeepers and instructors from the choral and gymnastic societies, and distributors of tracts, seditious papers and political slogans. Relying on a clandestine network, the radical propaganda denounced the misconduct of institutions long considered to be the most progressive in Germany and lyrically depicted the well-being that a republic would bring. Artisans and peasants in the process of becoming proletarians had imputed their difficulties, bit by bit, to a system based on particularism in internal affairs and impotence in external ones. A strong and democratic Germany would defend the "rights" of the Germans of Schleswig-Holstein against Petersburg and London, as well as the material interests of the nation. National, political and social aspirations tended, under the influence of radicalism, to become confounded in the minds of simple men. The parliamentary liberalism dominated by the *Akademiker* had paid little heed to the political and social emancipation of the working classes but passionately looked forward to a Germany which would be under its effective control. The sensation produced by the Offenburg meeting led it to take part publicly. Eminent members of the Chambers of the west and south—the Rhinelander Hansemann, the Hessian von Gagern, the

Wurtemberger Römer, the Badeners Bassermann, Mathy and Welcker—met on 10 October at Heppenheim in Hesse-Darmstadt in the heart of liberal Germany. Inspired by the standing of the participants and by the resolutions voted, historians have overestimated the importance of these discussions. The deceptive experience of the *United Landtag* had not dissipated the deep-held illusions of the Rhineland liberals about the will to unity of Frederick William IV. Camphausen succeeded in getting the meeting to declare in favour of a *Zollvereinsparlament*, that is to say a parliament representing the States of the *Zollverein*. From customs union would emerge a political Germany dominated by Prussia but amputated from the Hanseatic towns, from Mecklenburg, from Oldenburg, from Hanover and from Germanic Austria.

This programme was too Prussian for a king of Prussia respectful of the historic superiority of Austria! A month after Heppenheim he tried to shake Frankfurt out of its torpor; his plan for the reform of the Federal Act revived ancient proposals, especially that of introducing Austria into a *Zollverein* henceforth controlled by the Diet. Happily for Prussia, Metternich remained an obstinate supporter of the *status quo* in Germany. The attitude of Frederick William in any case dealt a mortal blow to Camphausen's idea. The liberals of the south quickly forgot the Heppenheim dream. In his famous motion to the Baden Chamber (12 February) Bassermann proposed, on the model of the men of Offenburg, a representative assembly of the people and not of the princes; he had to be contented with a parliament appointed by the local Chambers, to which he won over Hecker and even Struve. Turning on the princes who resisted the forces of nationalism, the veteran Welcker once more revived the language of the members of the Convention wielding the threat of revolution: "To-day there is still time to give you warning. Tomorrow it will be too late!" Before a month had passed the prophecy was fulfilled. An import from France, the revolution was to break out in the south, where social structures were still archaic but political tendencies were advanced.

ITALY: FROM LIBERAL REFORMS TO "REVOLUTIONS"
(JUNE 1846—JANUARY 1848)

In 1847 Italy was the scene of an unrest unknown since 1831. Far from following, as formerly, Parisian stimuli, it was Italy which gave the signal for the European commotions of 1848. Doubtless a considerable section of the peasant masses had not felt, even vaguely, the influence of the Risorgimento. But never had so great and so diversified a section of the population condemned with such passion the tyranny of governments, the fractioning of Italy and the domination of the Tedeschi. Unemployment and the high price of foodstuffs increased the power of the progressive elements and incited the moderates to demand reforms which would bar the way to adventurers.

Since June 1846 Rome, the traditional target of the enemies of reactionary régimes, had become the capital of liberal and national hopes. The resurrection of moribund neo-Guelphism was linked to the advent of a Pope whose name would remain associated with the *Syllabus*, with the doctrine of papal infallibility and with the obstinate refusal to accept the incorporation of the Papal States into the kingdom of Italy. For two years no one doubted the good will of Pius IX to reconcile the Church with the modern world in all domains. Metternich's sour remark is well known: "A liberal Pope! That's really something new!" Alexandre Dumas, echoing the delirious enthusiasm of vast sections of Italian opinion, wrote in March 1848: "Italy has found the stuff of a new Gregory VII. . . . So each day the cry is heard beneath his windows: 'Holy Father, be careful of the chocolate!' [poison]." Assuredly the former cardinal Mastai was to be, up until his defection in 1848, a patriot and a liberal, but he would never consent to despoil the office of Pope and sovereign. On his advent, Pius IX remarked that despite a despotic régime Gregory XVI had left the Papal States in the same revolutionary situation in which he had found them in 1831. To break the cycle of insurrections and reprisals, he promulgated a decree of political amnesty (July 1846) which, after so long a period of blind repression, seemed almost a revolutionary measure. Prisoner of his prodigious popularity,

of which the *Hymn to Pius IX* was a touching manifestation, the
Pope went far beyond his original intention of reforming a
sclerotic administration; a law of March 1847 entrusting the
censorship to a commission made up chiefly of laymen was a
step towards freedom of the press. With the institution, four
months later, of a civic guard, two of the principal demands of
the European liberals were satisfied in one of the bastions of
reaction.

Leopold II, made uneasy by the agitation in the university
of Pisa, introduced similar reforms in Tuscany in May and
September. Charles Albert even modified the censorship
régime, promised elected municipal councils and in October
removed some ultrareactionary ministers. But nothing was
changed in the Two Sicilies where Ferdinand II relied on the
loyalty of his army and his Swiss mercenaries, nor in the duchies
of central Italy. At Parma, the successor of Marie Louise,
Charles II of Bourbon (1847–9), who had been forced to
abandon Lucca to Leopold II after a riot, and at Modena
Francis V d'Este (1846–59) resisted the liberal contagion, with
the thought that Austria would intervene in time to spare them
the misfortunes of Marie Louise and of Francis IV in 1831.

Their hopes were not misplaced. At the moment when, in
the *Sonderbund* quarrel, Metternich had started an international
crisis, he unleashed another one, infinitely more serious. In
Switzerland the old Chancellor carried out purely diplomatic
activities; in Italy he had recourse, as in 1821 and 1831, to
military action. The Austrian forces were installed on 13 August
1847 at Ferrara in the Papal States. These preoccupations of
Metternich were not wholly ideological; if the liberal democrats
were sapping the friendly conservative régimes, their schemes
in Milan and Venice, above all those of a clergy won over to
neo-Guelphism, might well be preparing the succession of
opulent provinces whence the imperial treasury extracted
abundant resources. This was the underlying reason for a
decision in which Metternich, unable to win over London or
Paris, was supported by Russia alone.

In fact, the policy of *fait accompli* in Italy, even more than
his tortuous manœuvres in Switzerland, clashed with the

opposition of Palmerston and the disapproval of Guizot. The two ministers, though at variance with one another, pursued similar policies, the former openly, the latter with the reserve suitable to an unavowed friend of Metternich, to restore peace to men by forcing the Italian governments to make opportune concessions. Lord Minto, a member of the British cabinet, went to Turin, Florence, Rome and Naples. He was lavish of words of wisdom to the sovereigns, of encouragement to the liberals, while discreetly begging the Pope to use his influence on the hierarchy to restrain the revolutionary ardour of the Irish peasants! His mission foreshadowed those of other noble mediators which were to contribute to the catastrophes on the continent which they aimed at preventing! For the delirious mobs which cheered Lord Minto the moral support of London was the prelude to a military aid very far from the intentions of Palmerston and of English public opinion. In Italy (the intimate ties between the French ambassador Rossi and Pius IX are well known) the advocate of moderate reform, Guizot, as at one time Casimir Périer, was the butt of furious attacks from the opposition which accused him of complicity with Metternich. However, his prudent firmness, added to the thundering declarations of Palmerston, induced Austria to abandon Ferrara on 18 December. The presence of the Tedeschi at Ferrara had in four months caused the ideal of Italian unity to make rapid advances. Far from soliciting, as had his predecessor, the armed intervention of Vienna, Pius IX solemnly condemned it, which increases his popularity more than ever. From London, Mazzini, the anti-clerical, advised his followers to support the Pope! Rome, Florence and Turin discussed a proposal for a customs union.

Metternich's climb-down in Italy, as well as his diplomatic setbacks in Switzerland, started up the agitations once again. The Kingdom of the Two Sicilies had been, during the summer, the scene of riots, fomented by cries of "Long live Pius IX!" On 12 January 1848 an insurrection broke out at Palermo in which all classes took part, as in 1820. By 27 January only the citadel of Messina remained in the hands of the Neapolitan army. A committee presided over by an old

admiral, Settimo (1778–1863), convoked for 23 March a
parliament charged with modifying the 1872 constitution,
never accepted by Naples. For the time being it demanded
neither the overthrow of the Bourbons nor independence.
Historians therefore contest, contrary to the opinion of contemporaries, the particularist character of the movement.
However that may be, the essential cause of the first revolution
of the year 1848 was rooted in popular passions: hatred of
Neapolitan domination momentarily united the diverse
elements of a class-ridden society.

The triumph of the revolution in Sicily increased the boldness
of the liberals in the peninsula and weakened the resistance of
the reactionary forces. The time for piecemeal reforms had
passed. Against the return of abuses, the oppositions demanded,
as at one time in the Germanic Confederation, written
guarantees; the panic-stricken sovereigns accorded them. At
Naples, Ferdinand II, after having formed a new government
in which the Minister of the Interior was a former Carbonaro,
published a constitution on 10 February. In Tuscany Leopold II
decided, despite the proximity of the Austrian forces, to follow
his example (17 February). The news from Sicily and Naples
stirred up an effervescence in Genoa and Turin by which the
Albertists knew very well how to profit. Uneasy at the unforeseen popularity of the Papacy, Cavour and now also Balbo
and d'Azeglio tirelessly demonstrated that the national destiny
of the House of Savoy depended on a transformation of the
régime. Enlightened at last, Charles Albert promised on 8
February a Constitutional Statute. While the King of Sardinia
won the favour of a section of the Italian opposition, the
reformist enthusiasm of the initiator of the liberal explosion
seemed to have been cut off: Pius IX contented himself with a
council of ministers presided over by the Cardinal-Secretary
of State and by a *consulta* formed of members nominated by the
Pope. Under pressure from his disappointed subjects, he
announced on 14 February the institution of a commission
of reform.

Only Parma and Modena, allied to Austria by secret
treaties of protectorate (December 1847) were apparently not

affected by the breeze of liberalism which the revolution in Vienna was to transform into a tempest.

Austria first became aware of these symptoms in Lombardy-Venetia in January. The patriots organized a boycott against an increase in the price of tobacco, a state monopoly; they attacked the Austrian troops who, out of bravado, smoked in public. The "cigar riot" (2–4 January) of Milan was harshly repressed. As the agitation continued, Marshal Radetzky proclaimed a state of siege in Lombardy on 11 February. At Venice the lawyer Manin (1804–57) and the writer Tommaseo who had plotted an anti-Austrian and republican uprising were thrown into prison.

Assured of having maintained order in the north, Radetzky reported to Vienna that only force would be able to restore the former authorities in the south. An armed intervention similar to that of 1821 was decided on. This expedition, which would have carried the unpopularity of the July régime to a climax, was frustrated by the fall of Guizot and of Louis Philippe.

# [ Chapter Nine ]

## The Parisian Revolution

THE FEBRUARY DAYS in Paris staggered France and Europe, especially those peoples who were searching for their national unity. East of the Rhine and south of the Alps, rulers were seized with panic fed by recollections of 1792–3; a France republican in the Parisian manner could not be other than bellicose. Would it not be better to yield to the demands of subjects whom it would doubtless soon be necessary to ask to take up arms against the new helmeted missionaries? The provisional government was to do its best, without much success, to dissipate these alarms. Subjected to the pressure of small groups of enthusiastic revolutionaries, skilled at demonstrating to the Parisian proletarians that the emancipation of the Parisian workers and the liberation of oppressed peoples were complementary obligations for their missionaries in the Hotel de Ville, the government itself lived in constant fear of being overthrown. With the defeat of the Parisian revolution (16–23 April), which was to be confirmed by the days of June, the majority of Frenchmen and all the established authorities in Europe felt the time of great political and social upheavals had passed.

THE BIRTH OF A REVOLUTION: FROM "LONG LIVE
REFORM!" TO "LONG LIVE THE REPUBLIC!"

The different phases of what Girard[1] has called "the scenario
of a revolution" are well known. A campaign of banquets (it
was a question of challenging the legislation affecting the right
of assembly and demonstration) organized by opposition
parliamentarians (dynastics and liberals who regarded the
republic as a distant ideal), anxious to dictate mild reforms to a
servile Chamber without recourse to the streets, ended in a
democratic and social revolution. From 9 July in Paris until
25 December in Rouen, several banquets brought together a
total of 17,000 participants who, by virtue of a high subscription,
had agreed to hear "before the cold turkey" (Flaubert) Odilon
Barrot, Lamartine, Ledru-Rollin and to listen to all and sundry
proposing toasts to "electoral and parliamentary reform" and
to "the July revolution". As alongside those with property
qualifications (there were 246,000 in 1846) many petty
bourgeois without voting rights had taken part in these
reformist reunions, it was extremely likely that this campaign
was riding for a fall. It was also an occasion for the opposition
to display its divisions; even if in the heat of the banquet some
of the radicals attacked the person of the King and preached
universal suffrage, Barrot's dynastics appeared reconcilable at
the cost of modest concessions. But, sure of his throne, Louis
Philippe confounded them all in a common public censure,
stigmatizing in them their "blind and hostile passions".

By a sequence of false moves and unforeseen reactions, the
prohibition of the Seventy-first banquet was to lead to extraordinary events which none of the promoters of the reformist
campaign would have dared to envisage a week earlier. In
December, in one of the most revolutionary of the Paris
districts, the XII arrondissement, some officers of the National
Guard, elected by men whom the success of electoral reform
concerned most closely, decided to hold a final banquet before
the opening of the parliamentary session and to solicit the

[1] *La II<sup>e</sup> République*, Calmann-Levy, 1968.

patronage of republican (the denomination "radicals" was to disappear with the monarchy) and dynastic deputies. The former accepted; the latter were hesitant. On 14 January the banquet was forbidden. The republicans decided to hold it nonetheless. However, anxious to avoid any confrontation with the authorities, they took a number of precautions; the site (Chaillot, far from old Paris), the postponed date (22 February, a Tuesday) and an increase in the price of attendance, inspired by a desire to exclude the more extreme participants such as students or workers. Some clever Orléanists proposed a trial, in agreement with Guizot, intended primarily to save the face of the opposition and also of the Government (why should the Seventy-first banquet alone be illegal?) They would attend the banquet; at the entrance a police superintendent would take down all details and everything would end before a police court! When they got wind of this plan, the republicans were indignant. Marrast, the oracle of the *National*, an impetuous disciple of General Lamarque, then took an initiative which we now know changed the whole course of events. He drew up a detailed programme for the demonstration. It appeared on the 21st. The banquet was almost forgotten; the stress shifted to the procession which, from the Place de la Madeleine, was to accompany the parliamentarians and the subscribers as far as Chaillot. As well as students and the populace, national guards "in uniform"—a bold stroke!—were invited to take part. The ministry replied to this challenge by forbidding both procession and banquet. The republican deputies were abandoned by all their reformist allies, save for Lamartine and half a dozen trusties. On the evening of the 21st the banquet was cancelled, though the workmen, who had not been told, continued to set up tents and trestles. The procession was pointless.

At the Tuileries everyone was in good humour; surely 20,000 troops and 3,000 guards would be enough to control a few trouble-makers? It had been known since 1840 that the National Guard was not unanimous in approving the refusal of political reforms and the policy of peace at any price; but could anyone the next day pick out the subversive elements who would respond to the invitation of the agitators?

On the morning of the 22nd the readers of the *National* read, with mixed feelings, Marrast's appeals for calm. The majority of the enemies of the Government and the idlers who crowded the Place de la Madeleine awaiting the organizers of the banquet did not know that they were not coming and were astonished to see the soldiers there. A particularly excited procession of students passed, which drew the crowds towards the Palais-Bourbon. Municipal guards cleared the Concorde. Agents of the secret societies provoked scuffles here and there. The dragoons intervened brutally. That evening, though order had not yet been re-established, it seemed at least that the régime was no longer in danger. In the disorderly movements of students and the populace, slogans repeated a thousand times since 1847—"Down with Guizot! Long live reform!"— could scarcely be heard. Thiers believed that his rival would emerge from this trial stronger than ever.

The 23rd was the prologue to the drama. Faced with events which were disconcerting men looked back for inspiration to the days of 1830 and to the revolution, where in the royal set-up they saw the events of 20 June and 10 August. In a city filled with unrest appeals to the troops and recourse to the National Guard created an anarchic situation. Out of twelve legions of the Guard (one for each arrondissement) one only, the First (Champs Elysées, Place Vendôme), displayed an undeviating loyalty to the Government. Far from co-operating with the troops, as in June 1832, the National Guard under arms limited themselves to shouting: "Long live reform! Down with the ministry!" More and more of them placed themselves between the soldiers and the demonstrators. Once made uneasy, the troops began to fear lest they be attacked from behind. The idea never even occurred to the King to include in the same repression the mob and the National Guard, now disloyal to its oath but nonetheless recruited from those social classes which had for so long been loyal to the régime. "I have seen blood enough!" said Louis Philippe. He wished to be more subtle than Charles X, of whom it was said that he had lost the game by keeping Polignac to the end. Since the "grocer janissaries" were filled with hatred for Guizot, he must be sacrificed and thus a wedge would be driven between the National Guard and the rebels. In the afternoon the King off-handedly dismissed his minister and replaced him by Molé, who prepared the formation of a new Government with the prudent slowness of an expert in parliamentary crises. Thiers, overcome with joy at once more having a portfolio, agreed that the old monarch had once more skilfully rounded a dangerous cape. By the end of the afternoon the appearance of the streets suggested optimism. The announcement of Guizot's fall produced a lessening of tension on which all witnesses agree. Whereas the National Guards envisaged a peaceful return home, crowned with the laurels of victorious warriors, enormous crowds poured on to the boulevards. Strangers kissed one another. Thousands of lights twinkled in the windows. Candles were stuck in rifle-barrels. Two songs replied to one another: the Marseillaise and the Song of the Girondins (To die for the country . . .), which triumphed every evening in A. Dumas' play, the *Chevalier de Maison-Rouge*.

The obscure leaders who took command on the barricades erected in the centre of the city certainly did not share this euphoria. Far from appeasing them, the withdrawal, under pressure, of the "old scoundrel" who in 1830 had stolen their republic from the people increased their courage. Would they have been able to overthrow the monarchy no matter what happened? Historians argue about it. But contemporaries agree in seeing in the fusillade of the Boulevard des Capucines the tragic incident which transformed a riot into a revolution.

A little after nine o'clock that evening two hundred resolute men from the Faubourg Saint-Antoine made their way towards the Madeleine. At their head, dressed despite the winter cold in shirt and trousers, one of them, like that other unknown at Lamarque's funeral, held a red flag. On the Boulevard des Capucines, roughly level with the Ministry of Foreign Affairs, the procession clashed with a detachment of troops entrusted with the protection of a building which Guizot's long presence there had rendered odious. An isolated shot rang out. The troops fired. A score of dead, including two women, and about fifty wounded lay on the pavements. The responsibility, as in all killings which have been the cause or the pretext of great popular movements, was an "historical enigma". Was it an act of provocation by Lagrange, a veteran of the insurrection of 1834? Was it the unthinking gesture of Sergeant Giacomini who thought his chief in danger? Survivors among the demonstrators piled seventeen corpses into a dustcart. Spontaneous reaction? Macabre stage-setting? Now transformed into a funeral procession, the column marched off to the light of those torches lit only a few moments before as a sign of rejoicing. It stopped before the offices of the *National*, chanting: "To arms! They are massacring us!" which led to a moving but prudent address by Garnier-Pagès! In the dark alleys of the Faubourgs Saint-Denis and Saint-Martin, sowing hatred and calling for vengeance, they erected more barricades.

As it continued its march, Louis Philippe learnt of the incident. He could hardly have been unaware of the worsening of the situation. A compromise would have suited him best, but, if it should fail, then a solution by force. His choice of men and his reactions up until late in the morning of the 24th revealed a judgement always a step or two behind the quickened rhythm of events. Decidedly anachronistic, Molé and Louis Philippe thought they were doing something new by putting forward Thiers, who was considered sure of an immense popularity. With great difficulty Louis Philippe swallowed "that snake" Barrot whose prestige, acquired during the banquet campaign, was expected to work wonders. Booed by the insurgents whom he had thought to appease, Barrot was soon to return home "to reassure his wife".

If the idea of substituting for these two incapables a single commander-in-chief of the troops and the National Guard was forced upon him, the appointment to this post of Marshal Bugeaud, whose name was closely linked with the massacre of the rue Transnonain, was an unfortunate choice. To break the resistance of thousands of rebels keeping watch behind fifteen hundred barricades and firmly resolved to oust Louis Philippe, Guizot, Thiers, Barrot and everyone associated with them, Bugeaud had ten thousand harassed and demoralized men. During the night he had played the braggart, but he realized that to clear the environs of the Hôtel de Ville would lead to a slaughter for which quite certainly he would have to bear the responsibility. Already the army, which was not stimulated by the passivity of the King, of the princes and of the ministry, felt abandoned to its own resources. The generals bickered among themselves in inextricable confusion. The National Guards, at least those who had not returned home, showed, as on the day before, proofs of a hostile neutrality or passed squarely to the opposing side. The soldiers, finally, let themselves be disarmed. At nine o'clock Bugeaud ordered a withdrawal from the Tuileries which became the objective of a motley crowd of National Guards, armed civilians and inquisitive onlookers. The courage of two companies entrenched near the Palais-Royal held back the decisive assault until midday. For Louis Philippe this 24 February was his 10 August! As amenable as the insurgents to the lessons of the Revolution, which he had lived through, the son of Philippe Égalité did not imagine that he could, even with the loyal troops in barracks in the provinces, appeal against the verdict of Paris. Before fleeing (he was to die in England in 1850) he abdicated, without anyone trying to stop him, in favour of his grandson the Count of Paris.

His abdication brought to a close the first act of the drama of 24 February. A discredited Chamber, of which only a few hours before Thiers had vainly proposed the dissolution and which was still sitting in the midst of a triumphant revolution, was asked to proclaim the accession of a ten-year-old child and to confer the regency, of somewhat doubtful legality (who worried about the Chamber of Peers, co-author of the law which guaranteed the rights of the Prince of Nemours?), on his mother, the Duchess of Orléans, at one time so esteemed by Lamartine and the deputies of the Left. Much courage was needed to approve on the 24th a solution which would have stopped everything on the 22nd, much courage, much loyalty ... and many illusions. A group of Orléanists bore witness to this, primarily Barrot, doubtless conscious of his role as sorcerer's apprentice. As minister, perhaps on paper even as Prime Minister, he had put up at the entrance of the Ministry of the Interior a proclamation in favour of the duchess and her son. After stating that "law and order is entrusted to the courage and wisdom of the people of Paris and its heroic National Guard" (sic!) he rushed to the Chamber. Already the idea of a provisional government had been mooted, in an atmosphere which irresistibly recalled 1793. Brushing aside the ushers, some National Guards had broken down the doors of the Assembly. Behind them were more and more armed men, increasingly noisy and impatient. Barrot threatened, rather anachronistically, to resign. After a gallant homage to the duchess, Lamartine proposed the nomination of a provincial government called to consult the country. At the end of his peroration, he was confronted by fresh intruders who demanded if the parliamentarians were preparing, as in 1830, to hoax the victors at the barricades. The president declared the meeting closed. The deputies vanished, except for the small group who knew in advance the main outlines of what was going on. In the hemicycle of national representation transformed into a people's club (Lamartine was seated between the legitimist deputy La Rochejaquelin and an unknown man with a long beard, a dented hat and a threadbare jacket) the names of the new leaders were acclaimed: Dupont de l'Eure, Lamartine, Arago, Ledru-Rollin, Garnier-Pagès, Marie and Crémieux, all republicans of the day before or from that same day! The list had been hastily drawn up at the end of the morning when the respectable bourgeois of the *National* were at last agreed that there was a risk that power might fall into impure hands. It was above all a question of barring the way to their adversaries of the *Reform* and, through them, to those obscure leaders of the secret societies who, on the night of the 23rd–24th, had launched the insurgents on the assault of the monarchy. The operation was carried out rapidly; it resulted in a strictly parliamentary combination, with a majority of moderates, with Ledru-Rollin, the sole hostage of the *Reform*, Crémieux, that same morning still a warm supporter of the Count of Paris, and Lamartine, totally won over to the republic a few minutes before the opening of the Chamber!

Third act! To obtain the approval of the streets, the sole effective authority, and not to be outwitted, the seven notables, as soon as the encumbrances of the street barricades permitted, reached the Hôtel de Ville, that "Tuileries of the people", surrounded by a noisy crowd and occupied by strong young men, armed and vociferous. They found an office there and began, in indescribable tumult, punctuated by rifle-shots, to share out portfolios. An easy task among comrades! But about eight o'clock in the evening four men arrived unceremoniously who called themselves ministers chosen after discussion by the secret societies in the haunts of the *Reform*; three journalists, Marrast, Flocon and Louis Blanc and an unknown Albert. Disgruntled, the others had to push themselves forward a bit! Then the eleven passed into the municipal council hall, packed to the ceiling, to receive there, in a more or less official manner, their investiture by the people. They were acclaimed. The new leaders when the list was read out "offered themselves in the window recesses to the admiration of the crowd" (Duveau) and heard shouts of "Long live the Republic"! One thing was certain; the barricades had abolished the régime of property qualifications and brought in the experience, perhaps premature, of universal suffrage.

But was France republican? Has one the right, is it sensible, when one has been nominated by a revolutionary procedure, to run the risk of a repudiation? Hence after a laborious discussion, this little masterpiece: "Although the provisional government . . . prefers the republican form, neither the people of Paris nor the provisional government can claim to impose their opinion on that of the citizens who will be consulted about the final form of government. . . ." Who then would dare to read this proclamation to men becoming more and more impatient, and whom memories of July predisposed to sniff out betrayal everywhere? Then, resolutely, Lamartine launched from the balcony the magic formula: "The Republic is proclaimed!"

Thus ended at the Hôtel de Ville a drama which had commenced that morning at the Tuileries and had continued at the Palais-Bourbon. Its speed and its culmination had upset all calculations. The *National* of the 25th said: "Never has a revolution been so swift, so unexpected." And Barrot, towards the end of his life: "We were . . . very far from suspecting with what ease this government which had claimed to be so strong could be overthrown." From the monarchy to the republic, by the intermediary of a regency, everything had given way to the pressure of the mob. Up until the elections of 23 April, for the 16th was already a warning, the Parisian revolutionaries claimed to rule France by the agency of authorities regarded as executive organs of "the will of the people".

## THE "SEVEN-WEEK REVOLUTION"

### A Government Disarmed and Torn Asunder

Party spirit has not been kind to the guardians of the Hôtel de Ville who had never envisaged recourse to violence; they have often been judged traitors or incompetents. They represented a majority current among the forty-eighters of France and of Europe; they believed in Fraternity. They were men of 1792 or of 1789, rarely of 1793! On the example of the poet who fascinated them and dominated the crowd, they were Girondins rather than men of the Mountain; they held the Terror in hatred.

But who were these illustrious persons who had been enthroned by the workers? Dupont de l'Eure (1767–1855), the nominal president, was a symbol; the people's imagination liked to link the doyen of the parliamentary opposition under two monarchies to the Revolution, improperly associating the Assembly of the Five Hundred, where he sat, with the Convention. Lamartine (1790–1869) enjoyed among the uncultured masses a prestige conferred on him by his mysterious gift. The educated artisans admired his work as historian of the Revolution. During those few weeks when the art of government was to become confounded with the art of oratory, action with poetry, he was without a rival. Minister of Foreign Affairs, he resisted the seductions of dreams and showed a surprising realism. The presence of François Arago (1786–1853) demanded attention; the Republic always had a weakness for revolutionary savants. The famous astronomer had for decades been regarded as a model of uprightness and political integrity. He was to show himself particularly hostile to the workers' demands, but exceedingly attentive to the interests of his family; he himself was Minister of the Marine, his brother Étienne was entrusted with control of the Posts and his son Émmanuel would be successively government commissioner in Lyons and a diplomat at Berlin. Like Arago, Garnier-Pagès (1803–73) belonged, through his half-brother who died in 1841, to the radical aristocracy; this honest broker, having become Mayor of Paris on 24 February, was installed on 6 March in the Ministry of Finances which the Jewish banker, Goudchaux, a friend of James de Rothschild, relinquished with relief. His memory is burdened with the "45 centime" tax. Insisting on the mediocrity of his personality and recalling the shouted comment of some street-urchin when his name was read out from the list of the Provisional Government, "He's no bloody good!", historians do not explain his entry, despite the anathemas cast at the "greybeards" of 1848, into the Government of National Defence of 1870. Crémieux (1796–1880), also called upon to link the Third Republic with the Second (his decree in favour of his co-religionists in Algeria is famous), Marie (1795–1870), a republican deputy under the Second Empire, Ledru-Rollin (1807–74), all of them lawyers, administered respectively Justice, Public Works and Internal Affairs. The first two were able moderates, the third a bombastic leader of a purely verbal social democracy. The conservatives reproached him for the looseness of his morals and above all for his cynical interventions in the electoral campaign; they forgot, once their fears had passed, the outstanding services rendered to the cause of law and order by a revolutionary Minister of the Interior.

The latecomers of the evening of the 24th were only to take a full part from the 28th onward in the work of the Provisional Government, a group of colleagues representing the State, but they were not to get portfolios. Marrast (1801–52), a person of some importance as editor of the *National*, played a clever trick on his friends by rejoining them under the standard of the *Reform*; soon successor to Garnier-Pagès as Mayor of Paris, he was to act like a sworn enemy of the extreme Left to which his three eleventh-hour companions belonged. Flocon (1800–66) probably played an important part in the insurrection. Louis Blanc (1812–82), a contributor to the *Reform*, was a historian of talent and the theoretician of European reputation of the Organization of Labour. He burned with the desire to avenge himself on the fate which had ordained for him, a child of the well-to-do bourgeoisie, a life of trials and had endowed small stature on a great man. He wished that a proletarian would symbolize his mission. Alexandre Martin (1815–95), a humble mechanic, made an impression on the bourgeois; once recovered from their surprise, they soon grew accustomed to this silent young man who reassured them by his presence. After the fall of the Government, this former militant of the Seasons was to find his own milieu, that of the secret societies. He was to know the fate of the losers by 15 May and ended his long life as an obscure employee of the gas company.

The cohesion of a Government divided among all shades of republican ideology and split by personal conflicts remained the major fact of spring 1848. Masonic ties (Dupont de l'Eure, Crémieux, Ledru-Rollin, Garnier-Pagès, Marie and Louis Blanc were all freemasons) no doubt contributed, as Duveau loves to point out. But the real cement of the February Government was the conviction that rallying around Lamartine was for each of them the sole means, in the midst of gathering storms, to reach without too much leeway the sea of tranquillity, that is to say the elections.

The situation in Paris on the evening of 24 February was far from reassuring; it was to improve slowly. Order was not really restored in the streets until after the days of June. Workshops and businesses closed by the insurrection reopened, but there were no orders, for capital was hiding. The business slump, born of unrest, nourished it. Paris became a city of idlers and armed unemployed, which anyone who saw the city in 1944 can easily imagine. But in 1848 there was no regular force to guarantee the security of persons or goods; the defeated army had vanished and the police force faded away. At the police prefecture the giant Caussidière (1808–61), "an official cap, two pistols in his belt and an enormous bandolier supporting his sabre", had carved out a fief independent of the Mayor of Paris who was, moreover, a member of the Government. His Men of the Mountain, recruited from former political prisoners, made property-owners uneasy and did not even reassure the men who, at the Hôtel de Ville, deliberated under the impotent protection of Saint-Cyr cadets and Polytechnicians (cadets of the Artillery School). As for the National Guards no one could, on the morrow of the insurrection, distinguish amongst them which were the guardians of law and order and which the fomenters of discord. The absence of settlings of account and the extraordinarily small number of acts of looting were also remarkable. No one dreamed of hunting down "collaborators" of the régime which had been overthrown. Doubtless, from time to time, someone took advantage of the chance of destroying machinery or attacking railway lines in the outer suburbs (these were the only gestures, as we have noted, taking place throughout Europe, which the victims of progress could accomplish with an easy conscience).

This good-humoured aspect of the explosion of 1848 was inseparable from the romantic atmosphere. The people of Paris were a prey to "lyrical illusions". "At last there will be formed a society based on justice, in which all members will be free and equal. . . . Then, who knows, aided by the contagion, all Europe will soon be transformed into a federation of free peoples. After all, all that is necessary is uprightness and energy on the part of the provisional government. . . ." Shooting in the air and kicking up a row had at first been for the insurgents merely the naïve expression of triumph over the past. To wander about rifle in hand, pistol at the belt, was to prove to oneself and to others that one belonged to the *avant-garde* of the republican party. Ex-combatants became more numerous as 24 February faded into the past, and these more inclined than the genuine insurgents to form escorts for their leaders when they went to show themselves off to the authorities.

Never had the people of Paris so many guides eager to assure their well being. The suppression of surety-bonds and stamp duties led to an astonishing burgeoning of the press. Between February and June more than three hundred, cheap, often ephemeral papers were started. The one-sou newspaper made its appearance. They were cried in the streets and advertised on the hoardings. Their founders did not behave as businessmen but as apostles. Written for the masses, as their sensational titles attested (*The Voice of the People*, *The Spirit of the People*, *The Constituent People*, Lamennais, *The Representative of the People*, Proudhon), this press aimed less at information than at education. The condemnation in the emphatic language of the time of "abuses and social privileges" was its principal theme. It was not accomplished by any practical plan. Association, based on the brotherhood of workers and the propertied classes, rarely questioned, was the miracle-remedy. Catholicism, if we are to believe certain authors, and freemasonry should have marked the course of the French revolution of 1848 and should have helped, through a handful of intellectuals, to spread the doctrine that the solution of social problems was largely a matter of good-will; in *The New Era*, Lacordaire, the abbé Maret and Ozanam were regarded by the middle classes as the advocates of the poor. There was, also, a violent press, for which the audience increased the more dreams clashed with realities. It drew its force from the tradition of 1793 (1848 had its *Père Duchesne* and its *Vieux Cordelier*). Under the patronage of the "great ancestors" it attacked the "bourgeois", the "Girondins of our time", and denounced the supposed fraternity as a reactionary intrigue. By its excesses it created in the provinces and throughout Europe the impression that the capital was in the hands of new terrorists.

In Paris the activities of the press were eclipsed by those of the clubs, of which the name alone, recalling the Jacobin period, was enough to arouse the mistrust of the country people. Their prodigious scope was the expression of a feeling of relaxation or liberation. Pure idealists, but also lovers of direct action, the outcasts long compelled to go to earth or to keep silent took possession of hastily erected rostra whence they preached vast schemes of social and political reconstruction. The crowd of idlers, sometimes armed, sometimes not, flocked to these unaccustomed spectacles. The people, well meaning but ignorant, burned with the moving passion for self-instruction. Those who had been nothing on 24 February felt a delirious joy at being in the forefront of the foundation of a new world. In a few weeks more than four hundred clubs were founded. Feminism, a product of literary Romanticism, made its appearance on the public forum. Disciples of George Sand undertook to educate French women and to eliminate the prejudices of French men. Public opinion was to welcome Eugénie Niboyet's Club for the Emancipation of Women with ironic sympathy. The clubs of foreign refugees, to which we shall return, worked in liaison with the progressive clubs to modify French policy even if it should be at the cost of internal unrest. The greater number of some hundred and fifty such clubs enjoyed, quite wrongly, a terrifying reputation. Such was the case of the Central Fraternal Society of the mild Cabet (1788–1856). Really formidable were those which emerged from the secret societies that had preserved the habits of clandestinity in a régime of liberty. The Society of the Rights of Man had been, since its foundation, preoccupied with recruiting trusty agents ready to respond without equivocation to the first call to insurrection. Blanqui's club and that of Barbès had, because of the personality of their founders, attracted the attention of a vast public. Imprisoned since 1839 (he was to pass more than thirty-three years in prison), Blanqui (1805–81) was liberated on 24 February; on the 25th he founded the Central Republican Society! At first celebrities (Baudelaire, Sainte-Beuve) and ladies of good society came with shuddering curiosity to hear this little man promulgate with courtesy a sort of theory of "permanent revolution". When it became evident that this was not a vague proposal the social world deserted a club which was to be more and more frequented by revolutionary artisans from the suburbs. Also freed by the February days but chilly towards Blanqui since the setback of 1839, Barbès (1809–70) opened the Club of the Revolution on 21 March. The title had no doubt been chosen to entice away adherents of the rival club. Unlike Blanqui, harsh and bitter, Barbès did not recall the tradition of 1793. He was a man of forty-eight, sentimental and charming. At first he dreamed, as did many other popular leaders, of making his club a forceful central electoral committee in agreement with provincial clubs for the constitution of electoral committees in the departments. Rivalry with the Republican Society turned the initial position of the Club of the Revolution "Left". This outbidding, fruit of disunion, was to mark all the enterprises of the spokesmen of the people of Paris. The government was to learn little by little how to make good use of the clubs, but on several occasions the clubs were to endanger its existence.

### A Government Confined: the Seven-Day Social Revolution (25 February–2 March)

From 25 February to 2 March the Government lived in constant fear of being swept away, either by the crowds massed before the Hôtel de Ville which, according to the latest rumours, either acclaimed or booed it, or by the delegations which invested it and demanded an immediate hearing. The important decisions taken, especially in the social field, did not make up, as pedagogic imperatives have led us to believe, the elements of a concerted policy. They were promises, marking out the calendar of riotous demonstrations.

On the 25th about midday a small group detached itself from an armed mob above which floated red flags; at its head was the workman Marche, holding a petition drawn up in the offices of the *Pacific Democracy* by Considérant (1808–93) which Louis Blanc might well have been able to sign. Slapping the stock of his rifle noisily, Marche commented laconically: "The organization of labour, *within one hour!* That is the people's wish. We are waiting!" What could be done, except to give way? And Louis Blanc drew up, with what joy we may well guess, the famous decree: "The Government of the French Republic binds itself to guarantee the livelihood of the workers by providing work . . . it will guarantee work for all citizens. It recognizes that workers may organize in order to enjoy the profits of their labour." In a few hours the Republic had become, on paper, socialist!

For a new régime a new symbol! About three o'clock in the afternoon men excited by rumours of an imminent regency chanted "The Red Flag" before the Hôtel de Ville. Lamartine

came forward and confronted the vociferous sabre bearers.
The astonishing self-confidence of which he had already given
proof on the 24th was stimulated by the fear, expressed in
whispers, that the adoption of the red flag would take away all
credit from his pacific policy as Minister of Foreign Affairs. Of
his lyrical effusion, admirably adapted to move popular feelings,
history has retained only the splendour of a peroration . . . a
false one! "The red flag . . . has made only the circuit of the
Champ de Mars, dragged in the blood of the people . . . the
tricolour has made the circuit of the world, with the name, the
glory and the freedom of the country." An eye-witness states:
"The people, who rose like a tide, who rumbled like thunder,
stopped and were silent."

What the eloquence of a poet could do, the eloquence of a
demagogue could undo. During the night the intractable
Blanqui had again stirred up his partisans; a fresh manifestation on the 26th in favour of the red flag! An ingenious compromise, which Louis Blanc accepted, provided that "the
authorities will wear a red rosette which will also be placed on
the haft of the flag." On the 27th, a Sunday, the new masters
left the heavy atmosphere of the Hôtel de Ville for a few hours.
The solemn proclamation of the Republic at the foot of the July
column had a double effect: it flattered the taste of the Parisians
for ceremonies which recalled the great civic festivals of the
Revolution and it gathered together enough people to impress
on the trouble-makers the support given to the Government by
peaceful men. Behind the organized units, the men of Saint-Cyr
and the Polytechnic, were elements of the National Guard with
whom were mingled "other citizens whose arms and dress were
the living evidence of the accomplished revolution". The
members of the Government "with tricolour scarves and the
red rosette" bathed in the plaudits of the crowd which consoled
them for the discordant clamour of the previous days.

The following day, the 28th, two thousand workers (mainly
from the printing and building trades), drawn up in bodies
according to trade, came to demand the creation of a "Ministry
of Progress", that is to say of Labour. Whether in agreement
with Louis Blanc or not, this was the logical outcome of the

decree of the 25th of which the first practical application seems to have been, actually on the 28th, the revolutionary institution of the National Workshops (which were in fact charity workshops). To fulfil this the Government had to turn to the theoretician of the 'organization of labour' and confide in him the official mission of installing socialism. Once again the majority was outwitted. By a transaction which calmed the susceptibilities of the extreme Left, it was decided to form a "government commission for the workers" immediately. Sitting at the Luxembourg in place of the Chamber of Peers, under the presidency of Louis Blanc assisted by Albert and made up of employers' and workers' delegates, joined by socialist writers and economists, it had "for special and express mission to concern itself" with the fate of the workers. Having met on 1 March, it proposed the abolition of competitive wage-bargaining (in the building industry, above all, the foremen, veritable sub-contractors, shamelessly exploited their companions whom they engaged) and a reduction in working hours. The Government was to ratify it on 2 March. The decree fixing the hours of work in Paris at ten and in the provinces at eleven hours affected, unlike the English legislation, workers of all ages and both sexes and all enterprises. But after this good start, the commission became bogged down in endless controversies between intransigent doctrinaires.

Thus ended the "seven-day revolution". Seized by the throat, the Government had made promises whose fulfilment was regarded as certain; at the beginning of March why doubt the social efficacy of the workshops and the Luxembourg Commission for which Louis Blanc stood surety? Were not the undertaking to reform indirect taxation (taxes on salt, drinks, etc.) and the decrees of 2 March the final proof of an active sympathy for "the working classes?"

## A Government Under the Régime of Supervised Liberty
## (4 March–11 April)

On 4 March the funerals of "the citizens who had died for the Republic on the 23 and 24 of February" were the occasion of a fresh and very moving civic ceremony. After an immense procession in which the clergy of the Madeleine and the National Guards took part, the workers' delegations accompanied the relics of the martyrs to the July column (in the Place de la Bastille, commemorating the 1830 revolution). Marie expressed the hope that the "calm and grandeur of today's meeting would be a fresh proof of those principles of order which are the solid and durable foundation of the new Republic".

In fact, after 4 March, the Provisional Government passed from the régime of confinement to that of supervised liberty. Goaded by the press, organized by the clubs, a section of the populace abandoned itself passionately to politics; the preparations of the elections to the National Guard and to the Assembly were the problems of the day. The Government took advantage of this respite to forestall a repetition of the threats from the streets and to hasten the transference of its fragile authority to the representatives of the nation.

On the 25th it had been decided to open enrolment in the National Guard to all Frenchmen aged between twenty-one and fifty-five. This eminently democratic measure was to increase the effectives from 56,000 in February to 190,000 in March. On the 25th also the *garde mobile* was established. It was to consist, in principle, of twenty-four battalions of a thousand volunteers each, aged between sixteen and thirty and receiving 1·50 francs a day. Young workers who had had their baptism of fire on the barricades were tempted (service in the National Guard remained unpaid) to become the pretorians of legality. The attitude of the *garde mobile* in June was to prove that, following the example of Caussidière, the eleven men of the Hôtel de Ville had known how "to make order out of disorder".

On 5 March the elections to the Assembly had been fixed for 9 April. The many troubles reported from the departments (forest crimes, crimes against tax officials, anti-Semitic agitation in the east, machine-smashing, strikes) were linked to the difficulties of 1845-7; they had become explosive because of the disorder in the administration but were not aimed against the Government. From 25 February the immense army of "republicans of the day after" submerged, in the provinces,

the slender cohorts of the "republicans of the day before".
Thus at Chavignolles, on the 26th, the "proclamation of the
Republic was posted on the town hall. This great event stunned
the bourgeois. But when it became known that the Supreme
Court of Appeal, the Court of Appeal, the Exchequer Court,
the Commercial Court, the Chamber of Notaries, the State
Council, the University, the generals and M. de la Roche-
jaquelin himself had given their adhesion to the Provisional
Government, people began to breathe more easily . . . "
(*Bouvard and Pécuchet*, Flaubert).

The rallying of the great State bodies and of the army to all
régimes had become a regular thing since 1815; the clergy had
scarcely taken in the Voltairean atmosphere of the July
Monarchy, before it reproached it for having supported the
cause of freedom of secondary education very feebly. The
peasant vote opened wide perspectives to them. The legitimist
nobility saw in the fall of Louis Philippe the judgement of God,
and, as we know, had for some time past calculated the advantages of an extended suffrage. The local notables were not
prepared to play the role of Don Quixote. The fear of spreading
unrest in the provinces, and above all the spectre of Parisian
"communism", led them to rally to a republic which rejected
the heritage of 1793 and its symbols: the guillotine and the
promissory note. On 26 February the government took the
initiative of abolishing the death penalty for political offences.
Faced with a financial and monetary crisis, Garnier-Pagès
used the classic methods to gain the confidence of the propertied
classes and increased by 45 per cent all the direct taxes, which
provoked a discontent "in the countryside which was to prove
fatal to the Republic" (Pouthas). After a time it would, to be
sure. For the moment, the peasant, even when poor, believed
his patch of land threatened by the socialist writers and threw
all responsibility for the increase in his rates (levied only after
the elections) on loafers who strutted pompously in the National
Workshops. With his vote he was to contribute to the foundation
of a cheap and "honest" republic. This state of mind was well
known to the Minister of the Interior, Ledru-Rollin, and the
small groups of the "republicans of the day before". They tried,

by creating clubs and newspapers in the Parisian manner, to fashion these backward fellow-citizens in their own image. This man, Ledru-Rollin, supporter of an "interventionist and radical conception in the elections" (Kayser), replaced the prefects by "missionaries of new ideas", who were agents of the Government. Those historians who tried to judge equitably these "republicans of the day after" depict them as Convention members on circuit and stress spitefully that these gentlemen who were preparing themselves for a parliamentary career were lacking in disinterestedness! The ever more incisive circulars of Ledru-Rollin and the attitude of the members of the Parisian clubs demanding a postponement of the elections showed that the progressives had no faith in the efficacy of official propaganda.

The certainty of their impending victory incited men of good will to take to the streets; on 14 March the Government, with an eye to democratization, disbanded the crack companies of the National Guard (riflemen and grenadiers). On 16 March, 30,000 National Guards converged on the Hôtel de Ville to save their "bearskins". Amongst them were residents of the Faubourg Saint-Germain, but also petty bourgeois who, three weeks earlier, had been fighters for liberty. The split among the February insurgents had as its pretext this blow to their self-esteem, as its cause the social problem. The demonstrators, shouting "Down with Ledru-Rollin! Down with the communists!", were coldly received by the Government.

On the pretext of supporting the Government against this reactionary putsch, the clubs, in accord with Louis Blanc, next day assembled more than a hundred thousand persons, a rally such as had never been seen before! Its real aim was to postpone the elections. At the last moment, out of the fear of Blanqui who controlled the demonstration, the extreme Left rallied to the majority, which postponed the elections in the National Guard to 5 April and those in the Assembly to the 23rd. Once more the Government extricated itself from its difficulties, as the weak always do, by a compromise. It was a great temptation for its adversaries to misuse force against its impotence.

## THE DEFEAT OF THE PEOPLE'S REVOLUTION IN PARIS AND IN THE PROVINCES (16–23 APRIL)

On 16 April the extremists lost control of the Paris streets. On the 23rd the votes of Frenchmen condemned them without appeal.

On 16 April an unsigned extract from the *Bulletin of the Republic* of the 14th could be read on the walls of Paris: "If the elections do not lead to the triumph of *social truth* . . . there can be only one way of salvation for the people . . . to adjourn the decisions of a false national representation." To avoid recourse to the extreme solution which George Sand, the Egeria of the republic, put forward ingenuously in an official organ, the *Club of the Clubs*, a federation of about sixty clubs, it was resolved to postpone these accursed elections indefinitely. The occasion would be the meeting on the Champ de Mars on Sunday 16 April of thousands of workers invited there to elect the officers of the general staff of the National Guard, the pretext a demonstration for the application of noble principles: abolition of the exploitation of man by man, the organization of labour. Forewarned, notably by Louis Blanc and Albert in accord with the chiefs of the conspiracy, the majority decided, for the first time, to resist; it appealed to the *garde mobile* and the National Guard which Ledru-Rollin summoned, after an attack of conscience. The unarmed workers paraded under the bantering laughter of the "bearskins", shouting: "Long live the Republic! Down with the communists!"

An abyss separated the 16th of April from the 16–17 of March. The isolation of the revolutionaries was accentuated. In March the much-hated defection of the republican petty bourgeois had been compensated for on the following day by the fervent rally of the populace. A month later many workers, such as Colonel Barbès (since the publication of the Taschereau documents on 31 March his rival Blanqui seemed lost), rejoined their legion to support the Government. Just before his disappearance Blanqui had at last, thanks to the skill and courage of Lamartine, acquired his freedom (despite the whining of the clubs, he had allowed the first troops to return to the capital) and had reinforced his cohesion at the expense of the extreme Left. The exemplary attitude of Ledru-Rollin had isolated Louis Blanc and Albert. With the Festival of Fraternity of 20 April a period of unrest ended in apotheosis; hundreds of thousands of Parisians, impassioned actors or enthusiastic spectators, took part in the restoration of their colours to the National Guard, to the *garde mobile* ... and to the army!

The results of the elections of 23 April, marked by an 84 per cent turnout, surpassed the most sombre forecasts of the Parisian revolutionaries. France, and Paris, had rejected them! Tired of agitations which they did not understand, the provinces were irritated by the demonstrations of 17 March and 16 April which were intended to muzzle them. Their votes were a reaction due to fear and indignation. Out of nine hundred seats the candidates of the *Reform* and of Socialism obtained less than a hundred; the monarchists transformed into republicans won three hundred. To the legitimist majority were added some former dynastics (Barrot). The curés carried more weight than the instructors mobilized by their minister, Carnot. The undeniable success of the five hundred republicans (known as the *National*) relied on the prestige of Lamartine and on a régime ready to facilitate the activities of the Government agents. The scrutiny of the departmental polls ended, because of the multiplicity of lists, by giving an advantage to those which the Government agents had drawn up under official patronage; seventy-seven of these were to be ephemeral representatives of the people.

This strange outcome increased the bitterness of the revolutionaries; the greater number of the deputies were, as under the monarchy, rich landowners, while the percentage of lawyers increased. The twenty-six workmen elected were, generally speaking, moderates. In Paris the defeat of the socialist writers Considérant and Cabet was crushing, and Louis Blanc, the most recently elected of the members of the Government, received less than half the number of votes given to Lamartine (120,000 as against 260,000). The "seven-week revolution" (Labrousse) ended with the melancholy conclusion that the foundation and maintenance of a new society were incompatible with the free play of democratic politics; at the local elections and then at the legislative elections of May 1849 universal suffrage was to dispense its favours to the elect of the former electoral régime.

## THE LAST PARISIAN REACTION AGAINST THE VERDICT OF THE PEOPLE: THE DAYS OF JUNE

Between the lamentable political activities of 15 May 1848 and of 13 June 1849 against the national representation, the workers' insurrection of June 1848 was the last demonstration of despair and of hopes betrayed.

The composition of the Executive Committee, to which were appointed Arago, Garnier-Pagès, Marie, Lamartine and Ledru-Rollin, in that order, showed that the elected of the nation judged the concessions wrested from the Government to be excessive. On 15 May the members of the clubs accepted George Sand's threat to the letter. To drive out the Assembly and proclaim a derisory insurrectionist government they succeeded in mobilizing their adherents for the last time only by involving the liberation of Poland! Albert, Barbès, Blanqui, were arrested, Caussidière and Louis Blanc eliminated from public life.

The June days (23–26) were exclusively the work of a proletariat which despised the politicians of the Assembly and the organizers of vain political coups. The workers, and not only those who had benefited from these institutions, saw in the Workshops a memory, the people's victory in February, and a symbol, the right to work. For the Assembly, the interpreter of the country, the existence of the Workshops was a financial scandal (they cost 150,000 francs a day), a moral scandal (more than a hundred thousand men were enrolled and paid to do nothing) and a political scandal. Marie had favoured the creation of a Club of the National Workshops and the entry into the National Guard of workers whom he believed he could control; the penetration of "demagogic" propaganda into a milieu intended to combat it was one of the lessons of

15 May. The measures announcing dissolution sparked off spontaneous riots which degenerated into a strictly social war. Against the insurgents of hunger, the *garde mobile* and the National Guard fought with even more ardour than the army: several thousand dead among the insurgents as well as a thousand of their adversaries. The fear was not only, as it has been called, "a bourgeois fear", though it was recalled that the zone of barricades had been that of workers' Paris facing bourgeois Paris. Ledru-Rollin demanded that the prefects send contingents of the National Guard, and units of this people's militia got under way from the north, the east and from Normandy. The provinces were eager to combat, by force of arms, the perpetual agitators who refused to bow before the verdict of universal suffrage. How could one be astonished if, after so atrocious a repression (more than fifteen hundred shot and more than ten thousand condemned to prison or deportation) followed by the annulment of the social victories of the revolution (a law of September increased the working day to twelve hours but only in factories and workshops of at least twenty workers; in November the right to work was not included in the Constitution), the proletarians revived, over and above the dreams of February, the Bonapartist myth?

The crushing victory won on 10 December 1848 by Louis Napoleon was primarily due to the peasantry. But the workers too had a considerable share in it; with their five-and-a-half million votes, the "nephew of the little corporal" defeated the candidate of the bourgeoisie, the republican General Cavaignac (one-and-a-half million), leader of the executive and "prince of the blood" since his triumph in June and also crushed that of the Left-wing parliamentarian Ledru-Rollin (370,000), the socialist Raspail (37,000) and Lamartine (17,000), the symbol of a dead hope.

Universal suffrage had put an end to the revolution in April. Was it now to substitute the Empire or the Monarchy for the Republic? To this alternative the day of 13 June 1849 gave an answer of which the people dimly perceived the anachronism. The "assassination of the Roman Republic" drove Ledru-Rollin to attempt against the legislative conservative majority elected a month earlier a new 15 May which foundered in ridicule or indifference. The leader of the Mountain escaped the repression by taking refuge in London. . . .

## THE FRENCH REVOLUTION AND EUROPE

### The French Republic Repudiates Revolutionary Messianism

While in internal affairs the Government, driven by fear, took improvised measures, it courageously fixed the main principles of an external policy which it did its best to put into force despite the most lively opposition and which its successors, prince-president included, were to adopt until the Rome expedition. At the beginning of the "seven-weeks revolution" Lamartine rejected the temptation of going to war in order to give the oppressed peoples their freedom and France her "natural frontiers".

This policy clashed with that of the extreme Left, in which the "pacifists" Considérant and Leroux were considered eccentrics; within the Government Ledru-Rollin and Louis Blanc were fervent partisans of "the crusade of the peoples". Lamartine, one of the few writers who had not been carried away by the enthusiasm of 1840 (his *Marseillaise of Peace* countered both Becker and Musset), succeeded in getting his views shared by the majority of his colleagues because republican France, it is sometimes forgotten, was threatened until mid-March by a "crusade of the kings". Nicholas I nurtured the hope of realizing, with Austria and Prussia, the dream which the Polish insurrection, the German unrest and the Italian troubles had dissipated after July 1830. Even more serious was that the German liberals approved the Prussian mobilization on the Rhine, fearing lest France should once again invade peaceable Germany.

The manifesto of 4 March, which appeared before the fall of Metternich and before the Berlin days which made all fears of a coalition similar to that of 1815 vanish, was not merely the work of chance; it was also in a noble style the statement of a long-term policy. Revolutionary Messianism was repudiated:

"As all the world, we too want to go forward in fraternity and peace." Attempting to appease the apprehensions of the chancelleries without exacerbating the Parisian revolutionaries, Lamartine recognized *de facto* the treaties of 1815 which he formally condemned *de jure*. His revisionism in principle only envisaged recourse to diplomacy. Deeply enamoured of peace, France declared that she was none the less willing to fight if she were "constrained or threatened" or if Austria tried to crush the liberal and national movements of Italy or Switzerland on her frontiers. By looking forward only to "the proselytism of sympathy and esteem", the manifesto achieved its essential purpose: to woo the good graces of London. Palmerston, to whom Lamartine made it known that France cherished no designs on Belgium, appreciated the efforts of the French Government to free itself from the romanticism of the barricades. Close understanding with the United Kingdom was for Lamartine and his successors the condition for the maintenance of peace.

This policy, which revived that of the July Monarchy on the morrow of 1830, had nothing stirring in it for a Left-wing interventionist and Anglophobe whose activities were linked with those of several foreign clubs: the Club of the Polish Emigration, a resurrection of the Polish Democratic Society, three German clubs (especially the German Workers' Club, an offshoot of the Federation of the Just) soon merged into the German Democratic Society presided over by Herwegh, the Italian Exiles Club, the Iberian Democratic Club, the Belgian Patriotic Society, etc. These groups were supported by the delegations rushing to Paris to act as spokesmen for their compatriots. Under pretext of expressing to the new leaders an admiring sympathy, they pressed them to help to export the revolution. From 4 March to 2 April there was a procession of Poles, Germans, Swiss, Greeks, Magyars, Rumanians, Portuguese, Spaniards and also deputations who criticized the policy of friendship with Sardinia (the Savoyards) or of understanding with the United Kingdom (the Chartists and Irishmen). The ceremony was immutable: Garnier-Pagès, Cremieux, Lamartine, expanded vague formulas which nonetheless the

Governments concerned considered unseemly for "they comprised some sort of judgement on the affairs of another country" (Lord Normanby).

Even more than imprudent utterances, the existence of armed bands which openly organized, with the complicity of high administrative authorities, free corps intended to foment revolution in Belgium, Savoy and Germany, cast suspicion on Lamartine's good faith, though he was without authority in internal affairs. On 29 March fifteen hundred men were marshalled, with the support of the Government commissioner in the north and in accord with Ledru-Rollin, near Mouscron, at Risquons-Tout. The Savoy expedition assumed another aspect since it appeared, rightly or wrongly, to be the result of a considered policy. On 20 March Lamartine had suggested the possibility of Savoy being one day "reunited with France". On 3 April the Savoy workers, supported by the Lyons republicans, the *Voraces*, who had paraded on 30 March before the Government commissioner Emmanuel Arago, took possession of Chambéry, whence they were driven out on the 4th by the country people who reacted in a similar manner to the provincial National Guards when faced by the June insurgents. Charles Albert even proposed a defensive alliance with Switzerland! The mad adventure of Herwegh created between republican France and Germans of all persuasions an atmosphere of profound mistrust. The German Democratic Society was openly and apparently preparing an invasion of Germany. On 18 March six thousand Germans assembled in the Champs-Élysées. Between 24 March and 3 April five battalions left, heading for Strasbourg. Everywhere along the route the champions of German democracy, who were joined by Poles and Frenchmen, were fêted. Finally, the German Legion, formed in Strasbourg on 14 April, announced its aims through the pen of Herwegh: "To fight for the freedom of the German people . . . to rush to the aid of a revived Poland . . . to commence the struggle for German rights in Schleswig-Holstein." The German princes, in terror, pleaded for weeks with the Provisional Government to keep its undertakings, while the press announced an imminent invasion of French workers.

During the night of 23–24 March, at the news that the French had crossed the Rhine, a "great fear" (*Franzosenlärm*) seized the Baden and Wurtemberg countryside: a Tübingen professor seriously advised young persons of the fair sex to wear men's clothes ... to preserve their virtue! Hecker and Struve, who had launched an appeal for insurrection, refused, anxious not to be compromised by foreign agents, the aid of the Paris Legion, a tendentious translation of the German Legion. Having crossed the river on 23 April, the legion was wiped out at Dossenbach on the 27th. It was only on the 26th that a decree dated the 19th appeared in the *Moniteur* (the demonstration of the 16th had strengthened the authority of the moderates) pronouncing the dissolution of meetings held by Germans.

Even as the raid on Savoy made the Italians indignant, so Herwegh's enterprise did not facilitate diplomatic intervention in favour of Poland. Lamartine had thought to profit by the popularity of the Polish cause in Germany to encourage the King of Prussia to transform the Grand duchy of Posen into an autonomous Poland. After a few weeks of idyll, Poles and Germans confronted one another in Poznania; in Germany, by the end of April, the Polish effervescence decreased. The question was asked as to what was the role of these Poles who swore only by France; were they not, as their participation in the Paris Legion seemed to suggest, the tools of French ambitions? On 26 April Frederick William IV incorporated the German districts of the Grand duchy of Posen into Prussia.

Nationalism, which had proved so sensitive in Germany and Italy, little by little dissipated the illusions of the majority of the Provisional Government about the fraternity of peoples and encouraged Lamartine to keep to the policy laid down on 4 March. This passivity, which the Parisian revolutionaries condemned, was, as we have seen, the cause of tumultuous demonstrations. But the provinces, hostile to adventure, approved it. At the April elections the peasants voted against those whom they considered enemies both of property and peace.

## Abortive Revolutions

Despite the abstention of official France, the wave of revolution broke over the constitutional States bordering on the Republic. Everywhere it was halted, either by opportune concessions or by threat of force.

The influence of the February days on Belgium was not limited to the unfortunate affair of Risquons-Tout. An explosive economic and social situation (we must recall the harsh conditions of the workers' lives and the misery of Flanders) would doubtless have produced in 1848 serious convulsions if Belgium had not carried out in 1847 what d'Hondt had called "the Belgian revolution". The authoritarian Leopold I was accustomed to more and more conservative Catholic Governments, the liberals having little by little been forced into opposition. In 1846 the liberal organizations had become grouped in a real party with a programme: progressive reduction of the property qualification for franchise and reforms in favour of "the working classes and the poor". The new party won the elections of 1847; its leader Rogier (1800–85) formed a homogeneous government which was still hesitant on 14 February 1848 to increase the number of electors by more than a thousand! On the news of the fall of Louis Philippe, panic seized the governing classes. Cash disappeared; without credit, industry ground to a halt. The Government called up the reservists and laid down a proposal on 21 February which, approved on 12 March, reduced the property qualification to the constitutional minimum. The electoral body suddenly increased from 55,000 to 79,000! The working classes stirred; at Ghent on 1 April the troops killed two demonstrators. Advances were made to the industrialists to revive industrial activity, aid was distributed to 400,000 unemployed (a tenth of the population), for the most part Flemings, and charity workshops were opened. To provide for such enormous expenses "the propertied classes did all that they could for themselves" (d'Hondt). With the agreement of the Catholic opposition the Ministry had two forced loans voted. It may be understood that these political and social measures, together with the actions of the army and the police, cancelled all the efficacy of a republican and socializing propaganda too obviously inspired by Parisian annexionist circles.

In the Netherlands the proclamation of the French Republic, the Parisian demonstrations and the attempt at Risquons-Tout frightened the middle classes who had not forgotten either the French domination of the revolutionary epoch or the consequences of the days of July. The spectre of 1793 which the nobles and the Protestant conservatives evoked to thwart the revision of the *fundamental law* and the emancipation of the Catholics on the contrary encouraged William II to pursue reforms. He dismissed the reactionary ministry. The new ministry was based on the liberals of Thorbecke, for the most part tolerant Protestants, and on the Catholic admirers of Lamennais and the readers of *The New Era*, strong in the resistance of their Limburg co-religionists to Germanic appetites. The work of the "Catholic-Liberal" union resembled that undertaken in 1830–1 in the Belgian State by a coalition of similar views. The constitution of October 1848 guaranteed, together with freedom of the press and the right of assembly, the free exercise of religion. The re-establishment of the Catholic hierarchy was promised (it was to become effective in 1853). The provincial Estates nominated the members of the Upper Chamber; the Lower Chamber to which ministers were responsible no longer represented the "orders" but the qualified electors. Thus in a few weeks a state of the *ancien régime*, through fear of French subversive doctrines, achieved at the same time its 1789 revolution and its 1830 revolution! In 1848 William II also endowed the Grand duchy of Luxembourg with a constitution based on qualified electors.

The Scandinavian States were only affected by the events of February through the nationalist unleashing of the "German revolution". The great problem for the Danes, supported by public opinion in Sweden and Norway, was the survival of the Danish State, for which absolutist Russia was a guarantor; in Copenhagen, as in Stockholm, the Germans were considered the most bellicose disciples of the February insurgents. The non-recognition *de jure* of the 1815 treaties had ended by discrediting democratic ideas; at the cost of a few concessions (freedom of the press) the nationalist bourgeoisie became reconciled to the absolutist monarchy in its struggle against the external peril; from this loyal collaboration was to emerge the constitution of 1849 which suppressed representation by "orders".

In Sweden the liberal vacillations of Oscar I lasted only a short time; the property qualification régime was not to be introduced until 1865. The menace of Germanism against Jutland relegated to the background the nationalist claims of Norway, which did not obtain its independence until 1905.

Nowhere did the proclamation of the republic arouse such enthusiasm as in Switzerland. The press was at first almost unanimous in praising the virtues of the insurgents, who found imitators at Neuchâtel; on 1 March the aristocratic Government there was overthrown (it was not until 1857 that the King of Prussia recognized the *fait accompli*). But the denunciation of the treaties of Vienna soon created uneasiness. Lamartine found it hard to retort that far from concealing any intention of violating Swiss neutrality the manifesto affirmed the will to respect it. The difficulties of Austria and Prussia, the German unrest, the war in Italy, delivered the victors over the *Sonderbund* from the threats and recriminations of the conservative Powers for a year. The German republicans prepared, with the more or less open connivance of the Rhenish cantons, the movements of April and September 1848 and of May 1849. Finally, a programme drawn up in an atmosphere of civil war was realized in independence and civil peace. The constitution of 12 September 1848 transformed the Confederation, whose anachronistic name was perpetuated, into a federal State modelled on the United States; two Chambers, one representing the people, the other the cantons, nominated the executive: the federal council. Marked by the recent struggles (the Jesuits were excluded from federal territory) and still impregnated with medieval prejudices (Jews were not full citizens), the constitution of 1848 was the origin of modern Switzerland, whose wisdom was henceforth to preserve it from internal troubles and external conflicts.

Accustomed to live dangerously, the Iberian dictatorships were the most apt to resist the revolutionary contagion. The ministerial press depicted the February days in the most sombre colours and aroused in peoples jealous of their independence the memory of French invasions. In a State of alert, the army took preventive measures. In Portugal nothing happened; the opposition renounced an armed coup which the French Government refused to support. In Spain, in the first days of March, Narvaez suspended even the appearance of constitutional guarantees. The ultra-reactionary "Carlists" did not succeed in getting the Basque peasants to rise. Serious troubles fomented by the liberals and the republicans burst out in Madrid on 26 March; the state of siege raised, a demonstration of civilians and soldiers led, which was something new, by their non-commissioned officers took place on 7 May in the capital to cries of "Long live the Republic! Long live the sovereign people!" Seven soldiers and five civilians were executed. The two days of Madrid ended with fifteen hundred individuals sent to penal servitude and the detention or deportation of eight hundred others. The provinces remained calm with the exception of Seville where, on 13 May, part of the garrison revolted, amid popular indifference. In Spain as in Portugal the revolution of 1848 did not modify the course of an evolution which obeyed its own laws.

Irish nationalism and English Chartism were overstimulated by the February days. Irish and Chartist delegations rushed to Paris to solicit aid and advice. The alliance concluded in the spring of 1848 under the auspices of O'Connor seemed for some weeks to menace the unity of the United Kingdom and the political privileges of the propertied classes. After a cordial homage to the Irish cause, which irritated London, Lamartine, receiving Smith O'Brien on 3 April, declared that France wished "to remain on good terms . . . with the whole of Great Britain". The defection of Paris, soon followed by the Chartist setbacks and the display of internal quarrels in the face of Orangist solidarity, demobilized a great part of the opposition. John O'Connell (1810–58), who was the perpetuator, as far as the Government was concerned, of the "peaceful agitation" of his father, recommended the use of violence against his Irish rivals; on 30 April his partisans attacked the members of the Irish Confederation in Limerick. This had been torn between Smith O'Brien and J. Mitchell, who was favourable to the general insurrection which failed miserably (August) since its instigator two months before had been sentenced to fourteen years' deportation. The arrest or flight of the leaders and the drain of emigration (between 1846 and 1850 more than a million Irishmen had left for the United States) helped to restore peace for almost fifteen years.

The fall of Louis Philippe coming after the Palermo revolt reinvigorated Chartism. O'Connor shared the enthusiasm of the internationalists in the movement. On 26 February the *Northern Star* lyrically celebrated "the men of Paris". Meetings in favour of the People's Charter became more frequent as in 1838 and 1842; at Newcastle (2 March) moving addresses to the Parisian insurgents were approved. The increase in unemployment created by the reduction of demand from abroad led to spontaneous disorders on a scale unknown on the continent. At Glasgow, on 5 and 6 March, the army fired on about ten thousand rioters who were looting shops. Manchester, Birmingham and Nottingham were centres of unrest. For the first time the capital played its part. Would the United Kingdom, already profoundly shaken by the July barricades, turn to revolution under the impulsions of the February rebels? It was, however, decided to have recourse to legal methods which had already failed twice; the People's Charter supported by a petition for which it was hoped to collect six million signatures would be presented to Parliament by a delegation followed by several hundred thousand demonstrators! What was to be done after the certain rejection of the Chartist pro-gramme? Only an insignificant minority envisaged following the Parisian example. To the traditional Six Points the addition of a seventh, demanding the repeal of the Act of Union, clashed with the anti-Irish prejudices of public opinion and more especially of the workers. With the advantage of hindsight 10 April seems like a grotesque farce: O'Connor brought the petition with more than two million signatures in a cab, while the troops and a police force of 170,000 volunteers advised some tens of thousands of persons to go home peacefully across the Thames! However, the announcement of the Chartist demonstration drove the royal family and many wealthy Londoners to flight. The setback of 10 April encouraged (it was enough to evoke 16 April in Paris) the forces of reaction to begin a process of redress which the days of June were to accelerate.

There has been much discussion of the reasons for the collapse of the Chartists. The "1846 revolution"? The workers could not appreciate the benefits of free trade until the second half of the century. The influence of the Churches? Countless witnesses stress the decline of the practice of religion among the lower classes; in any case no one can seriously hold the view that English Protestantism would have been more conservative than German Protestantism or French or Italian Catholicism. The importance of the middle classes? Certainly these had won two resounding victories with electoral reform and the triumph of Cobden's League. Halévy, who insists on their "immensity", does not, however, deny the existence of two antagonistic classes, "the extreme wealth of some, the extreme poverty of others". Perhaps the preceding setbacks can throw some light on the downfall of 1848. The powerful weapon which the British proletariat alone in Europe possessed had, even at the time of Owen's revolutionary hopes, disdained the political struggle. Reserved in 1838, trade unionism had, in 1842, kept aloof from Chartism. The passing of the Factory Act of 1847 had probably contributed to accentuate this indifference to politics; in 1848 trade unionism was the enemy of Chartism. In a country where meetings could be held and petitions drawn up, and where there was a hope that concessions could be obtained by popular pressure, as in 1832, the spirit of insurrection after the fever of 1819–20 continued to decline. The Jacobin ideology, which never formed part of the workers' dreams, remained alien to the majority of the Chartists, of whom O'Connor was a good representative. Hence the mechanical repetition of unimaginative enterprises.

Resistance to the tide of revolution in the United Kingdom must be associated with that in other States (Belgium, the

Netherlands, Spain, Portugal) of differing social and economic structures and of diversified political institutions. Exported, the people's Parisian revolution only assumed explosive form (in the German and Italian States and in the Austrian Empire) where the peoples were seeking for their national unity.

# [ Chapter Ten ]

## The Crest of the Wave (March–July 1848)

AFTER THE NEWS of the proclamation of the Republic in France, the unrest in Italy increased and southern Germany, naturally enough, took the lead in the liberal, social and democratic movement in the Confederation. In Austria the Magyar aristocrats increased their demands, the Czech democrats spoke out and Metternich was overthrown. The Viennese riots (13 March) led to the Berlin insurrection (18 March). In the Confederation and Italy the movement towards liberalism and unity and in the Austrian Empire and eastern Europe the demands of the nationalities were strengthened.

### AUSTRIA ON THE DEFENSIVE IN THE EMPIRE

While the Italian "revolutions" were threatening to expel her from Lombardy-Venetia and the German revolution to dismember her, Austria was paralysed from within. On 3 March the Hungarian Diet demanded, on the instigation of Kossuth, the complete autonomy of the Crown of St Stephen and a ministry responsible to it. On the 11th a popular assembly at Pressburg (Bratislava) elaborated a plan of reform for the Czechs, inspired by a minority of bourgeois democrats grouped around Havliček, which included a Chamber common to all the lands of the Crown of St Wenceslas. Such demands were incompatible with the maintenance of absolutism personified by Metternich.

## The Viennese Revolution (13 March)

Metternich was soon to disappear, victim of an unpopularity which the diatribes of Kossuth had brought to a head. At Vienna, on 13 March—a Monday, the day which the workers only too willingly regarded as a prolongation of Sunday—a crowd of bourgeois, students and workers massed before the seat of the Diet of Lower Austria and demanded a constitution for the Empire and the dismissal of Metternich. The demonstrators were dispersed. Barricades were set up and the suburbs rose. Abandoned by most of the archdukes, notably the Archduke John, who advised against the continuance of armed repression, the old chancellor, like Louis Philippe, fled. Ferdinand I aroused great enthusiasm by conceding, together with freedom of the press, the creation of a National Guard and promising a constitution (15 March).

For the liberal nobles and the rich Viennese bourgeoisie the revolution was over. But the radicals (students, professors of the Academic Legion, petty bourgeois of the progressive clubs, proletarianized craftsmen) considered the concessions of 15 March only as a point of departure. They were, like the members of the Parisian clubs and for a longer time than they, to exert an irresistible pressure on weak Governments faced by insurmountable difficulties. The publication of a constitution applicable to the "Hereditary States", with a Chamber recruited on a basis of stringent property qualifications, led to a series of riots with the watchword "a universal Chamber elected by universal suffrage". After 15 May, the Government capitulated; a Constituent Assembly would draw up a new constitution. As in France, the action of the revolutionaries of the capital was to be submitted to the judgement of the peasantry. Already by the beginning of June observers noted the growing popularity of the Emperor who had thought himself obliged, the day after 15 May, to take refuge in

Innsbruck with his court, leaving the popular Archduke John to represent the imperial authority in Vienna.

## The Magyar Revolution

The "dualism" of 1848, which foreshadowed that of 1867–1918, was at first applied to Hungary. The Emperor entrusted Count Batthyany (1809–49), a liberal, with the formation of a ministry which would be responsible to the Diet, The first Government was a Magyar national Government, with Deak, Eötvös and Kossuth. Under the pressure of Kossuth and the Pest democrats the Diet passed a number of liberal measures (freedom of the press, trial by jury, a national guard) and social measures (equality of taxation, abolition of serfdom and suppression of seigniorial rights against compensation). In practice peasant emancipation was a mirage; lands were taken back from the serfs on the pretext that they had already been leased and the rents on vineyards were maintained; the penury of the majority of the country people prevented them from being able to pay the compensation. The constitutional laws approved on 11 April reinforced the hegemony of the Magyars. Hungary became a unitary State by the absorption of Croatia, of Transylvania and the Banat. The Diet, henceforward transferred to Pest, was made up of a Lower Chamber protected against the intrusion of non-Magyars; the complicated property qualification régime was matched with a cunning electoral distribution and with the obligation on those eligible to speak Magyar. Involved in the task of bringing to an end the settlement of problems of common interest, the imperial Government, hard pressed, was to remain deaf until the end of June to the complaints of the other nationalities of the Empire for whom 1848 meant no more than the reinforcement of a secular oppression.

## The Czech Movement and the Slavs of Austria

On the other hand, it gave satisfaction to the demands of its loyal Slavs directly under its authority. The Charter of Bohemia of 8 April ratified the most contentious of the demands of the

Assembly of 11 March (equality of the Czech and German languages in education and administration). However, solution of the fundamental political (organization of the future autonomous State) and social (emancipation of the peasants) problems was adjourned. The National Committee which, with the new governor, the liberal Count of Thun, played the role of a consultative council was dominated by the moderates, of the type of Palacky and Rieger. It repudiated the Vienna revolutionaries and sent an address of loyalty to the Emperor at Innsbruck. The invitation to Palacky to participate in the work of the Commission of the Fifty provided the Czechs with an opportunity of defining their position with regard to the new Germany and Austria. In his famous reply (11 April), widely broadcast, the historian repudiated the pretensions of the Germans at Frankfurt to absorb the Czechs. However, he did not conceive the future of his people in any other framework than that of an Austrian Federation separated from Germany: "If the Austrian State had not already existed for a long time, it would be necessary for us, in the interest of Europe and of humanity, to hasten to create it." "Austroslavism" was adopted by the radicals, who exhorted the Czechs to abstain in the elections for the Frankfurt parliament. Among the Germans of Bohemia, enthusiastic partisans of Germanic unity, it aroused the most lively reactions in that they in no way appreciated the imperial promises of 8 April concerning the equality of the two languages. The cohabitation of Czechs with the "Sudeten Germans" posed, from the year of the "fraternity of peoples", an insoluble problem which was to weigh heavily upon the destinies of the first Czechoslovak republic! The Viennese democrats, German patriots, applauded when Windischgrätz (1787–1862) put down the Prague riots of 12 June in blood. Once the state of siege was proclaimed and the National Committee dissolved, Vienna forgot its promises of 8 April; the "Czech revolution", the work of timid radicals in social affairs and intellectuals prone to negotiations, was ended. It was from the Constituent Assembly meeting in Vienna that Palacky and Rieger awaited the autonomy of the countries of the Crown of St Wenceslas.

In Galicia the fruitful policy of 1846 was continued; the Polish nobility was isolated by favouring the passions and interests of the Ruthene peasantry (half of the 4·6 million inhabitants according to the census of 1850). Serfdom was abolished and a Ruthene council set up, which demanded the division of the province into two parts, Ruthene and Polish. The Slovene demands in favour of their national language were the work of a minority, indifferent to the demands of illiterate peasants and which sent repeated declarations of loyalty.

### Austria Sacrifices the Loyal South Slavs to the Magyars

The spirit of revolt was evident among the Slavs and Rumanians, who rose against the Magyar dictatorship. The Slovak movement, whose recent efforts to resist Czech cultural influence are well known, was thrown into the arms of Prague by the refusal to grant autonomy to the *comitats* of Slovak speech; Stur and Havliček became reconciled. The Southern Slavs, who could count on many patriots among the priests and officers, took their destiny into their own hands. Under the leadership of Rajačić, Metropolitan of Karlovitz (Karlovci), more favourable than his predecessors to the newly revised Serbo-Croat language, and of Colonel Šuplikac, the restored Voivodina declared itself an autonomous province within the framework of the Empire and Šuplikac was proclaimed Voivode (13 May). A Serb legion prepared for the struggle. Strong in powerful supporters at court, the Croats obtained, without the authorization of Pest, the nomination as *ban* (governor) of Colonel, soon to be General, Jelačić (1801–59). A Croat delegation went to Alexander Karageorgević, who had replaced the Obrenović dynasty after a *coup d'état* in 1842 and who was more ready to round off his principality than to nourish vast dreams. Though the dream of a Yugoslav kingdom, under the leadership of the prince of Serbia, embracing Bosnia, Bulgaria, Croatia, Dalmatia and southern Hungary was opposed to the resolutions approved in June by the Croat Diet, a co-operation was sketched out between Belgrade and the

Serbo-Croat coalition; Alexander agreed to let his subjects enrol against the Magyars.

They (the Magyars) received the support of the imperial Government which on 10 June confirmed the integrity of the kingdom of Hungary and dismissed Jelačić. The promise to send Hungarian contingents into Italy probably explains this *volte-face*. At Vienna a division of authority between Germans and Magyars had been admitted, but no one was prepared to accept, for the benefit of a Yugoslav kingdom, a "tripartite" solution which on the eve of 1914 still had its supporters. Above all, there was fear of the advance of "pan-Slavism", uniting the Slav peoples of the Empire and those outside it. The intervention of Windischgrätz at Prague had as its aim not only the destruction of the Czech national movement but also the closing of the Slav Congress.

## *The End of the Czech Movement and the Dispersal of the Congress of Prague*

Opened on 2 June, interrupted on the 12th by the riots and dispersed on the 28th by Windischgrätz (whom the death of his wife, born a Schwartzenberg, killed by a stray bullet, did not incline to leniency), the Slav Congress, intentionally summoned at the moment when the Frankfurt parliament began its work, had from 1848 been represented in Germany as the instrument of a peril at that time imaginary pan-Slavist tsarism. (Let us recall the invectives of Engels.) Even if the Congress had brought together Poles, Ruthenes and South Slavs (Gaj, Karadžić), it was two-thirds composed of Czechs (Šafarik, Palacky, Rieger, Havliček) and Slovaks (Stur). It vigorously denounced the proposals of a "Grand Alliance" and the hegemonist pretensions of the Magyars. But a vote in favour of the reconstitution of Poland aroused suspicion in Viennese ruling circles. However, this was a prudent pan-Slavism. It rejected the Pan-Slav Federation proposed by Bakunin (1814–1876), the sole Russian delegate, and recourse to force. In the *Manifesto to the nations of Europe*, drawn up by Palacky, it wished to summon a congress of all European States from which the

Slavs expected recognition of their right to control their own destinies! Such chimeras bear the hallmark of the "springtide of the peoples"! Nonetheless, the historical importance of the Congress of Prague should not be underestimated. Faced by the German and Hungarian menace, the Slavs of the Empire for the first time displayed a solidarity which went far beyond linguistic and literary affinities.

### The Rumanian National Movement in Transylvania and in the Principalities

The Transylvanian peasants, subjected as serfs to the economic exploitation of the great Magyar and German landowners, formed, under the leadership of the patriotic clergy, one of the most turbulent classes in the Empire. At an assembly held at the "Field of Liberty" near Blaj, metropolis of the Uniate church and cradle of Rumanianism, forty thousand of them, under the leadership of two bishops, one Uniate, one Orthodox, acclaimed Barnut the apostle of political and social equality (15 May). They protested against the reunion of Transylvania and Hungary and demanded recognition of the "Rumanian nation", the creation of Rumanian schools, and, finally, the enfranchisement of the peasants. Loyalty to Ferdinand I took the form of vivats to the "Grand duke of Transylvania". Delivered by the imperial decree of 11 June to the oppression of the Magyars, the Rumanians too as allies of the South Slavs (the Serbs had recognized the rights of the Rumanian minority in the Voivodina) refused to bend the knee.

In the principalities the movements of 1848 were the work of intellectuals, isolated from the peasant masses who were abandoned to a clergy devoid of national feeling. Over them hovered the shadow of the Sultan and the Tsar, the protector. At Jassy, on the news of the February revolution, Kogalniceanu demanded the union of the principalities; on 27 March a liberal conspiracy miscarried because the *hospodar* Sturdza called on the Russians to intervene. On 23 June at Bucharest his colleague Bibesco abdicated without fighting. A provisional

Government was inspired by the Bratianu brothers and Balcesco, a progressive, who had rushed there from Paris. As Balcesco obtained nothing for the peasants, the rural masses remained inert. The Turks, whom the Russians were to replace in November, penetrated without resistance into Valachia and occupied Bucharest in September. The Russo-Turkish treaty of Balta-Liman (May 1849) was for the principalities a regression. The "constitutionalism" set up by Kisselef was abolished. The *hospodars*, formerly nominated for life, were nominated for seven years and the *divans* ceased to be elected. If the revolutions of 1848 had not hastened the birth of a "Great Rumania", they had at least taught the Valach revolutionaries exiled in Europe that the union of the principalities was impossible without the aid of France.

## THE ITALIAN "REVOLUTIONS"

The proud Italians, who had been restive even before the unrest in France, thought themselves strong enough to repulse with arrogance an offer of aid from the French Republic. In a matter of weeks the Viennese revolution had transformed the liberal movements localized in the Italian States into a great patriotic movement with somewhat imprecise aims which was opposed by the particularism of the princes.

### *The Acceleration of the Reformist Movement and the National Anti-German Revolution*

The February days accelerated prodigiously the fulfilment of the promises of the King of Sardinia and of the Pope. On 5 March, Charles Albert promulgated the Constitutional Statute, the future constitution of a united Italy: the Chamber of deputies was to be elected by property-qualified electors (the qualification of 40 francs was not to be lowered until 1882). On the 8th Balbo became Head of Government. On 14 March the Papal States received a constitution which created a Legislative Council with property-qualified recruitment. Thus the fall of Louis Philippe led to the endowment of two further States, other than the Two Sicilies and Tuscany, with constitutions modelled on the Charter of 1830.

The flight of Metternich led to insurrections in Lombardy-Venetia whose rapid success created dangerous illusions. In Venice the mob liberated Manin and Tommaseo on 17 March; on the 22nd Manin seized the arsenal while the Austrians withdrew without firing a shot. His Government caused a tremendous stir; it declared itself republican and included, following the example of Paris, a workers' representative! From the 18th to the 22nd (the Five Days) the streets of Milan were covered with barricades; twenty thousand men under Radetzky (1766–1858) were forced to retreat towards the Quadrilateral. The moderates took power; the provisional Government of Count Casati was composed of aristocrats and great landed proprietors, partisans of the House of Savoy, but the Committee of War, recruited from the people and animated by the republican Cattaneo, kept a watch on it. The defeat of Radetzky caused the collapse of the weak supporters of the Emperor. The Dukes of Modena and Parma fled.

*From the Patriotic Crusade to the Piedmont War*

The Italians were eager to take part in the expulsion of the Tedeschi, judged to be imminent. The "crusaders", as they called themselves, set out for Milan. Cavour, the chilly realist of the fifties, was swept into the dream. On the 23rd, in his *Risorgimento*, he urged the King to enter the war at once. This was soon an accomplished fact. In his proclamation "to the peoples of Lombardy and Venetia" Charles Albert announced that he counted on the aid of ... "God ... who made it possible for Italy to act for herself [*in grado di fara da se*]". God could not, like the French, approve the development of republican ideas nor exact compensation in Savoy! Turin lived in a fantasy world; the mustering of 60,000 men, the "army of the Alps", ready to support their Italian brothers aroused a Sardinian protest! The Ministry of Foreign Affairs declared publicly: "The French army will not enter, at least unless we ask it to do so, and as we will not ask it, it will not enter." In fact, with the exception of a handful of republicans who renounced their obedience to Mazzini, the greater number of the patriots adopted the Piedmontese *fara da se*, symbol of an ingenuous nationalism.

Charles Albert was concerned only with the enlargement of his kingdom; he was consumed by a desire to extend it to northern Italy, which Palmerston, for his part, already imagined to be under a British protectorate. The proclamation of 24 March had nonetheless unleashed a force against which the princes were unable to struggle. The Grand duke of Tuscany allowed volunteers to leave; General Durando marched towards Venetia at the head of papal troops and volunteers. Ferdinand II entrusted Pepe, leader of the revolution of 1820, with a corps of 15,000 men who were to fraternize in the north with a Sicilian contingent! The appearance of these "crusaders" kept the enthusiasm alive. But they were at the most 40,000 men. The basis of their recruitment was essentially urban (petty bourgeois, artisans) and members of the universities; the contribution of the masters and students of Pisa and Florence is well known. At the end of June, in Bologna, Gioberti exhorted "the curés ... to rouse the people of the countryside". In fact, the Sardinian army had an incontestable superiority in numbers, but it was badly commanded. The minor success of Goito (10 April) was not taken advantage of; the time lost was to allow Austria to rally its forces against a movement weakened by the defection of the princes.

In his address of 29 April which followed his disavowal of Durando, Pius IX spoke as Pope and no longer as patriot-prince; by formally condemning the war he forfeited his popularity and weakened the national resistance. Durando's troops were disbanded. Soon those of Pepe were also, for the attitude of Pius IX encouraged Ferdinand II to throw off the mask. On 13 May the progressives had fomented a riot at Naples. With the aid of his loyal mercenaries from democratic Switzerland, the King harshly repressed it, drove out the liberal Government of the historian Troya (1784–1858), dissolved the Chamber and recalled his contingent. Pepe had only two thousand men left when he reached the Po. The contradiction between the limited Sardinian war aims and a war supposed to be national now became clear.

The military inaction contrasted with the ardour of the Albertist propaganda. Modena and Parma eagerly accepted it. At Milan the "fusionist" Casati, opposed to Cattaneo who was willing to accept the continuance of Lombardy-Venetia in a federal or democratic Austria, received the support of Mazzini, the doctrinaire of unity. At the end of May Lombardy was united to Sardinia by 561,000 votes as against 681! In Venice it was more difficult. The new republic of St Mark wished to make Venice an autonomous State in a free Italy. But the populations of the *mainland* saw in the Government of Manin a revival of the despotism of the doges. On 4 June the schism was complete; the four continental provinces which were still free proclaimed their allegiance to Charles Albert. The assembly elected by the province of Venice followed suit on 3 July.

Meanwhile the King of Sardinia won a great prestige success in particularist Sicily. In March the provisional Government had not obtained from the Neapolitan liberal ministry the extensive autonomy which it had demanded. In April the parliament at Palermo pronounced the dethronement of Ferdinand II and his dynasty and discussed a proposed constitution (electors had to know how to read and write, which excluded very many!) while it set out in quest of a king. Very hostile to Charles Albert, Lamartine's successor Bastide, a friend of the Italian republicans, canvassed the choice of the eldest son of the Grand duke of Tuscany. The influence, traditional since 1812, of British liberalism, which the navy of His Gracious Majesty supported by its friendly presence, won the day: a son of Charles Albert, the Duke of Genoa, was elected on 10 July.

The egoism of Charles Albert, and the defections of Pius IX and Ferdinand II had relegated the unitary idea to the domain of myth. On the other hand at the beginning of July a "great kingdom of Sardinia" seemed realizable on paper, while the Austrians clung to the Quadrilateral and made progress in Venetia. The time had passed when the imperial Government, on the invitation of Palmerston, considered abandoning

Lombardy! Reassured by the attitude of the Magyars, who agreed not to recall their troops from Italy and even promised to send more, it could, after the repression at Prague, reinforce Radetzky. What a general had accomplished against the Czech movement a marshal could accomplish against the anaemic Italian movement, while in Germany the elections on 29 June of the Archduke John to the provisional presidency of the *Reich* was a proof of the imperishable prestige of the Hapsburgs.

## THE "GERMAN REVOLUTIONS" AND THE GERMAN REVOLUTION

The revolutionary days of Vienna and Berlin only fed the conflagration which, beginning in the south after the news of the February revolution in Paris, spread in all directions. The unrest ended with concessions which, according to the character of the prince or the vigour and pugnacity of the opposition, varied from a liberalization to a democratization of the régime. Such were those local movements of strictly political character known traditionally as "the German revolutions" whose full history has been ably summarized in the valuable works of V. Valentin and J. Droz. The real, the only, German revolution was a national revolution. In the more advanced States the pressure of public opinion sufficed, Metternich being still in power, to annihilate the action of the Diet and to prepare for the meeting of a constituent assembly by illegal methods which no authority dared to contest. The German revolution reached its apogee when, under the direction of the Archduke John, a government of the *Reich* was formed responsible to the parliament at Frankfurt.

### The March Unrests and the Agrarian Riots

Contemporaries did not have as clear an awareness as historians of the distinction between liberal aspirations and hopes for unity. In this regard the four "demands" (*Forderungen*) voted by the People's Assembly at Mannheim on 27 February are significant: "Arming of the people under elected officers, unlimited freedom of the press, establishment of a jury system on the English model, a German parliament." Like the fourth, the second also threatened the existence of the Diet, a federal institution which, as we know, set up censorship in all the States. By ceding to these behests, the Grand-ducal Government was acting illegally! After the fall of Louis Philippe, it seemed impossible to stand out against the popular current which the ephemeral union of the liberals and radicals had made irresistible. Too often local in conception, these first popular manifestations of revolutionary character had adopted four slogans acceptable both to the moderates and to the Left-wing extremists and which, from one meeting to the next, would soon go the rounds of the whole Confederation.

In Baden a small-scale modification was sufficient to reconcile the Government to the rhythm of events. In the other constitutional States of the south, the princes invested, with more or less good will, the "March ministers". In Hesse-Darmstadt the insignificant Louis II associated his son Louis, of liberal reputation, with him in power. Von Gagern (1799–1860), who had taken part in the Heppenheim meeting of 1847 first demanded a Hessian *Landtag* in the manner of Bassermann (1811–55) but after the Parisian barricades demanded the creation of a German parliament, became the head of the new Government. The menace of a jacquerie hastened the capitulation of Adolph I of Nassau, the last sovereign of a State which Prussia was to annex after Sadowa. In Wurtemberg, William I entrusted the control of affairs to Römer (1794–1864), head of the opposition and also a participant at Heppenheim; Pfizer (1801–67), who had in 1831 conceived the surprising idea of a Prussified Germany, was Minister of Cults. In Bavaria, for so long calm under Louis I, friend of the arts and of the Greek insurgents, touchy defender of the independence of his kingdom and enthusiastic German patriot, the situation by 1847 had become explosive. In the old conservative provinces, as in the distant Palatinate of a political temper almost as ardent as that of Baden, the King's passion for the dancer Lola Montez, an adventuress who meddled in State affairs with a cynical lack of deference, provoked rising indignation. On 8 February the students of Munich had risen and on the 11th Louis had had to agree to send away his favourite. Assailed by demands, he abdicated on 19 March rather than give way; under his son Maximilian II, Bavaria in its turn peacefully accomplished its "revolution".

In central Germany, the February revolution produced even more sudden conversions than that of July. Only Frederick William I of Hesse-Casel, who had never sincerely applied the constitution of 1831, tried to stand fast against the new wave from the West, but the famous *Turner* (gymnasts) of Hanau who, like those of Baden, formed the shock troops of unitary democracy, called on him to submit; on the 11th Hesse-Cassel was endowed with its "March minister". Ernst-August of Hanover had enjoyed an execrable reputation ever since, in 1837, he had suspended the constitution and dismissed the eminent professors of Göttingen; adapting himself easily to circumstances, in mid-March he called upon Stüwe (1798–1872), a moderate reformer. The privileges of the nobility were reduced and a constitution drawn up for study. Frederick Augustus II had, until 1848, governed Saxony with moderation. In March, like all cities whose living depended on the presence of the court, Dresden continued to give proofs of loyalty, but Leipzig, an industrial city, metropolis of German publishing and the seat of a brilliant university, became the centre of a fervent opposition divided as in Baden: the liberals were led by Professor Biedermann (1812–1901), the radicals by the journalist Blum (1807–48), head of the "German Catholic" community, whose tragic death was to turn him into a national hero. An "appeal to the German people" launched from Leipzig on 12 March led to an immediate formation of a liberal Government. The Grand duke of Mecklenburg-Schwerin promised, on 11 March, to modify at long last some medieval institutions. In the Hanseatic towns and in Frankfurt, the oligarchic régimes underwent a transformation.

The first fortnight of March was not only a stirring period when middle classes, artisans, factory workers and even peasants joyously experienced the apprenticeship of liberty (how many processions, public meetings, clubs, newspapers!), it was also the period of agrarian riots, of a seriousness exceptional for Europe. Baden was in the thick of it. On 4 March the peasants of the Kraichgau, who wanted to get hold of the receipts for debts held by usurers, seized the possessions and the persons of the Jews. From the 6th onward, the fury of the rural masses turned against the *Grundherren* and the *Standesherren*; the search for documents which stipulated the seigniorial dues still in force was accompanied by scenes of pillage and arson. On the 10th the area between the Main and the Neckar was prey to a delirious mob. From the Baden Odenwald the contagion spread to the Hessian Odenwald, to Wurtemberg and to the principality of Hohenzollern-Sigmaringen. Nowhere was the authority of the sovereign contested, nowhere was there any sign of subversive ideas. Inspired by strictly economic motives, these disorders should not have astonished the Left nor the extreme Left which had always supported the demands of the peasants and encouraged their anti-Semitism. When the capitulation of the State offered a chance to abolish the last vestiges of feudalism by force, the proclamation on 1 and 2 March of the civil and political equality of the Jews shocked the country people. But by suppressing the seigniorial dues, the Baden Chambers, which those of the turbulent States imitated, contributed to restore peace in the countryside; long before the meeting of the Frankfurt parliament, the revolution was ended in the Odenwald and the northern part of the Black Forest.

### The German Revolution: from the "Heidelberg Revolution" to the Vorparlament. Republic or Monarchy?

Before the explosions of Vienna and Berlin, southern liberals and radicals in close alliance had set in motion a revolutionary procedure for German unity, the will of the peoples replacing that of the princes.

The inaction, the "shirking" of Frederick William IV will always astonish the victims of the French myth of the "Prussian plot" amiably denounced by Minder, or the German myth of the "Prussian mission". His representative at the Diet did his

best to advise him to take the leadership of the national movement by convoking the delegates of all the German Chambers
immediately in Frankfurt, but the King persisted in his eternal
project of extending the *Zollverein* to Austria! Thence,
with Metternich's approval, the conference of the German
princes which was to be held at Dresden ... on 25 March!
Quite won over to the Prussian cause, but convinced that the
unitary current risked the sweeping away of all thrones, von
Gagern took action; at his instigation, his brother Max (1810–
89), counsellor to the Duke of Nassau, undertook to persuade
the sovereigns of the urgency of forming, under the patronage
of Frederick William IV, a provisional Government of the
*Reich*. His welcome, for the most part lukewarm, was
enthusiastic in Berlin where the insurrection had just transformed the King into the champion of the unitary idea. But,
since the "Heidelberg revolution" and the activities of the
Commission of the Seven, von Gagern's proposal belonged to
the past.

"*The Heidelberg Revolution*" (*5 March 1848*). What the supporters
of the putsch of 1833 had tried in vain to do was accomplished
in Baden on 5 March. On the initiative of Römer and Itzstein
(1775–1855), then in close accord with the radicals, fifty-one
persons, for the most part members of the Lower Chambers of
the Southern States, met at Heidelberg to decide on the best
means to achieve German unity. The Assembly included only
four Rhinelanders, Hansemann amongst them, and one Austrian.
Liberals and radicals (Hecker, Struve) agreed on the need to
elect rapidly a "national representation". This violated the
constitutional rights of the Diet and considered as null the
sovereign powers of all the princes. Men with no mandate
whatever gently set in motion the national revolution. A
permanent commission of seven members, amongst whom
were von Gagern, Welcker (1790–1869), Itzstein and Römer
were to call together a "pre-parliament" (*Vorparlament*)
entrusted with preparing for the first German parliament.
Although no one except diplomats any longer paid any
attention to them, the stupefied Diet counter-attacked weakly;

on the 10th it demanded that the Government add to its members seventeen persons "enjoying the confidence of the public" who would aid it in reforming the federal institutions. Unperturbed, the Seven decided that the *Vorparlament* would be made up of former, or present, deputies of all the German "countries" (not "States"), that is to say including the Prussian provinces outside the Confederation (Eastern and Western Prussia, Poznania and also Schleswig!). Did this expansionism, still theoretical, conceal those pro-Russian intentions which, according to some, had inspired the historic decision of 5 March? But why attribute conceptions to the liberals of Baden, Wurtemberg and Bavaria when they were more suitable to Gervinus and his *Deutsche Zeitung* than to von Gagern and a few Rhinelanders? In any case, on the eve of the meeting of the *Vorparlament*, set for 31 March, who would have dared to work for the King of Prussia? Since the bloody days of Berlin (16–18 March) never had the German people so hated Prussia and detested its King.

*The Berlin Revolution (18 March) and Prussian Disrepute.* To give way, as did so many princes, to the demands of refractory subjects was for Frederick William clamped to his absolutism by right divine, or for his brother William, the future King-emperor, unworthy of a Hohenzollern. The news which reached Berlin on 16 March of the fall of Metternich, and the capitulation of the Hapsburgs, stimulated the contentious spirit of the Berliners and drove the King to an "agonizing revision".

In a State where continual pressure from above had accustomed its people to obedience, the activities were at first limited, in the provinces, to the sending of petitions to some of the urban centres of the east (in Breslau the army dispersed the demonstrators) and the west. At Cologne, on 3 March, many thousands of workers added to the usual political demands social demands (security of work, free education) which Baden radicalism had formulated in September 1847. Unusual in the Rhineland, this demonstration scared the liberals and has held the attention of historians because of the personality of its main instigator, Gottschalk, the active president of an important

*Arbeitersverein* (association of workers) and founder of a section of the Federation of Communists.

With its four hundred thousand inhabitants, Berlin was an ideal parade ground for a revolutionary party. The radicals of the *Zeitungshalle*, which were moderately subscribed, could easily publish petitions and tracts! But nothing predisposed them to lead an armed rising. If the capital, profoundly attached to the dynasty, knew nothing of the clandestine formations of Parisian type, it would have been sufficient, once the insurrection had broken out, for a few guild artisans to recall the lessons learnt in Paris in the workshops or on the barricades.

The revolution was born of countless royal blunders. Penury and unemployment had aroused a discontent which at first crystallized in political demands. At the beginning of March, the people of Berlin were noisily astonished to find that they did not enjoy, as did other Germans, the elementary freedoms which a constitution would guarantee. The King, irritated, strengthened the garrison; on the 6th he decided to abolish the *United Landtag*, already clearly anachronistic in 1847. On the 13th the cavalry dispersed unarmed demonstrators *Unter den Linden*. The conflict between the civilians and the soldiers, that is from the viewpoint of 1848 between free men and the instruments of despotism, became embittered and resulted in a violent clash on 16 March, at the news of the Vienna revolution. On the 17th the democrats were emboldened to organize for the following day a great meeting to demand the withdrawal of the army and the creation of a civil guard. During the night the King thought that he could avoid this humiliating confrontation by proclaiming the abolition of censorship, the imminent formation of a new ministry and the elaboration of a constitution, subject, it is true, to the anti-democratic *United Landtag*. On the morning of the 18th Prussia seemed to have accomplished, in its turn and without too much harm done, its "March revolution".

In the afternoon the hatred of the populace for the army on the one hand and the spirit of revenge of the court and the high command on the other transformed a manifestation of loyalty to the monarchy into an insurrection. Informed of the King's

concessions, an enormous crowd which had come to acclaim
him found in the castle courtyard those troops which were
now odious. The crowd vociferously demanded their departure.
But it was with Prince William's approval that General von
Prittwitz gave the order to clear the square. As on the Boulevard
des Capucines on 23 February the panic-stricken soldiers fired.
The civilians suspected a trap; hundreds of barricades were set
up and defended fanatically (more than two hundred insurgents
were killed). Since popular fury was principally directed against
the military caste and the camarilla, the King of Prussia could,
as the "King of the French" could not, give way without
risking his crown. On the 19th he ordered the withdrawal of
the troops, placed himself under the protection of a civil guard
and sent his brother away to England. On the 21st he promised
freedom of the press and of assembly, religious equality in
favour of the "German Catholics" and the Jews, as well as a
constitution of parliamentary type. Meeting for the last time on
2 April the *United Landtag* ratified these concessions and decided
that a national assembly elected by universal suffrage should
draw up the statute of Prussia, which had now taken the
democratic road, in agreement with the King. After a far from
glorious *volte-face* accompanied by humiliating scenes, where
in the presence of thousands of demonstrators the King had to
salute the long funeral procession of the victims, there followed
the conversion for which the Rhineland liberals had hoped for
so long. In his pompous proclamation of 21 March, "to my
people and the German nation", the defeated monarch of the
19th announced his intention of leading Germany to freedom
and unity.

In the principal towns of Prussia, above all Berlin, this
grandiloquent appeal came too late. Outside the kingdom, the
bloodshed revived anti-Prussian hatred; the loyal *Deutsche
Zeitung* advised Frederick William to abdicate. At Karlsruhe,
Munich and Stuttgart his pictures were burnt in public. From
Cassel an anonymous writer fulminated against "this second
Nero": "You have massacred your people treacherously and in
cold blood . . . and now . . . that your acolyte Metternich has
been judged . . . you want to place yourself at our head. If your

people are so pusillanimous that they do not drive you out, know that we, we will not back you up." The Münchners too condemned "a king who, until 21 March, wanted to be head of a great power *without Germany* ..." and advised him: "Let us leave to our national parliament the task of deciding the form and extent of the central power called upon to assure to the German people the place which has for so long belonged to it."

*The Republican Thrust in the South-West.* In Baden the behaviour of the Berlin "weathercock" clearly illustrated one of the favourite themes of radical propaganda: "These princes, who cost us so dear, are imbeciles or criminals!" At the end of February the party had emerged from the background. Its clubs, its armed *Turner*, its ardent press, its numerous meetings, had made it a democratic organization without equal in Germany. The Offenburg meeting of 19 March bore witness to the extraordinary progress made since 12 September 1847; it was no longer a few hundred militants but at least ten thousand workers from the plain and the Black Forest who responded to the appeal of Hecker and Struve. Instead of vague aspirations, precise measures were demanded and acclaimed by the populace. After the initial convocation of a "German parliament" they demanded "immediate" application of a purge of the Government and the Lower Chamber, suppression of the Upper Chamber, fusion of the civil guard and the army, a progressive income tax, and separation of Church and State. To break down internal resistance in each commune a club was entrusted with the "political and social formation" and the arming of citizens, subject to a district club which in its turn was subject to a regional club which would receive instructions from a central committee with its seat at Mannheim: a real "shadow government" presided over by Hecker. Thus institutionalized, the Radical Party was prepared to set up a Baden republic, member of the first German republic. However, at Offenburg, Hecker and Struve had refused to proclaim the republic on the spot; before declaring war on all the princes, the republicans must organize everywhere on the

Baden model. An appeal was launched for this purpose from Offenburg itself to "all the provinces of Germany". Furthermore, there was nothing to show that the *Vorparlament* would not pronounce in favour of a republic within the next few days!

The more level-headed liberals, however, also envisaged this possibility. Faced with the social unrest and the progress of democratic propaganda in the Rhineland, Camphausen (1803–90) and Hansemann (1790–1864) began to regret having so thoughtlessly supported the operation of 5 March. Fearing "anarchy" and the republic, they offered their aid to Frederick William. On 29 March Camphausen became President of the Council and Hansemann Minister of Finance in a Government which considered universal suffrage as an unfortunate consequence of the Berlin insurrection! In Baden, the administration dared not proceed with the dissolution of the radical para-military forces; it was incapable of fulminating against the mayors who, with the connivance of those involved, advised the soldiers to return home and the recruits to stay there. Against the agents of subversion, the liberals rallied around the Grand-ducal throne and drew closer to the vacillating federal authority, so long detested. The Karlsruhe Government approved the entry of Bassermann into the commission of seventeen; Welcker was at the same time the very official Baden delegate to the Diet and the very active member of the illegal Commission of the Seven.

### The "Vorparlament" (31 March–3 April)

Those radicals who applauded and those liberals who feared the republican spirit of an assembly meeting at the instigation of a moderate majority were very short-sighted. The *Vorparlament* which sat from 31 March to 3 April at Frankfurt, first in Römer and then in the Protestant church of St Paul, was, on the model of the Commission of the Seven, an assembly of parliament-arians from the south and west, that is of *Akademiker*, attached to a familiar institution, the constitutional monarchy. Out of 574 delegates 304 were from Baden, Bavaria, Wurtemberg, Nassau, Hesse-Darmstadt, Hesse-Cassel. Under-represented

(141) the Prussian group included many Rhinelanders. As in Heidelberg, the Austrian participation (2) was symbolic. That of Schleswig-Holstein (7) represented the desires of men with no real power to settle a complex international problem to the benefit of a State which did not yet exist.

In agreement with the president, the famous Heidelberg jurist Mittermaier (1787–1867), the liberal majority was ready to vote, after several academic discussions, the proposals elaborated by the Seven, which foresaw a federal, imperial and parliamentary Germany. The extreme Left, a minority however (one eighth at most), tried, in the manner of the Parisian revolutionaries, to force the choice of the German people by imposing a republic upon it. Before an assembly which included opposition leaders of European reputation like the persecuted Professor Jordan (1792–1861) of Hesse-Cassel, and Ronge (1813–87), the "Pope" of German Catholicism, and resolute democrats like the Saxon Eisenstück (1805–71), Jacoby of Königsberg (1805–77), the pioneer of an advanced liberalism in East Prussia, d'Ester from Cologne (1811–59), a loyal supporter of Engels, Baden radicalism became for several days the guide of German radicalism. The plan for the democratization of the social and political life of the Grand duchy, drawn up at Offenburg on 19 March was to be found, sometimes word for word, in the programme set out by Struve. The constitutional innovations which its application to Germany presumed were of a type to arouse the fears of those who wished to reform but not to destroy! Germany would have an elected president on the American model, and twenty-three republics would replace the thirty-eight States. In referring back to parliament the task of determining whether the new Germany would be republican or monarchist, liberal Prussophiles or Prussophobes rallied in fact, under pretext of respecting the people's sovereignty, to the proposal of the Seven upheld by von Gagern, but avoided a split with the radicals who gave proof of an exemplary patriotism.

For the first time since 1815 the Germans were confronted— or at least so they thought—by a very serious problem for Germany and for Europe, that of the frontiers of the new State.

In the *Vorparlament*, as later in the parliament, divergencies were blurred when it was a matter of plunging into an arsenal of contradictory arguments based on ambiguous ideas, *Volkstum*, *Reich*, whose history has already been given. Struve, whom conservative historians were to declare un-*deutsch* (unworthy of being German) (he was a '93 enthusiast!), included in his Germany of twenty-three republics Vienna, Prague, Trieste and the Danish duchies. On paper, the *Vorparlament* unanimously proceeded to the annexation of Schleswig. Poznania, inhabited by a Polish majority, created a moral conflict which Struve set out with a certain cynicism. On the one hand, this Prussian province must be attached to the new Germany; on the other, could one overlook the rights of the Poles, enemies of barbarous Russia? Therefore, the promise made a thousand times must be kept, and the *Vorparlament* passed a motion to this effect, to re-establish Poland, but "without injustice towards the Germans". The reference of this matter to parliament, on the part of an assembly which included a majority of friends of Poland, presaged ill for the Polish cause!

Since the parliament was to meet in May, the *Vorparlament* was unable to draw up a uniform electoral law. It left the task of fixing not only the date but also the form of the elections to the Governments. It contented itself with stipulating that there should be one deputy for every fifty thousand inhabitants and granted the right to vote and to be eligible for election to every adult and independent (*selbständig*) German, which could result, according to the interpretation of that adjective, either in universal suffrage or in a caricature of it; in the States without political tradition, wage-earners were excluded!

Against the advice of Struve, who proposed the "permanence", until the meeting of parliament, of an assembly in which, moreover, he was a minority member, the *Vorparlament* chose from its ranks a commission of fifty members, from which the radical Left Wing was excluded, entrusted with watching over the interests of Germany.

*The Two Heads of Germany: the Fifty and the Diet (4 April–1 May)*

With a majority of moderates, but all the same including Itzstein, Blum and Jacoby, the Fifty gave, thanks to a cleverly balanced composition, a truer image of the real Germany than the *Vorparlament* or the Heidelberg assembly, since the six States of the south and west no longer held the majority (20). During the seven weeks of their brief existence, they found themselves faced with crushing tasks. Whereas the Baden republican insurrection intensified political cleavages, the affair of Poznania and, above all, the question of Schleswig-Holstein tended to efface them. The unleashing of nationalist passions afforded the King of Prussia the chance to rehabilitate himself in the eyes of the people, at a time when Austria was absent from the control of German affairs, now abandoned to the "diarchy" of the Fifty and the Diet.

The coexistence of a revolutionary organization and of a despised institution has never ceased to surprise historians, who denounce the feebleness and legalistic spirit of the liberals. Certainly it would have been easy enough to disperse the dignified plenipotentiaries of Governments which, in the euphoria of the first days of March, no one had even thought of overturning. What advantage would the "German revolution" have gained by this? Once the *Vorparlament* had agreed, on the proposal of the Badener Soiron (1806–55) soon called upon to preside over the Fifty, that the parliament would decide the constitution of Germany "entirely alone" (*einzig und allein*) the Diet stood condemned. Apparently regenerated by the addition of the seventeen, it did not cease to show a remarkable docility, as did its mandatories who were made numb by fear. After having "recommended" on 3 March that the States should abolish censorship, thus legalizing the violation of its own legislation, and having decided that the number of deputies in the parliament should be one for every 70,000 inhabitants on 30 March, was it now to fail to ratify the "resolutions" of the *Vorparlament*? While awaiting the meeting of parliament, it afforded the means, in fact the only means, of influencing the princely administrations.

*Union Against the Baden Republicans*. In this collaboration between
the moral authority and the symbol of material power, the
Baden republicans were the first to pay the price. Both because
of its promoters and the scene of its operations, the April
insurrection in Baden should not be considered as an episode
of regional history. It had its ramifications in the German
section of Switzerland, in Hesse-Cassel and in Hesse-Darmstadt.
It was directly linked with the refusal of the *Vorparlament* to
declare itself in favour of a federal and social republic. Bypassing
the Assembly, Hecker and Struve appealed to the masses. For
these enthusiastic forty-eighters, it would be enough to proclaim
the republic in the Grand duchy and all Germany would
follow! . . . The epic which began on 12 April today appears a
ridiculous escapade lasting a dozen days. One forgets the effects
produced by an uprising demanding the "right to work", the
confusion of the sovereigns, the fears of the "March ministers"
and the anger of the liberal politicians. The bourgeoisie of the
*Akademiker* who were making ready to govern Germany had no
intention of allowing the domination of the nobility, of the
cliques and of the bureaucrats to be replaced by that of the
working classes. After a vain attempt to induce Hecker and
Struve to renounce their enterprise, the Fifty ratified the
repressions which the Diet organized through the framework
of federal institutions. The anti-republican front invoked the
defence of the German fatherland. Memories of the *Franzosenlärm*
(23–24 March) were still sufficiently alive to be cleverly
exploited. By denouncing an imaginary collusion between the
Paris Legion and the radical leaders, the liberals justified the
appeal launched by the Grand duke to the forces of Hesse-
Darmstadt, Nassau, Wurtemberg and Bavaria. The victory
won at Kandern (20 April) by the Baden troops under the
command of a Hessian general, Frederick von Gagern (elder
brother of Henry and Max, he was to fall before the battle was
over) could be regarded as a triumph of the unitary idea over a
movement of separatist anarchists.

This propaganda seems above all to have influenced French
diplomats. Many partisans of Hecker and Struve did not feel
that they had been affected by the setback of an insurrection

for which, with the exception of young unemployed artisans and convinced radicals, they had refused their aid; for they considered it senseless to fight for a cause which was certain to win very shortly and peaceably, so great were the hopes placed in the first German parliament! A few weeks after Kandern the republicans in Baden were to win seven tenths of the seats; Hecker, then in flight, was to be triumphantly elected. From the deceptions of the year would arise, in May and June 1849, the great Baden republican insurrection. If the putsch which had failed in April had in no way weakened the republican idea in the south-west, it was, on the other hand, the origin of the final rupture between republicans and constitutional monarchists.

*Union in the Defence of Germanism: Poznania and the Duchies.* In agreement with the Diet against what Soiron called "anarchy", the Fifty did not succeed in overcoming it. They had, according to their mandate, demanded that the Austrian districts of the Confederation elect their deputies and, with a similar intention, asked Palacky to collaborate. The rebuff of the Czech historian is well known. On the question of Poznania, they wasted their breath in following, like the Diet, the evolution of an opinion less and less favourable to the Poles: when Frederick William founded a derisory duchy of Gnesen (300,000 inhabitants) which provoked the brief insurrection of Mieroslawski, the Diet decreed the union of these terrorists with the Confederation. Though they no longer dreamed of issuing a pious declaration in favour of the restoration of a nation whose unworthy spokesman dared to claim Danzig and refused to participate in the elections to the parliament, the Fifty, like the *Vorparlament*, left the task of resolving the prickly Polish question to the elected assembly.

The transformation of the "armed vigil" in the duchies to the fresh and joyous war against Denmark made the "Nero" of Berlin into the mandatory of the Diet and the defender of the rights of the German people represented by the Fifty. The unrest in southern Germany had had an immediate effect on the shores of the Baltic, where the liberal wave ebbed slowly as the nationalist tempest grew. Schleswig was the stake of two parties resolved, for reasons which we have already given, to trample upon the *Royal rescript* of 28 January and to annex the despised peoples against their will. In Copenhagen, on the 11 and 12 March, the "Eider party" demanded a constitution common to Denmark and Schleswig. At Rendsberg in Holstein the German opposition on the 18th demanded that the duchies should become an autonomous State, Schleswig in its turn joining the Confederation. To this the reactionary Frederick VII replied on the 22nd by forming with the liberals a cabinet of union which reflected "the Danish nationality in the duchies". On the 24th a provisional Government of Germans of all shades of opinion was set up at Kiel. On 3 April the Estates of the two duchies met at Rendsburg. Commandos, trained in the gymnastic societies, attacked the Danes who crushed them on 9 April.

Anxious to restore in the eyes of German opinion an authority which had been gravely compromised, Frederick William's advisers urged him to intervene. At the end of March the King, in an open letter to the Duke of Augustenburg, the pretender to the Danish succession, had declared that he would defend "German interests" in the duchies. On 8 April Prussian troops entered Holstein, which was federal territory. On the 12th the Diet recognized the revolutionary government of Kiel over which Augustenburg presided and proclaimed, as had the *Vorparlament*, the admission of Schleswig into the Confederation while the Fifty launched an appeal for the formation of commandos and sent the Baden Liberal Mathy (1807–68) to Berlin. Commander-in-chief of the federal forces, the Prussian General Wrangel (1784–1877) penetrated into Schleswig, defeated the Danes on 24 April and crossed the frontier into Jutland.

This success against a weak opponent created delirious enthusiasm in Germany. The press lauded the intrepidity of the commandos, the firmness of the Prussians and the strategic genius of Wrangel. Foreigners noted with stupefaction the brusque change of feeling in favour of Frederick William who, for his part, began to consider the serious consequences of an affair entered into in the heat of passion. Terrestrial Prussia discovered her impotence at sea; after seizing enemy ships in its ports, Denmark declared a blockade of the Prussian and Mecklenburg coasts. With the aid of its northern neighbour, Denmark would be in a position not only to stop the trade exchange of Prussia but to drive the Hanseatic republics to despair, by suffocating them. The state of opinion in Sweden and Norway made this eventuality more and more probable; since the beginning of April Scandinavianism was no longer confined to the literary world. It was now, according to a diplomat, "the movement of the Scandinavian races against the aggression of the German race". In Christiania, as in Upsala and in Lund, students enlisted. Military men in vain asked for permission to go and fight the Germans. The pacific Oscar I was swept along by an irresistible current. At the beginning of May he placed at the disposal of Frederick VII 15,000 Swedes and 3,000 Norwegians, as well as a naval squadron, certainly not to recover Schleswig but to preserve the integrity of Jutland.

To this threat of limited military intervention inspired by Scandinavianism was added growing diplomatic pressure from the two powers interested in maintaining the *status quo* at the entry to the Baltic. The threats of Nicholas I led Frederick William to accept the mediation of London, which foresaw a partition of Schleswig along the linguistic frontier. Wrangel evacuated Jutland; one side wanted to keep all, the other to conquer all. The question of the duchies, which was to complicate international relations right up to Sadowa, troubled from its birth the Germany which was still searching for its own identity. The State interests of Prussia had disappointed the aspiration of the nation and disdained the decisions of the Diet and the Fifty. When parliament met, the prestige of Frederick William was as low as it had been the day after 18 March.

*The Apogee of the German Revolution; the First German Parliament and the Foundation of a Provisional Reich (18 May–July 1848)*

From its first meeting in the church of St Paul (18 May) to the foundation of the first Government of the *Reich*, the Frankfurt parliament behaved as a sovereign body. The moral authority of its mission to bring well-being to the Germans and greatness to Germany was an invincible force. Who would dare to oppose the revolution born at Heidelberg on 5 March? Up until June not even Prussia, because of the unpopularity of its King and his contentions with the Prussian National Assembly.[1] Nor was Austria—whose Government, which had taken refuge in Innsbruck, was in conflict with the Viennese democrats, the Czech national movement (the Congress of Prague opened on 2 June), the Magyar demands and the Sardinian intrigues—in a position to influence the debates to which these ephemeral masters of German destinies devoted themselves rapturously.

Who, then, were these six hundred rhetoricians whom, a century later, we reproach for not having, by persuasion alone, forestalled the work which Bismarck carried out "by fire and the sword"? Out of the 573 deputies in November 1848 there was a weak representation of the great landowners (38, of whom 25 were nobles), of the great industrial (7) and commercial (13) bourgeoisie and the insignificance of the small traders (13) and the artisans (4) (not a single factory worker!) and the peasantry (3). On the other hand the preponderance of the *Akademiker* (about 400, of whom 49 were professors) is no matter for surprise. In a two-stage election, less favourable to the upper classes than the doctrinaires of direct suffrage imagined, the "great electors" had naturally chosen the most experienced candidates. The Frankfurt parliament, despite a more or less extended suffrage according to regions, was a watered-down reflection of the Lower Chambers of the constitutional States. If the *Akademiker* and the professors (Dahlmann, Welcker, Gervinus, Soiron, Mohl, etc.) proved in the end less effective than either their contemporaries or historians expected, this could not be imputed to a lack of political experience. The problems they had to face could only arouse a creative imagination. The Frankfurt *Akademiker* having become assimilated to the upper ranks of the reactionary bourgeoisie with whom, as we believe we have proved, German intellectuals had nothing

---

[1] A study of the political life of the Prussian State from the time of the meeting of the National Assembly (22 May) will be found in the next chapter.

in common, it remains to recall the reasons for the withdrawal of the representatives of progressive tendencies between the Heidelberg meeting and the *Vorparlament* and between the *Vorparlament* and the parliament. To invoke the fear of "anarchy", as has sometimes been done, is an explanation contradicted by the results of the elections in the more turbulent States. Dyed-in-the-wool liberalism and republican radicalism in the south-west had been progressively reduced in influence and, taken together, Prussia (200) and Austria (121) accounted for more than half of the parliamentary members. Each of these included scarcely more deputies of the Left and the extreme Left (19) than Baden and Hesse-Darmstadt (17).

In fact, the idea of party was only introduced little by little and not without meeting the stubborn resistance of men who were anxious to fulfil their exalted mission in complete independence. Gradually, parliamentary life was to force deputies to band together according to their affinities. In this way clubs or, if one prefers, parliamentary groups began to appear; the Bavarian Eisenmann (1795–1867) mentions nine of them, from the café Milani (Right) to the hotel Donnersberg (extreme Left). Centre of a political life upon which hopes and despairs converged (never had any assembly received so many petitions!) parliament was too new to modify the particularism of formations born within the framework of the States and was always heedful of the debates of the Chambers which continued to sit, as did the Prussian National Assembly. The first attempts to endow Germany with national parties were to emanate from the parliamentary democrats at Frankfurt; a network of clubs aimed at mobilizing the lower classes for the defence of the constitution voted in March 1849. The return in force of reaction was to make this tardy initiative illusory.

The first decisions of the parliament did not express the views of non-existent or embryonic parties but the deep feelings of the majority of Germans. The elections were still too near and the church of St Paul was situated in the heart of a region with too unitary and too democratic an opinion to allow the majority, made up of constitutional monarchists, to forget the clamours of March and April. The attitude of the Prussophile von

Gagern, brilliantly elected to the presidency of the Assembly, was in line with public opinion and Germanic tradition. He demanded that parliament, the sole holder of national sovereignty, should draw up the constitution of the *Reich* without consulting the princes, who were, however, the sole depositories of material power! And the parliament was to decide in the manner of the Diet of the thirties, but in a different spirit, the annulment of those local constitutional forms which were contrary to the federal constitution. As the agreement in principle for the creation of an executive endowed with authority until the setting up of new institutions had been followed by an incredible number of proposals, all of which were rejected, von Gagern proposed on 24 June the election of a Vicar of the *Reich* (*Reichsverweser*) and put forward the name of the Archduke John. On the 28th the law "on the provisional central authority [*provisorische Zentralgewalt*]" was approved; the *Reichsverweser* was to be assisted by a ministry responsible to parliament. On coming into force it would put an end to the existence of the Diet. On the 29th John was nominated by 436 votes against 53 for von Gagern, who was not a candidate, and 32 for Itzstein. An earlier vote on a republican motion, rejected by 355 votes to 171, showed that half of the Left had voted for the Archduke.

This election which, save for the King of Hanover, provoked no protest among the princes, aroused great popular enthusiasm. Even before a military parade had been ordered in each State, the Government considered it wise to allow the citizens to give public vent to their rejoicing; on 30 June there were parades at Karlsruhe, Freiburg, Rastatt and Baden-Baden through the beflagged streets led by bands, and the artillery fired salutes. The press of all shades of opinion displayed an uncharacteristic unanimity; there was no criticism of the election of an Austrian prince nor of the person of the *Reichsverweser*. The radical journals even protested against the irresponsibility of a provisional head of State! For the liberal papers, in the hands of Protestants or lukewarm Catholics, the fact that the man elected belonged to the oldest of reigning families marked both continuity, the setback to the republican party, and change, the victory of the unitary idea. Nobody condemned the ostracism which had struck the Hohenzollerns. The majority of Germans resented what the clerical and reactionary *South German Gazette* (*Süddeutsche Zeitung*) noisily saluted as "the scion of the ancient imperial family". To whom should the task of presiding over the foundations of a new *Reich* be better entrusted than to the most popular of the Hapsburgs? Thirteenth son of Leopold II (died 1792), brother of Francis II (died 1835), uncle of Ferdinand I, the Archduke John (1782–1859) was not the colourless individual who would have appealed, as is sometimes said, to the deputies because of his mediocrity and disinterestedness. Ambitious, patient, he had known how to win the sympathies of cultivated circles (he was notably the protector of the learned Slavs), of the liberals (an adversary of Metternich, it was known that he was instrumental in his fall) and of the common people. His marriage to the daughter of a postmaster and a simplicity which appeared unaffected gave this great lord the appearance of a democrat. For long excluded from the conduct of affairs, he assumed, at the moment of his election and in dramatic circumstances, supreme responsibility. In a capital which had become a prey to unrest in the streets, he had not only to confront the contradictory contentions of the nationalities but above all to accomplish two tasks essential to the peace and the integrity of the Empire: to prepare for the meeting of a parliament of the "Hereditary States" and to save, if not Lombardy, at least Venetia. Welcomed at Frankfurt on 11 July as a Germanic Emperor, he left again for Vienna on the 15th. In the midst of the universal rejoicings he had, on the 12th, formally drawn up the death certificate of that most hated of institutions, the Diet. His return at the beginning of August was to be triumphal; the man who, soon, would feign to refer to "his ex-sovereign, the Emperor of Austria" personified liberal aspirations and the appetites of Germanism. Opening on 22 July in the name of Ferdinand I a parliament elected by universal suffrage, he proclaimed the need for close co-operation between the Empire and the new Germany. The glory of Custozza threw its lustre upon him. This Austrian victory was hailed as a German victory by a number of deputies who saw in Lombardy-Venetia the bastion of a *Reich* which included Trieste, Trento and the Tirol.

After having installed at Vienna the first liberal ministry of the ancient monarchy, the *Reichsverweser*, according to the principles of a parliamentary régime, set up the first Government of Germany at Frankfurt. Monarchists attached to representative institutions, all the ministers except one belonged to parliament. Their leader the Prince Karl von Leiningen (1804–56), one of the richest *Standesherren*, whose liberalism in March had not saved him from agrarian riots, was convinced of the urgency of creating a strong central power. The apparent equilibrium between north and south was, in fact, to the disadvantage of Prussia; of the six holders of portfolios (Leiningen was without one) there were two Prussians, one of whom was a Rhinelander, two bourgeois from Bremen and Hamburg, cities opposed to the *Zollverein*, and two open supporters of a Germany unified under Hapsburg control, Mohl (1799–1875) and Schmerling (1805–93). The former, a Wurtemberger and an ex-*Burschenschaftler*, was a brilliant teacher of law at Heidelberg; he had, in a resounding article published just after the Berlin days, broken with the pro-Prussian policy of the *Deutsche Zeitung*. The latter, a magistrate whose opposition to Metternich after 13 March had led him to represent Austria in the Diet, began an extraordinary career—Minister of the Interior of the *Reich* in July and successor to Leiningen in September, then Minister of the Interior of Schwarzenberg (1849–51) and head of the Government of the Empire (1860–65). Beyond these political adaptations one senses in this adversary of the nationalities of the Empire the unbreakable will to strengthen the influence of Vienna in German affairs. On the whole this ministry, whose very existence was, after the meeting of parliament, a fresh miracle of "the spring", was welcomed by a public eager to see actions follow proclamations.

The power of the parliament rested on the approval of the masses and the embarrassment of the reactionary authorities. From July to November Frankfurt was to feel the effects of the ebbing of the revolutionary tides in Vienna and Berlin and the unequivocal signs of public disappointment.

# [ Chapter Eleven ]

## The Tide Turns (July–December 1848)

EVERYTHING went on as if the defeat of the Parisian workers in June had dissipated the "lyrical illusions" of "the spring" and had encouraged Austria and Prussia to make use of arms instead of ideas. The parliamentarians began to give way to the military. Austria re-established her position in Italy in July and destroyed the Viennese democratic movement in October. As the abolition in September of the seigniorial régime had ended the revolution in the countryside of the "Hereditary States", Austria, thanks to her loyal Slav and Rumanian subjects, was in a position to put an end to Magyar arrogance. In the struggle for frontiers, the Frankfurt parliament experienced a bitter setback in Schleswig-Holstein which nearly swept it away in September; only the intervention of Austrian and Prussian troops saved it. In November, following the example of the Emperor, though in easier circumstances, the King of Prussia eliminated in Berlin the consequences of March. After the crushing of the Viennese rebellion and the triumph of the counter-revolution in Berlin, what was to be the future of the German revolution?

### ITALY: FROM THE NATIONAL SETBACK TO THE DEMOCRATIC REVOLUTIONS

Custozza (25 July) marked the start of the re-establishment

of imperial authority just as it had existed before the first
assaults of the revolution. Charles Albert fled from Milan amid
the shouts and boos of a populace which, still believing in
Italian invincibility, suspected treason. Except in Venice where
Manin kept the flame burning, everything crashed, everything
was abandoned. The chimera of *farà da se* faded away, but how
slowly! On 4 July Mazzini was still exhorting the French to
concern themselves with the fate . . . of the Poles! Palmerston
had no intention of substituting a risky military intervention
for a diplomatic support which Piedmontese conceit had in no
way facilitated, so all that was left to Charles Albert was to
follow the example of his provisional Government in Milan
and to turn to France, whose Constituent Assembly had voted
a declaration in favour of Italian independence at the end of
May. The suppliant posed his conditions: France was to send
40,000 men into Lombardy and 10,000 into Venetia to fight
under the command of Charles Albert. She was to promise not
to seek any territorial compensation and to forbid all republican
propaganda. Cavaignac and Bastide who, as we have seen,
had recently been active in Sicily in countering the ambitions
of the House of Savoy, did not want to work for the King of
Sardinia or to help in restoring Austrian influence in Italy. On
7 August, Bastide replied mockingly to Charles Albert's
request: "We regret that a noble nationalist sensitivity did not
permit you to call upon us sooner"; and added that Paris and
London would propose their mediation. The policy of entente,
of which Lamartine had laid the foundations in March, was to
save Charles Albert. However, the armistice imposed on
General Salasco (9 August) wiped out Sardinian ambitions to
that Lombardy whose loss Austria had envisaged only a month
before. Charles Albert's troops must withdraw to the Ticino
and evacuate Parma and Modena. Strong in Italy but weak
in its internal affairs, the imperial Government did not press the
negotiations with the two powers which it knew were resolved
not to fight.

Political elements soured by disappointments of their hopes
for unity were inclined to throw the responsibility on the
princes and the liberal ministries. While the masses saw their

position made worse by the disorders and the military activities and took refuge in their usual passivity (the enlistment of "crusaders" had ceased after the end of May and in many States the indifference of the populace had forced the authorities to postpone the date of the elections), a handful of democrats supported by a following of artisans tried to seize power in order to unleash the war of the peoples.

In Piedmont the monarchy seemed to vacillate. Despite a peasantry eager for peace, the democrats vociferously demanded a denunciation of the armistice; far from numerous, except in Genoa, they succeeded in imposing their views on the political classes which had driven the King into this adventure. The question of war or peace became that of the continuance or disappearance of the monarchy. In December the rise to power of Gioberti reassured the monarchists who were anxious to spare the kingdom, by war, the destiny that seemed reserved for Tuscany and the Papal States.

Since the armistice, the concentration in Florence and Rome of the most impassioned democrats worsened an already explosive situation. In this Italy, in which historians of all schools of thought had noted the almost complete lack of class consciousness among the workers, Tuscany, the country of Buonarotti, was the exception: republican secret societies, communist in tendency, had demonstrated, as we have seen, during the "subsistence troubles" of 1847. In 1848 there appeared in Florence a review which propagated communism "founded by Jesus Christ". Livorno, above all, was the scene of strikes inspired by both political and social demands between September 1847 and September 1848. Defeat was resented even more bitterly in the Duchy where, relatively speaking, the war effort had been the greatest. The return of the vanquished, the republican agitation, the renewed outbreak of unemployment, all bred an atmosphere of anarchy. On 23 August Livorno rose in revolt and threatened to become, under the leadership of Guerrazzi, an independent republic! At the end of October Leopold II agreed to the formation of a ministry under Guerrazzi. Tuscany was now a monarchy only in name!

The divorce between Pius IX and Italian liberal and national opinion stemmed, as we know, from the resounding declaration of 29 April which condemned both the war and the revolution. To appease men's minds the Pope had called on Mamiani (1799–1885), a supporter of Italian unity and hostile to the administration of the cardinals, who was filled with the desire to alleviate the sufferings of the humble. On the news of Custozza, the reactionary prelates obtained Mamiani's dismissal and, by inaugurating a return to the *ancien régime*, unleashed a revolutionary process. In September Pius IX nominated Rossi, Guizot's former ambassador, who had once more become an Italian after he had been recalled by Lamartine! This moderate was in the bad books of the cardinals and was execrated by the democrats, for he had no intention either of abolishing the constitution of 14 March or of deviating in external affairs from the prudent guide-lines laid down by the Pope. On 15 November he was stabbed by former Carbonari just as he was making ready to enter the Legislative Council. This assassination was the signal for insurrection. As in Paris in February, the National Guard took part. On the 16th an ultimatum resulting from the threat of an assault on the Quirinal was presented to the Pope: it demanded the immediate formation of a democratic Government, the convocation of a constituent assembly and a declaration of war on Austria. Pius IX evaded the last two demands by observing that they lay within the competence of the deputies but immediately appealed to the liberals whom, under pressure from his familiars, he had recently dismissed: Mamiani, the abbé-philosopher Rosmini. . . . A few weeks earlier this combination might have saved everything; now it was too late.

The propaganda of the Mazzinians, finally joined in January by their leader who had always unfortunately been absent from any decisive action, met with a great response. Exasperated by "the foodstuffs crisis, the crisis of credit, the stoppage of tourism and the slump in the sales of *objets d'art*" (Bourgin), the working classes hoped for changes which would improve their lot; the social aspect explains the sudden outbreaks of violence on 16 November and confers on the Roman revolution a special place in the Italian movements of 1848. Refusing to play the part of a puppet subjected to the vagaries of the mob, Pius IX adopted a position which he had secretly envisaged since the end of April: "If they persist in demanding from me things which are repugnant to my conscience, I will retire . . . into a convent to weep over the misfortunes of Rome, delivered over to . . . this anarchy of which my withdrawal will be the signal." On the night of the 24th–25th he placed himself under the safeguard of Ferdinand II at Gaeta whence, on 4 December, he prayed the powers to re-establish his temporal authority since Rome had become, while awaiting the election of a Constituent Assembly (the Roman republicans were even more legalistic than the Parisian republicans), a *de facto* republic. The provisional Government established contacts with the Guerrazzi Government.

On the continent the stiff-necked protector of Pius IX had succeeded during the summer in wiping out "the spring". This prince, who not without humour compared his action of 15 May with that of the French republican executive commission on the same day, did not put into force the constitution which he prided himself he had been the first in Italy to concede; since the Chamber elected after the May dissolution was as little subservient as the former one, he did not summon it. As Charles Albert had, after Custozza, declined the crown of Sicily offered to his son, Ferdinand II thought the moment ripe to launch the mass of his forces against the rebels. In September 20,000 men, supported by a powerful fleet, attacked Messina with a fury which earned the sovereign the sobriquet of *Re Bomba*. Bastide, who would have looked without displeasure on the birth of a new republic, interposed the squadrons of Admirals Baudin and Parker. The armistice imposed on Ferdinand was followed by fruitless negotiations; in Naples a nominal autonomy would have been accepted, in Palermo a *de facto* independence was demanded. Time was on Ferdinand's side. Had not the events of September shown that the future of a particularist movement cut off from the great democratic and unitary conflagrations of the peninsula rested, when all was said and done, on the presence, assuredly temporary, of foreign fleets?

In the heart of the provinces over which Radetzky set up a despotism even more burdensome than that of the King of the Two Sicilies, Venice alone did not cease to live on a war footing from March 1848 to August 1849. Obsessed by the idea of autonomy, the ancient republic of the doges symbolized, in the eyes of the European democrats, the national and republican idea personified by Manin. This epic and its hero were born of Custozza. Attached in principle to Sardinia since 3 July, Venice only lost her independence for five days; on 7 August Sardinian officials took possession of the city in the name of the King. The armistice of the 9th made them clear out, bag and baggage, on the 12th. The assembly annulled its vote of 3 July, restored the power to Manin and prepared for resistance. Cut off from the *mainland*, threatened with suffocation by the Austrian fleet, and subjected to an armistice whose validity Vienna contested, Venice was nonetheless torn by factions. The triumvirate (in 1848 that curious institution covered, as at the end of the Roman republic, personal ambitions), had to stand up to the moderates, to repentant Albertists now resigned to the restoration of Austrian domination and, above all, to the members of the Mazzinian clubs, who were reinforced by the arrival of volunteers. At the beginning of October Manin expelled some agents who declaimed against the clergy and vaunted the merits of a unitary republic. Abroad, he benefited from the support of Bastide until 20 December, the date of the ministerial changes after the election of Louis Napoleon. Would Lamartine's successor repair the injustices committed by Bonaparte at Campo Formio? Even if he had, in the course of the negotiations with Vienna, accepted the idea of a return to Austria of a Venice enjoying, it is true, the autonomy granted to the Magyars, his personal inclinations were for a Lombardy-Venetian republic. This Catholic republican, hostile to any enlargement of the Sardinian monarchy, exhibited, despite the exigencies of the *entente* with London, an active sympathy for the Venetian republic and its head, the most Francophile of the Italian democrats. From the time of his accession to the control of foreign affairs he had provided 20,000 rifles. If he had not yet gone so far as to recognize the new republic *de jure,* he had at least received its envoys. When Palmerston refused an Anglo-French occupation of Venice, he sent two French warships to patrol in front of the city. Thus the blockade decreed by Vienna became derisory.

The forces of reaction which had already made progress in Naples and in Lombardy-Venetia were able, by December, to envisage soon putting an end to the republican régimes set up, or in process of being set up, in Sicily, in Rome, Florence and Venice. When he became Minister of Foreign Affairs in November, the energetic Schwarzenberg was quite determined to impose on Piedmont the peace of the vanquished and to re-establish the legitimate authority everywhere. There was no counter-measure to fear from the monarchists who presided over the destinies of republican France (Barrot was the Head of Government and Drouyn de Lhuys Minister of Foreign Affairs). As for Palmerston, his customary verbal demonstrations in favour of Charles Albert could be regarded philosophically.

## THE AUSTRO-HUNGARIAN RUPTURE AND THE CRUSHING OF THE VIENNESE REVOLUTION

Between July and November the imperial Government coped successfully with Viennese democrats and Magyar aristocrats. The setback to the Viennese revolution was the signal for a general counter-offensive, supported by the non-Magyar nationalities, against the régime in Pest and for a more active policy in German affairs. The Frankfurt democrats had followed passionately the hopeless struggle of their Austrian "brothers" and had passed ardent resolutions in support of the Magyars. For they saw clearly a truth which the statements issued sometimes from Berlin and sometimes from Frankfurt concealed; the fate of the German revolution depended, in the final analysis, on the maintenance or destruction of the Austro-Hungarian dualism which had arisen on 13 March 1848.

The meeting of the Constituent Assembly (*Reichstag*) on 22 July was, for the imperial Government busy restoring its prestige in Italy, a means of establishing its authority in the

"Hereditary States". In a *Reichstag* elected by universal suffrage
the Slavs were in a majority: 190 (of whom 55 were Czechs)
against 160 Germans. The president, a Viennese lawyer, was
flanked by two vice-presidents, one Czech, the other Polish.
The liberal professions, widely represented (50 per cent), were
dispersed among the various nationalities. The relative insignificance of the class till then dominant (12 per cent nobles),
the high proportion of the lower class (25 per cent peasants)
(for this reason almost 10 per cent of the deputies did not know
German and some were even illiterate), conferred its original
traits on the Vienna *Reichstag*. From an Assembly preponderantly
Slav and with a strong peasant representation, which begged
Ferdinand I to do it the honour of returning to Vienna (12
August), the Government had nothing to dread. It had a
comfortable majority against the German Left-wingers: the
Czech intellectuals (Palacky, Rieger) were just as conservative
as the German monarchists. The Slav peasantry paid little or
no heed to the reorganization of political institutions and no
one even thought of instructing them in the virtues of federalism!
Surprised by, even indignant at, the revolution, it wanted to
carry out "its" revolution. It knew, with extraordinary
perspicacity, how to seize the unique opportunity afforded it
to obtain, in the legality born of the revolution, the suppression
of seigniorial dues. The question of compensation ranged the
nobles supported by the Czech deputies against the peasants
who were supported by the Left wing which championed the
aspirations of the most numerous class. Promulgated on 7
September, the law voted on 31 August fully satisfied the
peasantry (serfdom, forced labour and feudal dues were
abolished; these last, according to their nature, were either
suppressed without compensation or redeemed either by the
State or by those formerly subject to them) who had never
envisaged the partition of the large domains. Bewildered by
purely political debates, the rural deputies began to desert the
*Reichstag*. The popularity of the "good Emperor" was at its
height in the provinces, whereas the opposition in the capital
(bourgeois democrats, workers, intellectuals) seemed about to
disintegrate; on 23 August the middle classes enlisted in the

National Guard had, as in Paris in June, harshly suppressed
the workers' insurrection which had broken out after the
threat of an enforced reduction in wages. An even more
encouraging sign was that the turbulent Academic Legion
remained neutral. The Government, therefore, seemed able,
for the first time since March, to concentrate its forces against
one enemy alone, the Magyars.

Forced by circumstances, Austria had abandoned to the
Magyars her natural allies, the South Slavs and the Rumanians.
Despite the promises of the President of the Council, Batthyany,
the Diet had refused to send reinforcements to Radetzky; the
Minister of Finance, Kossuth, made public pronouncements
supporting Italian independence and proclaimed that the
Hungarian army would not participate in a "German" war. In
short, the new Hungary, which tried to defend its unity by
forcing its subjects to obedience, failed to appreciate the moral
unity of the Empire.

The very serious decisions taken in July and August led to a
*de facto* secession. The Diet, elected according to property
qualifications, was in the hands of the nationalist middle
nobility. Kossuth dominated it by his eloquence and the support
of the Pest intellectuals. On 11 July he had had voted the
creation of an army of 200,000 men and a credit of 42 million
florins for its upkeep. The coffers being empty, he obtained, on
24 August, authority to issue paper money. The Emperor
refused his sanction to these laws, separatist in spirit, and, at
the instigation of Windischgrätz, very influential at court
since the events at Prague, replied with the declaration of 31
August. Summoned to negotiate the establishment of services
of common interest, the Hungarian Government raised volunteers, approved bank-notes blocks and sent delegates to Frankfurt and Paris.

To put an end to this insolence the imperial Government
called on the rivalry of the nationalities. That was the meaning
of the restoration of Jelačić as *ban*. On 10 September Jelačić
crossed the Drava, while in southern Hungary the Serbs rose,
supported by Colonel Mayerhofer, Austrian consul in Belgrade.
Considered too biased towards the Magyars, the Archduke

Stephen, Palatine (personal representative of the sovereign) of Hungary, resigned his post; a Magyar aristocrat, General Count Lamberg received, with the title of royal commissioner, the double mission of ending the hostilities and recalling the Magyars to a respect for legality. He hoped to isolate Kossuth and the extremists by negotiating with Batthyany, Eötvös and Deak, members of a Government which had thought it must resign after the non-ratification of the laws on the army and the currency. The Diet proclaimed Lamberg a traitor to his country and forbade the army to obey him. On 28 September Lamberg arrived in Pest and the same day was stabbed to death by a fanatic. On 3 October the imperial Government dissolved the Diet, proclaimed a state of siege in Hungary and appointed a new royal commissioner with full civil and military powers—Jelačić! The Diet refused to submit. A Committee of Defence led by Kossuth became the revolutionary organ of the Hungarian, that is to say Magyar, independence movement. The success of the young army which, to everyone's astonishment, drove Jalačić's forces back across the frontier, increased the enthusiasm of the Magyar extremists and caused the outbreak of revolution in Vienna.

From 6–31 October the alliance between the Viennese democrats and the Magyar nobility called in question the re-establishment of the imperial authority in Austria, in Italy and above all in Germany. While Kossuth's agitation shook Austrian absolutism, the German extreme Left as a whole, whether it was a question of Struve or of Marx, was infatuated with the Magyars. The oppression of "moribund nationalities" (Engels), or "the refuse of peoples" (Marx) unworthy of freedom, left them indifferent. A Magyar initiative transformed friendship into alliance. On 15 September a Magyar delegation begged in vain to lay the grievances of Pest before the *Reichstag*. The anti-Magyar majority was made up of Slavs and German moderates, the "black-yellow" supporters of a unitary Austrian Empire. The minority of democrats were the "black-red-gold" champions of the resurrection of the *Reich*. But the envoys of Kossuth got in touch with the revolutionary opposition, re-invigorated by the powerful anti-Slav fever created by the

return of Jelačić to favour. To weaken the pressure of the *ban*
on Hungary an insurrection was planned in Vienna. The
extreme Left-wing press systematically concentrated its attacks,
to all intents and purposes incitements to murder, on the
Minister of War, General Latour, an aristocrat of the old
régime (born 1780) and a friend of Jelačić. The announcement
of the imperial decisions of 3 October confirmed the impression
that the forces of reaction had deliberately undertaken to crush
liberty in Pest before destroying it in Vienna. At the news that
a battalion was about to leave to reinforce Jelačić, the workers
and students set up barricades on the morning of the 6th. A
section of the National Guard supported them; another section,
the "black-yellows" fought against them. The troops of the line
either fled or joined the insurgents. Latour was assassinated
and his corpse left hanging on a lamp-post. The rioters seized
30,000 rifles from the arsenal. The Emperor and his court fled,
to place themselves under the protection of Windischgrätz at
Olmütz (Olomouc) in loyal Moravia.

For the first time since March the German workers, on the
example of the Parisian workers, had overthrown the authorities.
But without a revolutionary tradition or clearcut political
objectives (no one dared to propose the abolition of the
monarchy!) the democrats showed themselves incapable of
forging in fire and steel institutions adapted to a revolutionary
situation which they themselves had created. The *Reichstag*,
which had become since the departure of the Slavs a rump-
parliament, set up a Permanent Committee of 25 members.
This remarkable "Committee of Public Safety", ever eager to
be on the right side of the law could not bring itself to call on
the aid of the Magyars! Like its conduct, its defence of the
revolution was marked by triviality and lack of foresight.
Because of the abstention of the moderates of the National
Guard and of the Academic Legion, the revolutionary army
only amounted to about thirty thousand men, of whom the
most combative belonged to the *garde mobile*, a corps of paid
volunteers recruited from deserters and the unemployed. The
commander-in-chief Messenhauer, a wit without energy, had
at least the merit of entrusting the functions of chief-of-staff to

the Polish general Bem (1795–1850), the future hero of the Magyar revolt. Bem had certainly nothing of the democrat about him; he placed his courage and his ability at the service of all movements from which he hoped that one day the resurrection of his country would emerge.

By its revolution Vienna had isolated itself physically and morally from the provinces. In a State where the apparatus and the mentality of the *ancien régime* still persisted, nothing recalled the leading role of Paris. Who held Vienna did not hold Austria! The power and the authority remained where the Emperor was in residence. The democratic ideology was incomprehensible to the rural masses and to a section of the middle classes. The replacement of the black-red-gold flag for the old imperial standard was a disservice to the cause of the revolution in the "Hereditary States".

In the rest of the Confederation who could remain indifferent to what was going on in a metropolis which, incontestably, formed part of the new Germany? The constitutional monarchists, following the example of the Archduke John and Schmerling, recently Head of Government of the *Reich*, did not want to have to repress an agitation which they condemned. The extreme Left and a part of the Left took fire from the revolt. Marx showed in the *Neue Rheinische Zeitung* that the fate of the revolution in Germany was linked to the destinies of the Viennese insurrection; he exhorted the German democrats and the forces of Kossuth to come to the aid of Vienna. The support of an already defeated revolution was to be the origin of the last great Berlin demonstration.

Two missions, one official and one unofficial, left Frankfurt for Austria in mid-October. If the former had a comic outcome, the latter ended in drama. The *Reichsverweser* had entrusted two deputies, one of whom was Welcker, with the task of preventing the threatened bloody confrontation; the commissioners of the *Reich* went to Olmütz. The civil and military authorities there told them that the internal affairs of the Empire were no concern of the "provisional central authority" and told them to clear out!

The setback to attempts to obtain a vote in favour of the

Viennese revolutionaries led the Left to empower two of their members to go to Vienna to express their active sympathy: Blum and Fröbel (1805–93), the moving spirit of the Zurich *Comptoire littéraire* of the forties. Blum launched, in the name of German democracy, ardent appeals for a life and death struggle and, with Fröbel, enrolled in the revolutionary army. The time for speeches had passed.

In his manifestoes of 16 and 19 October the Emperor entrusted to Windischgrätz, now raised to the rank of marshal, the task of restoring order and transferred the seat of the *Reichstag* to Kremsier (Kromerice) in Czech territory. The encirclement of the city was completed by the 23rd and Windischgrätz, who had a crushing superiority in men and guns, passed to the attack. Street fighting went on until the 31st, interrupted by a truce on the 29th which was violated on the 30th by rumours of the arrival of the Magyars. But the Magyars were not over-insistent and went back across the Leitha even more rapidly than they had crossed it. On November 1st Vienna was totally occupied and the imperial flag hoisted over the city.

Many facets of the Viennese insurrection recall the Parisian June days. The losses of the adversaries were as heavy on the banks of the Danube as they had been on the banks of the Seine: between two and five thousand insurgents, about sixty officers and some eleven hundred soldiers. In Vienna, as in Paris, the proportion of those massacred after the surrender was abnormally high. If the ruthlessness of the fighting and the cruelty of the victors were comparable, this was not true of their causes. Working class in its composition and social in its despairing aims, the Parisian revolt opened the floodgates to all the passions engendered in civil wars. With a large workers' participation, of which the proletarian *garde mobile* was the spearhead, the Viennese revolution especially reflected, despite a few diatribes against the rich who had fled the city, the political and national aspirations of the working classes. These workmen, whose backwardness Marx had remarked on at the end of August, yielded to a mirage of striking egoism; in a Germany united and free the Slavs would be respected and the Viennese workers freed from their competition. The presence of numerous Slavs in Windischgrätz's troops, especially the Croats and their abhorred leader, had aggravated the spirit of resistance among the insurgents. Jelačić and his men, still smarting after their ignominious rout in Hungary, had centred their hatred on the Germans, allies of the Magyars. On both one side and the other the conflict took on the character of a pitiless "racial" war.

The Vienna days of October, even more than the Paris days of June, had a considerable repercussion abroad as well as at home. If June had to some extent wiped out February, October totally annihilated March. The state of siege, which ceased in Paris in October, was to weigh upon Vienna with inexorable rigour until May 1849. The defeat of the Parisian workmen was, as we have seen, that of a certain conception of revolution; it did not, however, mean the return of the monarchy based on property. The crushing of the Viennese proletarians and democrats, cut off from all the peoples of the empire, immediately let loose parallel efforts for the restoration both of absolutism and the prestige of the dynasty in Europe. On 21 November Prince Schwarzenberg (1800–52), brother-in-law of Windischgrätz, became President of the Council and Minister of Foreign Affairs. On 2 December Ferdinand I, from whom circumstances had extorted many promises and signatures which were now embarrassing (especially the ratification of the Hungarian constitutional laws), consented to abdicate in favour of his nephew Francis-Joseph. Assured of the unconditional support of the young Emperor, Schwarzenberg needed only one more thing, the backing of the loyal army which, after Prague and Custozza, had just had another success. The days of the parliamentary type of régime were numbered, but the dispersal of the babblers who, at Kremsier, under the reassuring protection of the imperial Government, were preparing a constitution which would never be applied, was not urgent. Why indeed, before the Magyars had been reduced to obedience, bother about these guileless Slav deputies? On the eve of the general offensive in Hungary, the old German monarchy felt itself strong enough to launch a bloody challenge to the young German democracy.

The October repression provided the opportunity. Bem had fled, too well-informed to cherish any illusions about the meekness of a Windischgrätz. Ingenuously, Blum and Fröbel thought themselves invulnerable; were they not covered by the truce of the 29th, since they had not taken up arms again? Did not the parliamentary immunity voted them at Frankfurt guarantee their freedom? Arrested on 2 November, they were condemned to death. Fröbel was reprieved; this member of the extreme Left (*Donnersberg*) had had the foresight to publish a pamphlet in September disapproving of any system which aimed at the dismemberment of the Hapsburg Empire! Blum was shot on the 9th. Frankfurt protested and received a reply tinged with black humour; never promulgated in Austria, the law of 30 September was not applicable there!

The execution of Blum aroused universal indignation in Germany. Democrats and constitutional monarchists bombarded the local Chambers and the parliamentarians with petitions and the Government and ministers of the *Reich* with addresses. From the banks of the Rhine to Saxony "funeral ceremonies" took place spontaneously, in which pastors took part and also curés, despite the interdictions of the Catholic hierarchy (Blum had been a disciple of Ronge). In Baden radical opinion forgot the controversies in the *Vorparlament* which had ranged Blum against Hecker and Struve. Everywhere the press launched subscriptions to aid the widow and children of the martyr with success. The manufacture of plaster busts of the hero became a lucrative industry. This naïve and sentimental cult betrayed the confusion among the working classes. At the spectacle of a parliament impotent to make the rights of the nation respected or to ensure the safety and honour of its members, the anxious question was posed: had the hour of the German revolution passed?

## GERMAN UNITY. NATIONALIST DISILLUSIONS AND DEMOCRATIC DISAPPOINTMENTS

Having met on 18 May, it was not until towards the end of October 1848 that the parliament at Frankfurt began to discuss the constitution. The September crisis had forced it, in order to resist the violent pressure of the republicans, to fall back on the Governments. Soon Austria and Prussia would be in a position to bring influence to bear on the debates, whereas it could have dared all during the course of the summer. Is this reproach, with which historians have not ceased to encumber it for more than a century, well founded?

The parliament has been blamed for the time lost in legislating on all sorts of matters, especially the long debates on fundamental rights (*Grundrechte*) which lasted from May to November. However, these did not have, if one takes the trouble to read them, the abstract character for which they are so often condemned. In a country where the freedom of the individual (it is enough to recall the arbitrary expulsion of Itzstein and Hecker from the Prussian state) and civil and political equality (one thinks of the proletarians and the Jews) were generally disregarded, since the vestiges of feudalism were always alive, the German *Gründlichkeit* was intended to prevent the return of abuses which had been denounced in vain so many times. Surely the law on gaming-houses could have waited! It bore witness, in any case, to highly moral preoccupations. And it was public opinion, shocked by the crushing Danish superiority in the Baltic, which had forced the decision, so often criticized, to build a war fleet.

The weakness of Frankfurt lay in its lack of means. The Government of the *Reich* had at its disposal one weapon only, an official journal, more and more voluminous! In foreign affairs it had no diplomatic representatives (the powers continued to recognize only the multiple missions accredited by the States), the Ministry of War had no troops and the Ministry of the Interior no officials (witness the treatment by Austria of the *Reich* "representatives on mission" endowed with full theoretical powers), and the Ministry of Finance had no revenues except the contributions hitherto paid by the States to the Diet. When all was said and done, everything depended on the good will of the sovereigns who were excluded from all participation in the transformation of federal institutions. "By leaving the State apparatus in the hands of the Governments the men of Frankfurt were condemned to impotence" (Droz). But no one has clearly explained how and with what, the "German revolutions" having been what they were, the "German revolution" could have snatched in the summer what only a handful of southern radicals had demanded in the exaltation of "the spring".

Logic, at least the logic of historians, would have assumed that this power, without material support within the country, would have done its best to avoid trouble abroad. It is an uncontested fact that ambitions foreshadowing those of William II and of Hitler had disquieted both the holders of "the principle of nationalities" and the partisans of a territorial *status quo*. The discord between foreign countries and Frankfurt was fatal because it was founded on ignorance of Germanic realities.

Problems which we still consider today as part of the foreign policy of a minority of doctrinaires and rhetoricians were regarded by large sections of the populace as matters of internal policy and there was irritation when foreign powers became involved in them. Such a problem, the most important and complicated of all, against which the *Vorparlament* and the Fifty had butted their heads in vain, was the extent of the State which was being formed. A minority, nostalgic for the medieval *Reich*, made imprudent speeches about Alsace, Switzerland and the Netherlands! Did they deceive themselves that there was any chance of realizing their dreams? The immense majority of the delegates, above all the Left (it is enough to recall Struve's projects!), considered it impossible to exclude even the smallest parcel of the *Bund* from the new *Reich*. Why should the unity of Germany mean the "dismemberment" of Germany? The fate of Limburg and the Grand duchy of Luxembourg was cited. The King of the Netherlands, supported by St Petersburg, London and Paris, protested. Frankfurt refused to risk a second war of the duchies. On the other hand, the parliament worked with fanatical obstinacy to preserve the unity of the Austrian lands. It paid no heed to Italian or Czech aspirations! The Italian deputies of the Tyrol did not contest the sovereignty of the Hapsburgs, but demanded the formation, on linguistic grounds, of two zones: the north would be attached to the Confederation, the Trento region detached from it. The majority, which had applauded Custozza, repudiated these modest demands, invoking the glorious history of the *Reich*, and the interests of Austria. The Prussian Radowitz (1797–1853), friend and confidant of Frederick William, declared that the German frontier "should be on the Mincio"! The Charter of Bohemia, which provisionally put an end to the privileges of the Germans, was considered a dangerous weakness of Austria; by claiming the union of the Crown of St Wenceslas with countries "where the German tongue resounds", the old Arndt aroused a delirious enthusiasm. The events of June in Prague aroused passionate interest. By announcing on the 20th that the ministry of the *Reich* had just begged Prussia, Saxony and Bavaria to intervene in Bohemia at the first appeal of Vienna, Schmerling had irritated the Left which demanded immediate action!

The debates between 24 and 27 July concerning the status of the Grand duchy of Posen confirmed that "cosmopolitanism", that is to say the French conception of nationality, and "Polonism" were definitely on the wane in the Left. At the end of March Herwegh did not distinguish between the German cause and the Polish cause; at the beginning of April the *Vorparlament* had approved a pro-Polish declaration of principle. The Fifty had referred the matter to parliament; from the idea of not renouncing any territory, it went on, to quote a clear-sighted Frenchman, to the principle that "every foreign country subject to a German power . . . must sooner or later belong to Germany (Saint-René Taillandier). On the 27th the parliament, as the Diet before it, ratified by 342 votes against 31 the Prussian decision to annex the greater part of the Grand duchy of Posen (the "Polish" duchy of Gnesen had been progressively whittled down by a perpetual shifting of the frontier demarcation traced out by the Prussian military). Nearly two hundred deputies of the Left or former friends of Poland took refuge in a prudent abstention. The universities had not preached in vain for decades the mission vested in the most cultivated nation in Europe! Amongst a multitude of declarations let us recall the astonishing statement of Blum about "a nation predestined to dictate its law" to free Europe!

The vote of 27 July alerted France to the dangers of a Germany with inconstant frontiers. Despite the annexationist measures of Frederick William, the Constituent Assembly had on 24 May, in an address to the Frankfurt parliament, proposed "a fraternal pact with Germany, the reconstitution of a free and independent Poland and the liberation of Italy". French diplomats continued to cherish fond illusions, inclined as they were to find in the Germans sentiments analogous to those which they held themselves. The French *chargé d'affaires* had written from Frankfurt on 31 May that "deputies of the most opposite shades of opinion" considered that the parliament would soon adopt as its own the text voted in Paris! Bastide, who was, like most of the forty-eighters, a partisan of "a close alliance betwen France and Germany" but even more devoted to the destinies of the Poles having taken part in the Parisian insurrection of June 1832, had from the beginning of June perceived the real aspirations of Germany. On the 9th he denounced "a fourth dismemberment of Poland". Thenceforward convinced that the word "nationality" was untranslatable into German, this minister of a Government which repudiated *de jure* the treaties of 1815 reproached Prussia for having modified them at Posen without the consent of its cosignatories of the Vienna acts. His intervention did not go beyond this diplomatic démarche, for the former Carbonaro noted each day that Germanic bellicose nationalism was not centred on the old particularist monarchy but on the young unitary democracy.

When Prussia, under the pressure of London, St Petersburg and Paris (Bastide lumped in a single censure the designs on Schleswig and Poznania), agreed to conclude the armistice of Malmö with Denmark (26 August) she unleashed the fury of the provisional government of the duchies (all its revolutionary decisions were annulled), the protests of the Ministry of the *Reich* which had not been consulted and the indignation of a public opinion enfevered by the very names of Schleswig and Holstein. Appealed to by Dahlmann, the doctrinaire of the

German cause in the duchies, the Frankfurt parliament refused, on 5 September, its ratification by 238 votes to 221. The Left declared itself *en bloc* for the continuation of the war. Cries of hate resounded from its benches against Prussia, Russia, England and France. Leiningen resigned and Dahlmann was entrusted with forming a new Government. But the brilliant professor discovered the impossibility of avenging the "honour" of Germany without an army. At his instigation the Assembly rescinded on the 16th its earlier vote and Schmerling became Prime Minister.

Prussia, the parliament and the Frankfurt executive all emerged from the Malmö crisis with discredit. The press of all shades of opinion noted the deep confusion of a public opinion which had never separated in its aspirations the improvement of the conditions of the Germans from the greatness of Germany. The proletarians constituted for the democrats the most unitary and the most Prussophobe of the Germans (Meinecke has clearly brought out that the characteristic of the man of the Left was his hatred of particularism and his nationalist intransigence), the shock troops who must drive out unworthy figureheads. In the *Neue Rheinische Zeitung* Marx waged a vigorous campaign against the Danish oppressors and their friend Russia; far from dreading, he *desired* the armed intervention of tsarism which, according to his calculations, would lead to the outbreak of a great patriotic war from which social democracy would be the gainer. Marx stigmatized the double treason of the King of Prussia and the Frankfurt régime; Cologne became the scene of stormy demonstrations. In Frankfurt itself the republicans, supported by the local *Arbeiterverein*, proposed, in the manner of the Parisian clubs of 15 May, to purge the Assembly. On the 18th barricades were set up. Two reactionary deputies were assassinated. The three thousand insurgents would have forced their way into the church of St Paul if Schmerling had not appealed (an indication of the changes which had taken place since May!) to the Austrian and Prussian forces of the federal garrison of Mainz. At the news that the revolution had triumphed in Frankfurt, Struve, who had taken refuge in Basle (the discouraged Hecker had just left Switzerland for the United States, where many republicans were soon to join him), crossed the Rhine with about thirty supporters, who were joined by volunteers from Switzerland and the Black Forest. On the 21st the republic was proclaimed at Lörrach, but Struve was crushed by the Baden troops and was taken prisoner at Staufen on the 24th.

This repression of movements of extra-parliamentary origin was justified in the eyes of the immense majority of delegates, who had scarcely recovered from their great fear of the 18th; the state of siege at Frankfurt and the military occupation of Baden seemed measures of public safety against "anarchy". Execrated by the progressives, despised by the patriotic masses, the ministry of the *Reich* at last obtained, by its eager participation in the hunting down of the revolutionaries, the recognition of a contested authority; with what alacrity the local administrations, for so long sullenly hostile, replied to the questionnaires of the Ministry of Justice on the activities of the democratic associations (*Vereine*)!

The shams barely concealed the reality. The parliament was saved by the two great Germanic powers which it had, at its birth, affected to ignore. When the constitutional debate was opened, it had to take account of the power of an Austria now so assured as to reject a particularist régime in its "German" provinces and of a Prussia whose Government was preparing to liquidate the Berlin democratic movement and to drive out the turbulent National Assembly.

### THE TRIUMPH OF REACTION IN PRUSSIA (END OF MAY TO THE BEGINNING OF DECEMBER 1848)

On 5 December 1848 Frederick William dissolved the National Assembly and conceded a constitution. Doubtless the defeat of the revolution in Vienna encouraged him to make these serious decisions. But the parallelism between the evolution of Prussia and that of Austria went no further. After 18 March Berlin had been the scene of riots, but never of a full-scale revolution. That fervent passion for Germanic unity which inflamed the Austrian capital was lacking in the Prussian one. What has sometimes been called the crushing of the revolution in Prussia was only the brutal aftermath, approved by a large section of public opinion, of the check of the reformist movement born of the barricades of 18 March.

A Chamber resolved to limit forever the powers of the monarchy and its supporters, the great landed nobility, the bureaucracy and the military caste, and which was under pressure from a proletariat without political tradition nagged at ministers of good will, while the united strength of the most powerful reactionary forces in Germany was being organized. Though elected on the same day and by the same electoral procedure (two-stage universal suffrage), the Berlin deputies were basically more modest, of more progressive tendencies and of less notoriety than their Frankfurt counterparts. The leading personages were above all interested in the elections to the first German parliament. Also the lower classes (the peasants especially) were freer in their choice of members of the Prussian National Assembly. Out of 402 deputies there were sixty-eight peasants and twenty-eight artisans as against one and seven respectively in Frankfurt, where the Prussian representation numbered two hundred. There were not so many great landowners. The *Akademiker* formed scarcely a half of the Chamber; faced with a very weak Right wing (Prince William, returned from England, and the young Bismarck were its leading lights) hostile to the "March principles", they were the most ardent supporters of the Left-wing majority. Under the leadership of the democrats Jacoby and d'Ester they claimed for the Assembly the right of drawing up the constitution as a sovereign body; the ministers, supported by the centre, recalled that the law voted by the *Landtag* required the agreement of the king and deputies. This controversy concealed a basic problem; was 18 March an incident or a revolution?

The Berlin democrats, through their clubs and their papers, tried to stimulate the zeal of the Left wing. The *Zeitungshalle* was their principal organ; its most outstanding contributor was the young printer Born (1824–98), formerly a friend of Marx and Engels, who like so many of his companions had lived in Switzerland, in Lyons, Paris and Brussels. He pioneered an extensive workers' organization to cover all Germany, and founded a Central Committee (*Zentralkomitee*) in Berlin and a newspaper, *Das Volk*. Obscure leaders lacking the political intelligence of Born had a good chance of stirring up a simple-minded proletariat, a prey to unemployment, and whose dignity was affronted by the setting aside of the civil guard (the limitations of the "Prussian revolution" were obvious!). Tumultuous demonstrations (the red flag made its appearance in Berlin on 4 June) and acts of violence drove the Assembly to act, but frightened the urban middle classes and the peasantry. On 15 June workers and students pillaged the arsenal and the Assembly assumed constituent power by entrusting to a commission the task of recasting the Government proposal. Vituperated by the masses, disavowed by the deputies, Camphausen abandoned the control of affairs to Auerswald (1795–1866); Hansemann, who remained in control of the finances, envisaged measures capable of satisfying the rural population, whose fate was a matter of indifference to the Berlin agitators; a law was proposed to free landed property and to subject the nobility to land tax.

Threatened in its interests, the formidable aristocracy of the eastern districts regrouped in the Association for the Defence of Property Rights. With the financial support of Frederick William, who had gone to earth in Potsdam, and was waiting for the rupture between the Left and the workers of the capital in order to dissolve the Assembly, and with the aid of von Gerlach (1790–1861), friend of the camarilla, it founded the *Kreuzzeitung* (*Gazette of the Cross*) on 1 July. It played on the fears of the Berlin troubles and the apprehension of the absorption of the kingdom into the Germany which was being fashioned at Frankfurt under the leadership of a Catholic archduke and politicians of the south and west. It called upon the virtues which had created the greatness of the State in the past; loyalty to the monarchy and fidelity to the Lutheran church. The old provinces were horrified at the consequences of their electoral aberrations in May. Junkers, senior officials and officers were no longer isolated.

Hostility to the army, which had been at the root of the

insurrection of 18 March, remained the sole link still uniting
the Berlin agitators and the parliamentarians irritated by the
anarchic disturbances. The bloody clash at Schweidnitz (31
July) in Silesia between the civil guard and the troops drove
the indignant Assembly to declare a war on the military caste,
a contest in which it was itself to perish; on 9 August an order
of the day called on the reactionary officers to resign. From the
16th to the 19th the great landowners of the east met, out of
bravado, in Berlin; in reply to this *Junkerparlament* the Berlin
workers on the 21st set up several barricades. Accused by the
*camarilla* of encouraging disorder and becoming the accomplice
of an Assembly far from anxious to facilitate this task, the
minister Auerswald resigned on 10 September. That was the
end of the era of the pseudo-liberalism of Camphausen and the
sincere liberalism of Hansemann.

From 21 September to 5 December the reaction, secure in
the approval or at least the apathy of the provinces (the
opposition of the Breslau democrats or of the *Neue Rheinische
Zeitung* had little effect) methodically prepared the investment
of its Berlin enemies, the Assembly and the workers. It re-
furbished its arms under the Pfül (1799–1866) ministry (21
September–1 November). The choice of this general was a
clever one; his harshness towards the Poles of Poznania had not
reduced his popularity. The *camarilla* had not associated him
with the policy of force which had been transformed into
disaster in March. In fact, the reaction considered Pfül as a
"temporary expedient"; it revealed its real intentions after the
return of the troops made available by the Malmö armistice.
Wrangel, the King's man, the victor over the Danes, was
nominated commander of the Berlin garrison.

On 12 October the Assembly at last began to elaborate a
constitution of democratic type and particularist character;
the monarch would cease to be "King by the grace of God"
and the nobility would be abolished; but federal legislation
would only become applicable after approval by the Prussian
deputies! The Germanic national idea did not arouse the
enthusiasm of the most progressive Chamber in Germany. The
indifference increased the tension between the Assembly and

the working classes in the streets: on 16 October the civil guard opened fire on some workers whose dismissal had led to unconsidered action. The Congress of German Democrats, driven from Frankfurt by the state of siege, moved to Berlin from 26–30 October; it hoped to mobilize the masses to demand from the Assembly military and financial support for the Vienna insurgents. Protected by the civil guard, the Assembly contented itself with begging the ministry to carry out at Frankfurt a derisory move forward in favour of the freedoms threatened in Austria.

That was, however, too much for the reaction. The Brandenburg-Manteuffel ministry, formed on 8 November and stimulated by the victory of Windischgrätz in Vienna, did not hesitate to act openly. First, under pretext of sparing a hostile Chamber a fresh 31 October, the Government ordered it, on 9 November, to meet again on 27 November in the little town of Brandenburg, near Potsdam. The deputies, playing hide and seek with the authorities, continued their deliberations wherever they could find accommodation. Second, a state of siege was proclaimed; on the 15th Wrangel expelled the recalcitrants. The capital remained inert. From the provinces came only respectful addresses. The campaign of the *Neue Rheinische Zeitung* in favour of a boycott of taxes was without effect. It was in Frankfurt that the Prussian *coup d'état* produced the most lively emotion; friends and adversaries of Berlin set themselves vainly to defend the rights of the Prussian people. In this regard the defeat of the president of the parliament, von Gagern, was significant. When he allowed it to be understood that the formation of a liberal ministry would facilitate the accession of the House of Hohenzollern to the imperial dignity, the King snubbed this Prussophile sharply: "I hope that I shall never have need of your friendship." Third, on the 27th the Left won a last victory, for less than half (154) of the deputies went to Brandenburg. On 5 December the Assembly was dissolved and a constitution conceded. Thanks to Wrangel's soldiers, the King had wiped out the humiliating memories of March, but what he accorded of his own free will, to the great disappointment of the conservatives, was inspired by the demands of "the spring". Alongside an Upper Chamber, partly nominated, a Lower Chamber was elected by universal suffrage. The principle of ministerial responsibility was balanced by the sovereign's veto. On the whole, reactions in the country were favourable. The liberals would even have desired the exclusion from political life of those without property qualifications. The Left hoped, through the working-class vote, to reap its revenge.

After many vicissitudes Prussia completed its "March revolution" in December. The particularism of the royal entourage and the conservatives, the lukewarmness of the parliamentary liberals and democrats towards Frankfurt and Vienna, showed that they cared very little for the "German revolution". The idea of the German mission of Prussia had not become, at the end of 1848, a Prussian idea.

## [ Chapter Twelve ]

## The Downfall (December 1848–August 1849)

SAVED BY Prussian and Austrian troops, the Frankfurt parliament resigned itself to beginning the task for which it had been so enthusiastically elected. To whom could it confide the control of the Reich if not to the Austria of Schwarzenberg or the Prussia of Brandenburg-Manteuffel? But Austria demanded that the whole of the Empire enter the *Reich*, which would thenceforth be Germanic only in name! This increased the chances of the most detested of the German monarchies. Would a Hohenzollern accept the imperial crown from men elected by universal suffrage?

ITALY: THE ROUT OF SARDINIA AND THE DOWNFALL OF THE DEMOCRATIC RÉGIMES

At the beginning of 1849 Austria thought that she would be able, as in 1848, to speak loudly and confidently in Germany, since Schwarzenberg would by then have put an end to the Sardinian dreams and opened the way to the imminent destruction of the republican régime in Italy.

Up until March 1849 the armies of Radetzky had remained in armed readiness in Lombardy-Venetia, since the bulk of the forces of the Empire were involved in operations against the Hungarians. In Rome a Constituent Assembly legalized the

November revolution; it proclaimed a republic (9 February) which was to introduce "pure democracy" and a "state of social perfection". Controlled by Mazzini, a triumvirate (22 February) strove to give "the land to the peasants" and to organize, by arming the people, the defence of the new régime. For the Roman revolution had formidable enemies. The representatives of the four Catholic powers (Austria, Spain, France and the Two Sicilies), from whom Pius IX had demanded on 4 December the collective occupation of his States, met at Gaeta on 30 March. Even before the conservative Drouyn de Lhuys, Bastide had declared himself favourable to the restoration of Papal sovereignty. Austria, which on its own authority had as in the good old days occupied Ferrara, had just crushed the armies of Charles Albert on the 23rd.

In the meantime a Constituent Assembly was sitting in Florence. Leopold having also left for Gaeta, Tuscany had become a republic (8 February) which seemed to recognize the unitary vocation of the Roman republic. Had not Guerrazzi on 5 March inaugurated elections both for the Tuscan and for the Roman Constituent Assemblies, thus forming the embryo of an Italian Constituent of the Mazzinian type? The apathy and the sullen hostility of the populace (80 per cent abstentions) gave the republic a dictatorial character; Guerrazzi was invested with full powers.

At the two ends of the peninsula the republican régimes were directly threatened by their former oppressors. In Venice, the January elections had strengthened the authority of the intractable Manin. At the end of February Ferdinand II had called on the Sicilians to submit. As the armistice imposed by Baudin and Parker expired on 29 March, the Government of Palermo prepared for a struggle to the death and appealed to Mieroslawski.

By denouncing the armistice of August 1848, Charles Albert was to call down upon Sardinia a disaster which was to hasten the downfall of all the movements which had resulted, with the exception of the Sicilian, from the rout at Custozza. The romantic idea that a fresh catastrophe would be preferable to inaction had continued to gain ground in Turin during the winter. The tiny political class (from Cavour to the radicals), the court and the King abandoned themselves to a morose delight. Gioberti, overthrown, resigned on 20 February. A Government which included intellectuals like the radical Rattazzi (1808–73) rushed light-heartedly to suicide. The army was still what it had been eight months before. It was thought that the incapacity of the officers could be remedied by an undiscriminating acceptance of the aid of the "pilgrims". Ramorino, the tragic hero of the Mazzinian epic of 1834 against Savoy, was appointed regimental commander! Made responsible for the defeat, he was later to be shot. No less incapable was General Chrzanowski to whom the King entrusted the supreme command! Within the country, as abroad, Charles Albert's isolation was total. His muddle-headed attempts at an alliance with Ferdinand II and with the Sicilians had come to nothing; the era of the "crusaders" was over, the idea of unity incarnated even in the most revolutionary Governments went no further than inflammatory speeches. Already made antagonistic by the often repeated reproach that they had not obtained the cession of Lombardy by Schwarzenberg, Paris and London made very clear in Turin their censure of any act of folly. Such an act Charles Albert committed on 20 March. On the 23rd, twenty-eight years after the little band of Santarosa, his army was cut to pieces in the plain of Novara. The King, who had vainly sought the death of a romantic hero on the field of battle, knew that henceforth it would be impossible for him to negotiate with Austria. He abdicated and was to die in Portugal. His son, Victor Emmanuel II, obtained an armistice on the 26th and very mild peace conditions on 6 August; under the pressure of Palmerston and even of Bonaparte, Vienna had to renounce the annexation of Alessandria. According to this traditional policy, for the "springtide of the peoples" was already far away, France and the United Kingdom became the defenders of the *status quo* in Italy.

Repeating their military walkover of 1831, the Austrians, with Leopold II, Francis V d'Este and Charles III (Charles II had resigned in favour of this other Bourbon who was to perish

in 1854, assassinated like his father-in-law, the Duc de Berry)
in their train, occupied Tuscany, Modena and Parma.
Abandoned by the British and French fleets to the vengeance
of Ferdinand II, the Sicilians held out for another two months
against the hated Neapolitans. The absolutism of "King
Bomba", already restored on the mainland, was restored in the
island on 11 May. The victory of the Tedeschi aroused in
Brescia and in Venice a patriotic re-awakening, of which
Italians were to cherish the memory. On 23 March a handful
of men from the mountains encircled the Austrian garrison of
Brescia in the citadel and roused the town to revolt; caught
between the artillery fire of their beleaguered prisoners and
that of the reinforcements sent to relieve them, the populace
fought desperately until 2 April. Galvanized by the "ten days
of Brescia", the Venetian assembly proclaimed resistance at
all costs. The siege began in May; despite the shelling, the
famine and the cholera which the Austrian army brought with
it, the Venetians rallied around Manin, who gave proof of an
exemplary moral authority. Hatred of the Tedeschi and also
the assurance that their valiant Magyar allies would soon win a
decisive victory over their common enemy brought fresh energy
to temperaments which had been vacillating between
enthusiasm and despair. On 22 August, after the news of the
Magyar defeat on the 13th, Manin resigned himself to
surrender; exiled with about forty other revolutionaries, he was
to end his days in that France which, in accord with the United
Kingdom, had since April counselled him to renounce "the
illusions of a noble patriotism".

At the beginning of July the Roman republic had succumbed
under the blows of the French troops. But Austria, based on
Ferrara, appeared, after Novara, the best placed of the four
Gaeta powers to restore to his capital that Pope whose election
three years earlier had unleashed a wave of liberalism and
nationalism. Decided by an assembly with a republican
majority, an intervention of anti-Austrian character had become,
to the great joy of an assembly with a conservative majority,
an expedition against the Roman republic. Moved by the reflex
which had led the July Monarchy to Ancona in 1832, the

Constituent Assembly voted, on the news of Novara, a resolution approving in advance "the partial and temporary occupation of some place in Italy" (31 March). This attitude safeguarded the integrity of the Sardinian monarchy but also justified the despatch of an expeditionary force to Rome; according to the Government declaration of 16 April it was a matter of restoring Pius IX without recourse to force! The conservatives were delighted, the republicans reassured. A pontifical proclamation promising a generous amnesty and far-reaching reforms would guarantee an ambiguous policy, to which, however, 30,000 combatants of all origins could not subscribe, primarily the thousand men of the Italian Legion of the Niçois Garibaldi (1807–82) whose reputation as a legendary hero had first stemmed from the clashes of the spring of 1848! The five thousand soldiers of Oudinot were forced to withdraw (30 April). In Paris the Constituent Assembly, coming to an end, reproved their behaviour; in the expectation of legislative elections negotiations with the triumvirate kept the members amused. As the Austrians had taken Ancona, while the Spaniards and the Neapolitans had penetrated into the Papal States from the south, the Prince-president decided to satisfy the conservative majority, victorious on 13 May. On 3 June the siege began which led to the riot of 13 June in Paris which proved fatal to the leaders of the extreme Left. After a month of stubborn resistance Rome fell on 1 July. Pius IX had become another Gregory XVI. Despite pressure from Napoleon, he refused all reforms, while the presence of Oudinot's troops in Rome opened a long period of diplomatic complications. With Austria and the Two Sicilies "the French Republic had played its part in the Italian counter-revolution" (Girard).

At the time when the attitude of Pius IX finally condemned neo-Guelphism, the kingdom of Sardinia, despite its errors and the levity of its leaders, still preserved the prestige of a liberal and independent State. At his dramatic advent Victor Emmanuel II had taken oath to support the Constitutional Statute; in an Italy where the princes were Hapsburg clients, he came of a national dynasty which had taken a courageous stand against Austria. In the other States reaction had abolished not only the conquests of "the spring" but even previous concessions. Never had the foreign domination been more suffocating; the only change brought about by the revolutionary movements was the French occupation of Rome!

This helped to alienate the Italian patriots from France more than ever. In 1848 they had rejected with arrogance the aid offered them; in 1849 they reproached the France of Barrot and Bonaparte for not having backed up its strong diplomatic support by military aid. Mazzini dared to denounce the "French treason". In fact, the conviction that Italy was quite incapable, as Custozza and Novara had shown, of "going it alone" slowly germinated. The memory of setbacks, of smarting defeats, became blurred. After the Bandiera brothers, the heroes of the "Five days of Milan", the volunteer legions, the "Ten days of Brescia" and the siege of Venice were to become epic. Breaking with his "juvenile mentality" (Jacini) of a forty-eighter, Cavour was to be one of the first to understand that "ideas count less than facts".

### THE VICTORY OF VIENNESE CENTRALISM AND THE REPRESSION OF THE NATIONALITIES

March 1849 was the month of dramas and triumphs for the Hapsburg monarchy; it was the month of Novara and of the *coup d'état* which anticipated writing *finis* once and for all to the political and national consequences of the Viennese rising on 13 March 1848. It was also the month of the election of Frederick William IV as "Emperor of the Germans" and above all of the stupefying Magyar counter-offensive. The convalescent colossus tottered. Only the intervention of the troops of the Tsar prevented it from disintegrating and being expelled from Germany.

By the end of the winter the project for chastizing the Magyars seemed as if it would soon be realized. The promise to accord equality to all the nationalities had reinvigorated the ardour of the non-Magyar peoples. The war of the peoples had become the ally of the old monarchy. As soon as Windischgrätz crossed the Hungarian frontier, the Rumanians of Jancu, the Serbs of Stratimirović and the Croats of Jelačić hurled themselves on the Magyars. The imperial troops aided by the Rumanians and the "Saxons" took possession of Transylvania despite the stubborn resistance of the *Szeklers*. Windischgrätz occupied Pest on 5 January, and Kossuth and his Defence Committee took refuge at Debreczin. A fresh Austrian success at Kapolna (26 February) forced the enemy to retreat behind the Tisza. The collapse of the Magyar national revolution seemed imminent.

Schwarzenberg thought he would be able to put an end to the play-acting at Kremsier. Like Brandenburg-Manteuffel at the beginning of November 1848, he found himself, at the end of February 1849, faced by a Constituent Assembly which had almost completed its task. Amputated from the German democrats, the only element favourable to Germanic unity, the *Reichstag*, re-opened on 22 November, was more than ever anxious to maintain the integrity of the Empire while re-invigorating it. Compromises between the Slav majority cleverly led by the "Austrophiles" Palacky and Rieger and the German minority of "black-yellow" tendencies reconciled the centralizing aim of the State with the autonomist aspirations of the nationalities. Inspired by a liberalism which was a heritage of the July tradition, where a representation of the peoples would be elected not by universal suffrage but on a property qualification basis, the *Reichstag* approved several innovations which would have been acceptable in the disorder of March 1848 but were intolerable a year later: the Emperor would only have a suspensive veto, his allies, the nobility and the clergy, would lose some of their last prerogatives, even their privileges (Catholicism would no longer be the state religion). Finally established on 2 March, the constitutional proposal would receive, on the 7th, its parliamentary ratification in the course of a purely formal session.

But, in Olmütz as formerly in Berlin, when the ministers had drawn up their constitution, Schwarzenberg, following the example of his Prussian colleague, used peremptory procedures; on the 7th troops occupied the hall of the *Reichstag* and the deputies were dispersed without resistance. The same day a

constitution dated the 4th was "conceded". Never put into force
because of liberal measures (parliamentary régime) intended to
make the *coup d'état* more easily acceptable, it set out clearly
the principles of the new Austrian policy. The still-born
constitution of Kremsier aimed at settling the internal problems
of the "Hereditary States". That of 4 March was applicable
not only to the whole of the Empire, that is to the lands of the
Crown of St Stephen, but also to the Lombardy-Venetian
kingdom, hitherto regarded as an imperial colony; it instituted,
thanks to a corps of civil servants directly dependent on Vienna,
the political and economic unity of a centralized Austria. The
suppression of customs barriers with Hungary and Lombardy-
Venetia removed all reasons for complaint from the industrial
and merchant bourgeoisie. On 14 March, in order fully to
reassure the peasantry, the abolition of feudal dues was
confirmed and conditions of land repurchase were improved.
Finally, the unitary organization of the Empire was a double
challenge to the revolutionaries of Debreczin and the parliamentarians of Frankfurt. Hungary was reduced to the status of
a province. The idea of introducing into the *Reich* only those
territories which belonged to the *Bund* was dead. The new
Empire must enter, as a whole, into the new *Reich*!

The unexpected Magyar counter-offensive brought into
question for some weeks the spectacular successes achieved since
November by the arms of Windischgrätz and the cold determination of Schwarzenberg. Reorganized after the improvisa-
tions of the winter and reinforced by the ten thousand men of
the Polish Legion—all the "pilgrims" had rushed to help the
adversaries of the power which had annexed Cracovia and
kept the Poles of Galicia under its yoke—the *Honved* (Magyar
armed forces) had found two leaders of sterling worth: a Pole,
Bem, and a Magyar, Görgey (1818–1916). In March the
former reoccupied almost the whole of Transylvania; at the
beginning of April the latter forced Windischgrätz to retreat.
The extremists thought that victory was within their grasp.
Under their pressure, Kossuth led the reticent Diet to proclaim
on 14 April in the Calvinist cathedral of Debreczin the dis-
enthronement of the Hapsburgs and the independence of the

Crown of St Stephen. Without the word being pronounced,
a republic was *de facto* set up.

These decisions weakened the cohesion of the Magyar camp
and exasperated the non-Magyars. Already Deak, Eötvös and
Batthyany had refused to join the men of Debreczin. The
magnates, many members of the middle nobility which
controlled the Diet and many officers, of whom Görgey was
one, bound to the Emperor by an oath of loyalty had seen in
the revolt a method of imposing Magyar autonomy upon
perjured ministers. They did not accept a secession of republican
character. A latent conflict placed military men and civil
leaders in opposition to one another, both however giving
proof of equal nationalist blindness. The incessant demand of
the Polish volunteers for a grand reconciliation with the Croats,
Serbs, Slovaks and Rumanians was beyond them; the army
brought about the failure of talks carried on by some exiled
Valach revolutionaries. Kossuth repudiated his envoy in Paris,
Teleki (1811–61), who had promised a wide autonomy to the
peoples of Hungary at a meeting of international refugees.

In Kossuth this absence of a noble realism was associated
with extraordinary diplomatic illusions. The sympathy of the
revolutionaries was one thing, the attitude of the Governments
another. Louis Napoleon and Palmerston were hostile to a
Hungarian secession; the integrity of Austria must be preserved
in order to prevent a Russian drive in eastern Europe and the
Balkans. Also it alone was able to prevent the formation of a
Germanic bloc whose dangerous aspirations had been revealed
in the debates at Frankfurt. The Hungary of Kossuth had only
one ally, and that one purely formal, the Venice of Manin.

Austria, however, obtained, and that without compensation,
Russian aid. Ideological motives were the reason for the intervention of Nicholas I. For twenty years the Tsar had been
burning to play the role of guide to the European counter-
revolution. The presence of Poles in the Hungarian army, the
reticence of Vienna on the German question strengthened his
resolve. The supporters of a united Germany were, as we have
seen, fanatically anti-Russian. On 13 May Paskievitch (1782–
1856) (the choice of the executioner of Poland in 1831 was

symbolic) penetrated into Hungary at the head of 200,000
men. In July, under the double pressure of the Russians and
the Austrians supported by the Croats, the Magyars, who had
reoccupied Pest, retreated on all fronts. Meeting at Szegedin,
the Diet at long last conceded administrative autonomy and
linguistic freedom to the other peoples. On 10 August Kossuth
resigned and fled to Turkey. On the 13th Görgey capitulated
at Villagos.

A harsh repression crushed Hungary: thirteen generals were
shot, as well as Batthyany, although he had nothing to do with
the subversive activities at Debreczin. According to the
principles laid down by the constitution of 4 March Hungary
even lost the right of invoking, as in the times of Metternich,
respect for its ancient "constitution". Like Croatia, Transylvania
and the Voivodina, it was no more than an administrative unit.

Under this centralist and police-controlled "neo-absolutism"
which replaced the former patriarchal absolutism, Austria
gave to the Slavs and the Rumanians "as a reward" what it
had reserved for the Magyars "as a punishment" (Ancel).
Forced Germanization triumphed in the countries of the Crown
of St Stephen as in the "Hereditary States". This total setback
to nationalist claims has relegated the social importance of 1848
and the conditions of Austrian reconstruction to the background. Even if the repeal of serfdom and the abolition of
seigniorial dues did not destroy the economic power of the
aristocracy which preserved its immense estates, it meant the
first step towards the emancipation of the Slav and Rumanian
peasants. As for the myth of Austrian power, it resisted the
lamentable spectacle of the imperial armies unable to conquer
rebels surrounded by enemies. That was the lesson of the last
phase of the German revolution.

THE END OF THE GERMAN REVOLUTION : SETBACK
OF THE PARLIAMENTARY SOLUTION AND THE GREAT
REPUBLICAN INSURRECTION OF THE SOUTH-WEST

Between October 1848 and March 1849 the Frankfurt Assembly
at last succeeded, despite the reserves of Prussia and the

hostility of Austria, Bavaria, Wurtemberg, Saxony and Hanover, in drawing up the unitary constitution so long expected by public opinion. The refusal of Frederick William to accept the imperial crown made a laughing-stock of the parliamentarians but provoked in the south-west a great republican insurrection which despite the sarcasms of Marx and Engels, the embarrassed silence of the repentant democrats and the disdain of Bismarckian historians saved the honour of the men of 1848.

The meetings of an Assembly without power, its authority shaken since September, detested by the forces of reaction in the full tide of repression, are imbued with a melancholy majesty. This is not evident in the exposés which describe the vagaries of the pitiless struggle which had been going on since October between the partisans of a "great Germany", supporters of a decentralized *Reich* including a part or even the whole of Austria, and those of a "little Germany", that is to say a *Reich* dominated by Prussia. In fact, it was only at the beginning of 1849 that the parliament was divided into approximately equal factions on the Austrian question. The vote on Article II ("No part of the *Reich* can be united in a single State with non-Germanic lands") and Article III ("If a German country finds itself having the same sovereign as non-German lands, the relations between these two countries can only be regulated by a personal union") of the constitution should not be considered as the victory of a "little German" party still in limbo. The debates and their results, the two articles were approved by a crushing majority of 340 to 76 and 316 to 90, confirm that the parliament remained faithful to its minimum programme of the summer, that of men as different as Struve, von Gagern and Radowitz: the union of all the territories of the *Bund*. On 27 October, that is before the wave of indignation which followed the repression of the Viennese insurrection and the execution of Blum, did not the existence of a *Reichstag* competent only for the "Hereditary States" open the way to the incorporation of a part of the Empire into the *Reich*?

It was the policy of Schwarzenberg which was to confer a more and more anti-Austrian tone to Articles II and III. At

the end of October, at a time when he was still not officially in
charge of affairs, Schwarzenberg was resolved to introduce a
unified and powerful Austria into a Germanic Confederation
with a weak central authority. This plan, founded on the
destruction of the Kremsier *Reichstag* and the submission of the
Frankfurt parliament, assumed the previous subjugation of the
Magyars. While awaiting this, the constitutional debates must
be slowed down, the Archduke John and Schmerling would see
to this, and the large particularist States won over. In fact,
Schwarzenberg's initiatives discredited the Austrian cause in
Frankfurt and increased the number of those resigned to a
Germany delivered over to Prussia. On 27 November he
proclaimed his wish to "maintain Austria in its State form",
thus precipitating the downfall of Schmerling and his replacement by von Gagern. Von Gagern saw ranged against him not
only the Austrians, the Catholics (the episcopal conference of
Würtzburg was disturbed by the idea of a *Reich* under
Protestant control) but also the moderates of the south like
Professor Welcker and the democrats, enemies of reactionary
Prussia. Though he declared himself in favour of a special treaty
between Austria and a *Reich* implicitly subject to the hegemony
of Berlin, he obtained, on 13 January 1849, only a narrow and
uncertain majority (261 against 224). The shilly-shallyings up
until mid-March of an Assembly which was committed to the
project of the Seven, which von Gagern had made his own, that
is a federal, imperial and parliamentary Germany, showed a
feeble readiness to accept the Prussian solution. Many deputies
went on hoping for Austrian adhesion right up to the last
moment. The constitutional project voted at a first reading on
28 January provided for an Emperor to whom the right of
heredity was refused, but who was not yet designated! Von
Gagern at once submitted it to the Governments (how far we
are from the *einzig und allein* of the *Vorparlament* and the
peremptory declarations of von Gagern on the full and entire
sovereignty of parliament!) and, through them, to the judgement of public opinion. The divorce between the subjects
impatient to see the unitary aspirations of "the spring" at last
realized and the princes, little desirous of losing a part of their

prerogatives (control of the army, administration of the finances, customs dues), became clearly apparent. The press for the most part and all the Chambers pronounced for immediate approval. Fearing mass insurrections, twenty-six States, all the little ones, made their approval known on 23 February. To the indomitable opposition of Schwarzenberg were added the manœuvres of Munich, which in order to cancel the influence of Berlin suggested a Directory, the reticence of Wurtemberg and Hanover, and . . . the indifference of Prussia: the denunciation on the 26th of the Malmö armistice by Denmark and the building up of his influence within the kingdom itself were the main preoccupations of a monarch who, in November, had made clear by his retort to von Gagern the scant importance he paid to the work of the parliamentarians! In Frankfurt, however, the current in favour of the constitutional proposal had impressed the partisans of the maintenance of German Austria in the *Reich*. About a hundred and twenty moderates, for the most part Austrians and Catholics, formed the "great German" group on 15 February; their programme was that of the Bavarian Government. On the 17th two hundred deputies reacted by forming the "little German" party, with Professors Dahlmann and Droysen, fanatical adversaries of the Roman Church and the Hapsburgs. Was it not natural for the "great Germans" to draw closer to the Left, which would not be consoled for the loss of Vienna? Inclined, as were the majority of their antagonists, to deprive the working classes of the right to vote, the former consented to the election of the Lower Chamber by secret and universal suffrage; the latter prepared to "torpedo" the constitutional debates in the course of the second reading.

By its unitary constitution of 4 March, followed on the 9th by its extravagant proposal of a Confederation of central Europe placed, like the *Bund*, under its presidency, Austria dealt a mortal blow to the tactical combinations of its friends. Many "great Germans" considered, as did Welcker, that the choice was no longer between Austria and Prussia but between a Prussian Emperor and republican anarchy. Hence the sensational *volte-face* of the Baden professor who, on 12 March, proposed to offer the imperial crown to Frederick William. A section of the Left also dreaded uncontrollable mass movements in the event of a parliamentary setback. It climbed on the band-wagon; in return for a confirmation of universal suffrage and the transformation of an absolute veto into a suspensive veto, it declared itself in favour of imperial heredity and for the King of Prussia! On 28 March 290 voices elected Frederick William "Emperor of the Germans". The unitary current was so strong that twenty-eight States, small and medium sized, concurred. In Prussia the Chamber nominated in February, with less advanced trends than the turbulent National Assembly, recognized the constitution of the *Reich*. On 26 April the King dissolved it and on the 28th refused the crown. By that action he announced the break with the "Prussian revolution" (in May the three-class system was to reassure the Junkers; applied in Baden from 1831 in the municipal elections, it varied the burden of the vote according to the figure of the taxes; in Prussia it was to "get by" provisionally . . . until the universal suffrage of 1918) and dealt a mortal blow to the German parliamentary revolution.

The refusal of "a crown superabundantly dishonoured by the stench of carrion given it by the 1848 revolution" surprised, astonishingly, men like Dahlmann, Camphausen and von Gagern as well as almost all the deputies. However, it was in accord with the unshaken principles which the humiliations endured since March 1848 had reinforced. To take from the Emperor of Austria a dignity consecrated by history would suppose at least the acquiescence of the other mandatories by divine right (the circular of 23 January made it clear that Prussia would accept a preponderant role if that was conceded to it by the princes). But the Kings of Bavaria, of Saxony and of Hanover had condemned the Frankfurt vote. Furthermore, would not realism counsel Prussia not to brave Austria, in truth weakened, but which Nicholas I would assuredly not fail to support in Germany as he had already done in Hungary? These were not vain speculations; it was with the support of the Tsar that Schwarzenberg was to make in November 1850, against the modest attempt of a "restricted union" presided over by Frederick William, the threat which was to result in, together with the "climb down of Olmütz", the resurrection of the Diet of 1815!

By the evening of 28 April nothing remained of the work of Frankfurt except the text of a constitution and an electoral law recorded in the still-born official journal of the *Reich*. The parliament could no longer either vanish with dignity or take the lead in mass movements.

From the beginning of May Frankfurt survived as a figure of ridicule. On 4 May the parliament fixed legislative elections for 15 July, elections which obviously neither Bavaria nor Prussia would authorize, and the meeting of the *Reichstag* for 16 August. Von Gagern, it is true, spoke of forcing the recalcitrant States to respect the constitution. The Archduke John compelled him to resign (10 May) and invested an extra-parliamentary Government which was subjected to more and more violent assaults by a Left whose power increased as the number of deputies diminished. Following the example of Schwarzenberg, who had recalled the Austrian deputies on 5 April, Frederick William annulled the Prussian mandates on 14 May. By the end of May the quorum was reduced to one hundred. The troubles and the insurrection did not produce any practical measures from these wordy last-ditchers. Only fear of the Prussians who were preparing to move southward roused them from their irresolution; on the 30th they decided to transfer the parliament to Stuttgart, capital of that Wurtemberg still considered today by certain historians as the most democratic of the German States because, on 27 May, 30,000 citizens had, at Reutlingen, acclaimed the constitution of the *Reich*, which the King had accepted on 25 April, and then prudently returned to their homes! Up till then what remained of the parliament had sent commissioners of the *Reich* to the insurgent regions to serve as mediators between the revolution and the counter-revolution. Now installed in the heart of a region regarded as friendly, the deputies played at being members of the Convention. On 7 June they replaced the ministry by a Committee of Public Safety of five members, the Regency of the *Reich* (*Reichsregentschaft*); they dismissed the *Reichsverweser* (the Archduke was officially to resign his duties six months later) and decreed the raising of a *Volkswehr* (people's militia) as a guarantee of the application of the constitution. Were they about to identify their cause with that of the Baden republicans? The "March ministry" still in office in Stuttgart under the control of Römer did not intend to draw the Prussian generals on the wise Schwabian population. On 2 June it sent the emissary of Karlsruhe who was trying to inveigle the kingdom into revolution away to prison; on the 17th it ordered those deputies who were not from Wurtemberg to leave Stuttgart. The next day it had the recalcitrants dispersed by the troops. Under the leadership of the worthy professor-poet Uhland (1787–1862) the last members of the parliament, welcomed thirteen months before in Frankfurt by the vivats of the masses, filed sadly through the streets of Stuttgart before fixing . . . their next meeting at Karlsruhe on 24 June. Because of the threat of the Prussian troops on the capital of the Grand duchy, the first German parliament disappeared on the 18th, overthrown by the particularist reaction, of which it remains, for history, the "most illustrious victim".

The struggle for Germanic unity, of which the monarchist constitution of the *Reich* was the convenient symbol behind which loomed the" federative" and social republic, mobilized in May 1849 even more proletarians than in September 1848. Does a study of the "workers' movement" explain this large participation? The crisis of 1847, prolonged by the shortage of capital inherent in political unrest, had aggravated the condition of the workers. The demands of the artisans were openly expressed in the new atmosphere of freedom; but their inspiration remained fundamentally conservative, even reactionary, when it was a question of "masters" or of guild members. The so-called Artisans' Congress (*Handwerker und Gewerbekongress*) held in Frankfurt (15 July–18 August 1848) only united the masters; this ephemeral pressure group aimed at imposing on the parliament legislation reinforcing the corporative system. At the same time (20 July–20 September) the guild members also held their congress (*Gesellenkongress*) in the capital of the new Germany. Apart from the demand to break the family monopoly for entry into mastership, the "counter-congress" of the guild members was in agreement with the masters' congress on the essential point, that is to say the struggle against free enterprise. The parliament, for which liberalism was a dogma in all domains (it nonetheless felt obliged to support the most numerous class by confirming the abolition of seigniorial dues decided by the local Chambers), also demurred at restricting emigration, regarded as a remedy against the spread of pauperism, and at proclaiming the "right to work" which had been the slogan of the June days, and at generalizing medieval institutions. This economic abstention undoubtedly weakened the sympathy felt for the elect of the nation, but it would be excessive to find in it a crisis of revolutionary conscience. The masters stubbornly wanted to preserve *Bürgerstand*; the guild members dreamed of entering it.

Had the *Arbeitervereine* which grouped workers of all trades and which had proliferated since March 1848 prepared the way to violent political action? That of Cologne which had organized the impressive mass demonstration of 3 March, that of Frankfurt which took part in the anti-parliamentary riot of 18 September were, we must not forget, exceptions. Of a spirit sometimes paternalist, almost always particularist, the *Arbeitervereine* formed tiny "popular universities" marooned in the midst of the "working classes". Therefore Born's efforts to federalize them have, rightly, attracted the attention of historians. It was in Berlin that Born's activities began, with his Central Committee and his newspaper *Das Volk*. The royal defeat of 18 March then allowed the inventors of magic formulae to democratize the State and reform society, to say and write anything and everything. But it had not, overnight, transformed the mentality of a backward proletariat. Though he belonged to the élite of the working class (imitated only by the cigarmakers, the printers had founded in 1848 the first German trade union) the jobbing printer was too close to the world of the artisans to risk disorientating him by suddenly revealing doctrines which were beyond his experience. Even if he had learnt from Marx "the ineluctable necessity of the class struggle" (Droz), Born believed that first of all the class consciousness of the workers must be aroused and their political education taken in hand. The convocation of all the *Arbeiter-vereine* of Germany (in fact, only about thirty associations responded to his appeal) was dictated by this double pre-occupation. The Workers' Congress (*Arbeiterkongress*) held in Berlin from 23 August to 3 September proposed, unlike the *Gesellenkongress* which was about then ending at Frankfurt, to extract the guild-workers from their spiritual ghetto. It resulted in the formation of the Brotherhood of Workers (*Arbeiterverbrüderung*). Soon transferred to Leipzig, it tried, through its organ *Die Verbrüderung* which appeared from 3 October, to achieve the regrouping which had been sketched out at Berlin. In the long term it envisaged the creation of workers' production associations (Born was also an admirer of Louis Blanc!). In the short term it set out to collect subscriptions to assist guild members in founding sickness funds and, under this cover, strike funds. To this social activity which was in no way subversive (a simple change of emphasis made it possible for the paper to survive until 1850 in the floodtide of reaction) was added political activity in favour of Frankfurt legality. Born welcomed the *Grundrechte* as a great revolutionary victory. Contrary to Marx, he did not deride the constitution of the *Reich*; he admired it. When he tried to rally the south-west which was reserved towards a movement born in the reactionary north, he asked the deputy Fröbel to preside at the Congress of the *Arbeitervereine* at Heidelberg (28 January 1849). What was the audience of this unitary reformer? The *Verbrüderung*, "the most famous of the workers' journals" (Balser) had never had more than a thousand subscribers which, taking into account the habits of the time, represented about ten thousand readers. How many *Arbeitervereine* were affiliated to the Brotherhood? Two hundred at most in the urban centres of Prussia, Saxony, Franconia and Wurtemberg where the artisans did not display, at the critical moment, any great revolutionary propensity. Doubtless, time was lacking to convert these spirits moulded by centuries of servitude. In any case, Born was able to adapt his practice to his preaching; he was to take part in the Dresden rising, whereas his censor, Marx, was to be eclipsed.

The *Neue Rheinische Zeitung, Organ der Demokratie* (1 June 1848 –19 May 1849), admirably reproduced in 1928 (published by J. H. W. Dietz, Berlin) was in quite a different vein from the *Verbrüderung*. It has been quoted on several occasions because it reveals a forty-eighter too often overlooked sharing the passions, the prejudices and the illusions of the German Left. This Marx is more varied than his hagiographers usually depict him; faced with his friends, more Marxist in the circumstances than he was himself, he spoke out against the purely working-class candidates in the elections of February 1849 in order not to split the votes of the adversaries of the Brandenburg-Manteuffel ministry. Did he not prophesy on 1 January 1849 that the new year would be "the year of the rising of the French working class and of the European war"? It seems that he was aiming at playing the role of guide to a movement based on an alliance of the middle classes with the working classes. Had he not, while working for the dissolution of the Federation of Communists, broken with those who, preaching in the manner of Blanqui that force was a normal means of achieving power, had weakened the progressive opposition front? The reality seems to have been very far from the dream and also from the accounts by the loyal Engels, written after the coup. One finds no trace in the documents of the time of the Marx so sure of himself that at the end of May 1849 he went to Frankfurt and Karlsruhe, sharply reprimanded the parliamentary democrats and the Baden republicans and then, disgusted by the flabbiness of some and the particularism of others, went to London to prepare in the "dunghill of the emigration" the proletarian revolution! Certainly the influence of Marx was scarcely perceptible in Cologne in May in the behaviour of the masses in the Rhineland. There have recently been attempts to trace his progress in industrial Westphalia, in the region of Cassel and at Wiesbaden. These are interesting because they may reveal the first readers of the *Manifesto* (known in Germany in March or April, it was translated into French just before June and into English in 1850) and the isolated admirers of the *Neue Rheinische Zeitung*. But it would be too much to maintain that Marx and his paper exercised any considerable ascendancy over the democratic associations, whose multiplicity is one of the most original aspects of the German history of 1848–9.

It has been suggested that the spectacular nature of the congress, to which the fame of certain participants has conferred a fugitive lustre, was one of the causes of the popular reaction of May. The idea of creating a great party of unitary democracy had been, as we have seen, put forward in Offenburg on 19 March 1848. Deputies of the extreme Left brought the matter up again at the church of St Paul during the summer. They hoped to use the weight of a popular organization devoted to their views against the parliamentary majority. Thus was created the first Democrats' Congress which sat in Frankfurt from 14–17 June under the presidency of Fröbel. It made the constitutional monarchists uneasy and scared the Governments, of Prussia as well as of Baden, because of the presence of participants regarded as dangerous fanatics; the Badener Damm, a former priest who had become a fanatic revolutionary, and Kapp, a supporter of "permanent revolution" who was soon to resign from a parliament which he considered too moderate, the deputy Zitz (1803–77), leader of the Mainz radical party, Ronge the antichrist, Gottschalk and two other communists, loyal companions of Marx, Schapper, the former militant of the Federation of the Just, and the watchmaker Moll (1812–49), he too involved in all the secret movements of France, Belgium and Germany. ... In actual fact, the Congress brought together only a little more than two hundred delegates, with mandates from less than a hundred associations. The debates ranged the "politicals" against the "socials". The Baden radicals considered the setting up of a Central Committee, even a shadow one, in the Prussian capital as unsuitable, as well as the nomination of the *Zeitungshalle* and the *Neue Rheinische Zeitung* as organs of the movement, alongside the *Mannheimer Abendzeitung* the sole radical paper in Germany before 1848! Their abstention helped to make an empty farce of a detailed organization.

Circumstances determined that the second Democrats' Congress, which met in Berlin, was above all preoccupied with the fate of the Viennese revolution. The essential fact of its activity consisted, as we know, in providing the Prussian reaction with the long awaited chance to seize power openly. This composite assembly of men from the north and from the Rhineland showed itself even less capable than its predecessor of laying the foundations of a real party. In included, as well as the timorous who left the meeting in order not to hear the word "republic" spoken, communists of various obediences ready to tear one another apart (Weitling and his former disciple Dr Ewerbeck, who had rushed there from Paris, friends of Marx, Born, etc.) and Ruge, always peremptory but more and more alienated from the "philosophic radicalism" of the period of the *Franco-German Annals*. Cut off from the south, the Congress did not even succeed in laying the foundations for an *entente* between a political party of the north, still in its infancy, and the Brotherhood of Born, which was about to federate, by the intermediacy of the *Arbeitervereine*, the working classes of Prussia and Saxony.

The lamentable setbacks of June and October were followed by an apparently sensational success. The September crisis and the rise of reaction in Berlin and Vienna favoured the enterprise of the indefatigable Fröbel to create a mass party which could force the parliament to vote a unitary constitution and compel the sovereigns to put it into force. Founded in December in Frankfurt and controlled by a committee made up exclusively of parliamentarians, the *Zentralmärzverein* (Central March Association) was to number by the end of March 1849 almost half a million supporters, spread over about a thousand affiliated associations. The reference to the hopes of March and a programme limited from the end of January to the recognition by all the Governments of the constitution of the *Reich* explained this startling progress: many of the lukewarm who would never be seen behind a barricade hoped to be able at last to emerge from a provincial situation which seemed to be going on eternally. In fact, the *Zentralmärzverein* had not, because of its moderation, penetrated deeply into those regions where radicalism had, for more than a year, woven a graded network of well-organized clubs which spread hatred of Prussia and Austria, condemned the parliamentary recantations in the

Schleswig-Holstein affair and the feebleness of the parliament at the time of the September repression. Denounced in Baden as reactionary, it was on the other hand welcomed in Wurtemberg and Franconia where the already existing associations joined it in a body. But a change of nomenclature was quite incapable of transforming the state of mind of populations more inclined to talk than to act. The *Zentralmärzverein* campaign for the constitution of the *Reich* (which is, moreover, the title of the well-known work published by Engels in 1850) remained verbal. Marx would not have been wrong to scourge the orators of the Congress held in Frankfurt at the beginning of May, who dared not express their opinions either on the Dresden rising or on the insurrection in the Palatinate.

Logically, it was in the States whose rulers regarded the vote of the parliament of 28 March as null that the battle for unity should have been more significant.

At the end of April the Prussian opposition had formidable arguments; not only had the King destroyed in Frankfurt the fragile edifice of which he had been the keystone, but he had dissolved a moderate Chamber. The liberal parliamentarians, the democrats who had harangued the capital in October, and the *Arbeitervereine* associated with the Brotherhood did not make a move. The people did not contest the victory over the Berlin proletariat won by the Brandenburg-Manteuffel ministry. The promulgation, on 30 May, of the edict of the three classes aroused only occasional protests. At the June elections, it was by propaganda in favour of abstention, that weapon of the weak, that the democrats made their presence felt. In the Rhineland the riots which broke out on 9 May at Elberfeld, a large industrial town, made it possible to gauge the influence of the Marxist group; its democrat inspirers expelled Engels who had come as a neighbour, as he was by origin from Barmen, to overwhelm them with advice on revolutionary tactics! Nonetheless, the occasion was seized by the Government to suppress the *Neue Rheinische Zeitung*. In its last number, dated 19 May and printed in red, the paper, which had never ceased to report with sympathy the events in Saxony, in the Palatinate and in Baden, advised the Cologne workers to remain calm.

The passivity of the Prussian provinces allowed Frederick William to bring aid to the sovereigns threatened by "anarchy" and to sketch out, with the Kings of Hanover and Saxony (26 May) that "restricted union" which Schwarzenberg was to destroy the following year.

Encouraged by the example of both the King of Hanover, who had dismissed his Chamber twenty-four hours before Frederick William, and of the King of Prussia, the King of Saxony tore off the liberal and unitary mask. He dissolved the Chamber which had just recommended recognition of the constitution of the *Reich* and expelled the ministry favourable to Frankfurt. He thus created a profound dissatisfaction. The constitutional monarchists of the *Deutsche Vereine* (German Associations) as well as the democrats loyal to the memory of Blum and grouped in the *Vaterlandsvereine* (Patriotic Associations: in most of the States this denomination meant a conservative movement!) drew up petitions and sent delegations to the sovereign. At the news that Frederick Augustus, arguing that Saxon troops had participated in the operations against Denmark, had asked for military aid from Prussia barricades were set up in the capital on 3 May. The initiative for the rising came neither from the non-existent *Zentralmärzverein* nor from the many *Arbeitervereine* but from a lawyer Tzschirner (1814–70), a Frankfurt republican who had distinguished himself in the Saxon Chamber by his attacks on an imperial and hereditary constitution. For him, as for the proletariat, the defence of the constitution of the *Reich* was therefore only a pretext. His aim was the "social republic". With the participation of Bakunin and Polish agitators who had rushed there from Paris, and with the unfolding, alongside the black-red-gold flag, of the red flag the riots assumed the appearance of an international proletarian insurrection. That accounted for the hostile or indifferent passivity of the greater number of the unitary organizations and for the calm which prevailed throughout the kingdom. Abandoned, Dresden became another Vienna. Imbued with hatred of Prussia and of professional soldiers, the workers, commanded by Born, resisted until the 9th with a tenacity for which the Prussians made them pay dear: on the one side 250 dead, on the other 31, 23 Saxons and 8 Prussians! The French representative in Dresden, highly unfavourable to a movement of which "the success would have led, not only in Saxony but even more in Germany and perhaps even for all Europe, to the destruction of all the conditions essential for good order and social life", noted: "the effect of the fury of the troops has been terrible and the tales current among the Dresdeners are balanced by their satisfaction at having been saved from the tyranny of Tzschirner".

In the south-west also the Prussians were soon to give proof of their common sense. The insurrection of the Palatinate and the revolution in Baden, begun on the 2 and 12 May respectively, revealed, even more than the Saxon movement, the "ambiguity" of the "campaign for the constitution of the *Reich*", and attested the burden of history upon the behaviour of men. It is interesting to compare the reactions in Franconia and the Palatinate to the news that the Bavarian Government had refused to accept the constitution of the *Reich*. In these two provinces, recently incorporated, loyalty to the dynasty was weak and Protestant hostility to the old Catholic and conservative Bavaria was strong. Over and above these resemblances, what contrasts there were between a passive Palatinate and a revolutionary Franconia! One was a land of good-humoured wine-growers. In the other, where the artisans working for a powerful capitalism were concentrated in Nuremberg, Bamberg and Schweinfurt, the first symptoms of a class struggle could be discerned. It is, in any case, certain that the Brotherhood had taken root there and that the democratic movement had shown its vigour at the time of the elections to parliament and to the Munich Chamber. Is there any need to recall the success of the *Zentralmärzverein*? What came of all this "immense propaganda"? Doubtless the harshness of the repression in neighbouring Saxony had led them to listen to mediocre demagogues who had arisen by chance at the meetings. In the Palatinate radicalism was less a hastily formed party than a state of mind. The memories of the French Revolution and the Napoleonic Empire had created in this outlying province of Bavaria a nostalgia for a great and unified

State; it was not fortuitously that the first demonstration for Germanic unity had been held in Hambach in 1832 in the presence of Frenchmen and Poles! The proximity of France and the attraction of "the capital of the revolution" kept the flame of democracy alight. Symbolic of the Palatine particularism spurned by the Prussian historians, Savoye (1802–69), a lawyer at Zweibrücken, was at the same time a German patriot and a French patriot. A refugee in Paris from 1832, he was from April to September 1848 chargé d'affaires of the French Republic in Frankfurt; deputy of the Upper Rhine in 1849, he did not differentiate the cause of the friends of Ledru-Rollin from that of the republicans of the south-west. Thus it is easier to understand the reaction of the Palatinate to the negative attitude of the King of Bavaria (23 April). On 2 May an assembly meeting at Neustadt on the initiative of the popular associations elected a committee which aimed at forcing the King to submission. On the 11th the garrison at Speier joined the insurrection. On the 17th a provisional Government was formed at Kaiserslautern whose authority covered, in principle, the whole country except the fortresses of Landau and Germersheim. It was a spontaneous movement which totally disorganized the administration and the defence preparations. The recognition of the *fait accompli* by the *Reich* commissioner Eisenstück would have conferred, in the eyes of the undecided, a unitary legality to the revolution if the rump-parliament, always obsessed with legality, had not disowned its emissary! D'Ester of Cologne tried vainly to instil the spirit of 1793 into brave democrats who relied primarily on the friends of Ledru-Rollin and on the Magyars to get them out of a situation in which their expansive temperament had involved them.

The idea that an alliance of all the revolutionaries would make of a spring which was one of downfall a true "springtide of the peoples" was not peculiar to the imaginative German democrats. Kossuth, as we have seen, shared it also. The entry of the Magyars into Pest on 4 June strengthened the ardour of the German insurgents and dangerously excited the French extreme Left. It was, as much as the Roman expedition, the origin of 13 June. The setback of that day demoralized the

Magyars, disheartened the Germans and dissipated the fears of the European Governments, the French Government in particular. From mid-May to the end of June, police reports had described a vast Franco-German-Hungarian conspiracy of which the threads had been woven in Paris. The Hungarian Committee inspired by Teleki, Kossuth's delegate, plotted with the German committee of Dr Ewerbeck, who welcomed the envoys from the Palatinate and Baden. Savoye was the liaison between his compatriots and the Mountain. "The two committees saw Considérant and Leroux daily. Ledru-Rollin received Teleki frequently." Had not the Mountain, in an address to "German democracy" on 9 June, confirmed the rumours of an imminent Parisian insurrection, liberating at the same time France and Germany? "Brothers! Shall a power disloyal to its origins, a traitor to its duties, long enchain the generous impulses of France? No! It cannot fail in its noble instincts and is ready, for the common cause, to pour out the blood with which it has never been miserly in favour of the oppressed nations. . . ."

In fact, faced with the Bavarian and Prussian troops (on 4 June Maximilian had, on the example of the King of Saxony, implored the aid of Frederick William), the Palatinate insurgents could count only on the Badeners with whom they had signed a military convention in due order on 18 May. Over the whole territory of Baden, equivalent to half of Belgium, all classes, with the obvious exception of the nobles and the senior civil servants, had shown proof, even when faced with seemingly insurmountable perils, of an indomitable will to win and had, to an extent unknown elsewhere, rallied to the cause of the revolution: *Akademiker*, shopkeepers, craftsmen, factory workers and even men from the countryside. The lest ardent were the instigators of the jacqueries of March 1848; after the abolition of seigniorial dues, they had again become loyal subjects, above all preoccupied with trying to wrest a living from their tiny and infertile patches of land for their over-abundant families. On the other hand, the peasants from the south of the Black Forest and the region of Konstanz, the vast majority of them Catholics, displayed an exemplary fervour. The influence of the churches, hostile to radicalism, was scarcely perceptible. The Catholics (2/3) had been excluded from the organizations set up after the first Catholic Congress held at Mainz in October under the presidency of Buss whom the "spring" had compelled to fly from Baden. The cult of Blum, the "German Catholic", had, as we know, brought Catholics and Protestants closer together and had aroused, both in one and the other, the same desire for vengeance. Curés and pastors rushed, alongside their parishioners, into the revolution. As for the Jews, even if the men of a certain age feared lest the tottering of the State should be the prelude to pogroms, the younger ones had no such reticence.

Under one of the most liberal ministries of Germany, which had recognized the constitution of the *Reich*, a powerful party relying upon the masses which it had educated politically since 1847 had been trying to found in the south a republic which must, by force of example, become progressively extended to all the German lands. This idea, which had matured gradually as long as Frankfurt appeared able to respond to unitary and democratic hopes, had become strengthened by the reaction of the autumn and the bankruptcy of parliament. From the time of the state of siege, Struve and many militant radicals had been thrown into prison and the clubs founded in March had been closed. But they re-formed, at first secretly and later openly, when the *Grundrechte* which the Baden Government dared not ignore granted all Germans the rights of assembly and association. Stronger than ever because of its long existence and the sympathy felt for those who had been persecuted, the radical party was no longer, as in the times of the popular Hecker, the party of a single man. Its new president, the lawyer Brentano, a member of the parliament and of the Baden Chamber, would have been satisfied to become a minister. The leaders of the clubs, lawyers, doctors, chemists, teachers and innkeepers, imposed their views on him. They knew that the common people had lost all respect for the Grand duke "Leopold-Baden", that it hated anti-liberal Prussia more and more and that it disparaged the five (out of nineteen) Baden deputies who on 28 March had voted for Frederick William.

Finally, they had succeeded in creating clubs within the army, open to soldiers and NCOs. Thus it was easy to arouse the soldiers against their officers, who were nobles. The radicalism of the military was a reflection of the radicalism of the civilians, for which the men on leave had become the more or less conscious propagandists.

In a word, it was the massive participation of the army which gave the Baden revolution its peculiar originality. In the European revolutions isolated soldiers or groups of soldiers had sometimes defected, but in Baden all the garrisons without exception took the side of illegality. What is more, it was the most powerful of them, the garrison of the federal fortress of Rastatt, which despite the presence of two Austrian companies gave the signal for revolution! In a Germany where strained relations between civilians and soldiers were often the source of bloody clashes, in Baden civilians and military worked together in perfect accord. At Offenburg, where it was formed in March 1848, the party was to hold its congress on 13 May. At Rastatt, about fifty kilometres away, the garrison had, despite all the efforts of the Minister of War, mutinied the day before, and the garrisons of Freiburg, Lörrach, Karlsruhe, Bruchsal and Mannheim soon followed suit. Even before the opening of the congress the soldiers, arriving by train (the railway line parallel to the Rhine from Mannheim to the Swiss frontier played an important role in the revolution), marched joyously, the black-red-gold flag at their head. In the presence of Savoye the jubilant deputies added to their political demands (resignation of the Government, Constituent Assembly) a programme of social reforms (old-age pensions, etc.). The sedition of the Karlsruhe garrison as much as the Offenburg demands led to the flight of the Grand duke. The control committee of the radical party became *de facto* the Government of a republic. The Baden revolution was over.

Thus began the most powerful revolutionary movement in German history. Leopold, like Maximilian, appealed to Frederick William, whose soldiers began their attack on 11 June. An alliance between Karlsruhe and Kaiserslautern was essential. An attempt was made, no matter what Engels says, to incite Wurtemberg and Hesse-Darmstadt to revolution. The attitude of the democrats there was disappointing. From Frankfurt came only counsels of reconciliation with the Grand duke, relayed by the *Reich* commissioners! The rump-parliament was not to rally to the revolution except on the eve of its expulsion from Stuttgart. Despite their isolation the Badeners did not feel themselves abandoned. In an extraordinary enthusiasm, kept alive by the "good news" from Hungary and Paris with which the press was filled, there was a spontaneous enlistment of volunteers, soon reinforced by the mobilization of a part of the civil guard. Émigrés rushed from France and even more from Switzerland. The vanquished, eager for revenge, hastened from all the German States. Amongst them were ardent and noble idealists: the Bonn student Schurz (aged 20), a future American Secretary of State, Liebknecht (aged 23), a social democratic leader at the end of the century, Engels and his friend Moll, killed in the fighting, the Saxon lawyer Trützschler, a deputy from Frankfurt and a civil commissioner (Baden had borrowed this institution from the French Provisional Government) at Mannheim, who was to be shot in August, Professor Kinkel (1815–82), Schurz's master, former Prussian officers who were democrats such as Anneke (1817–66), a disciple of Marx, and Corvin (1812–86), as well as paladins of the revolution such as the Wiesbaden watchmaker Böhning (aged 51), a former fighter for Greek independence, who was soon to be executed. But also how many seedy intellectuals, cabaret revolutionaries, who battened on the unhappy country in search of lucrative sinecures! Loud-mouthed, they demanded an implacable purge and wise strategic movements within Germany! These blusterers who later denounced the "particularism" and "bourgeois spirit" of the Karlsruhe revolutionaries (Engels was to take part in this campaign of denigration with a talent which still has an effect today) weakened the internal front by espousing the quarrels of the Badeners; generally speaking, they supported the ideas of Struve against Brentano.

After the rapid defeat of the Palatinate (11–18 June) 40,000 men held out for a month against 100,000 Prussians and Bavarians commanded by Prince William. Other than the regular army which had passed over to the revolution, the republican forces included the Baden militia (*Volkswehr*), the German-Polish Legion (the "pilgrims" again), a battalion of refugees under Böhning and a foreign legion. Placed under the command of Mieroslawski, who gave his orders in French, they covered themselves with glory on the 15 and 16 June in the Mannheim region. Outflanked by Prince William, who crossed the Rhine at Germersheim, they abandoned their positions on the Neckar. On 25 June, after furious fighting near Waghäusel, Mieroslawski had to evacuate the capital and withdraw along the Murg, his support centre being the fortress of Rastatt. On the 29th and 30th the last line of defence was breached and by 11 July the Grand duchy was completely occupied with the exception of Rastatt. The citadel whence the revolution had started out on 12 May was to capitulate on 23 July for lack of food and munitions.

Order now reigned from Mannheim to Konstanz. Leopold re-entered his capital on 18 August. Repression was at its full. Whereas in the Palatinate the Bavarians behaved with moderation, in Baden the Prussians set up courts-martial which functioned until October. There were fourteen executions. Then the Baden administration took over; thousands of persons were uneasy. An official document in which 804 responsible leaders were enumerated reveals the scope of the movement.

If hatred for Prussia remained alive among the common people, the repression decapitated the democratic party for a long time to come. This facilitated the influence, till then derisory, of political Catholicism in this Catholic country. But by its victorious intervention in the struggle against "anarchy" Berlin won the gratitude of the upper classes, the professors and the timorous. Many of the radicals became, since they supported unity, national-liberals; admirers of the Prussia of Bismarck did their best to forget that the German revolution of 1848, born in Baden, had died in Baden. They were to throw a veil over their participation in a movement treated harshly by the future "German emperor". As for the socialists, they were to adopt the criticism of Engels against a revolution which had not developed along Marxist lines. In 1850 Engels, who was awaiting a new revolution, admitted its confusion; after noting that "before the insurrection there had been practically no class struggle in Baden", which was true, and affirming that "no experience of insurrection can make up for the development of class feeling which can only by attained by long years of practice in industry", he added: "It is none the less true that Baden, by its last insurrection and its consequence, has taken its place among the German lands which will play one of the most important roles in the revolution which is to come."

## Some Reflections

FROM THE SPRING of 1848 to the summer of 1849—how
many hopes, but how many setbacks! 1848—April: The
Chartist downfall in London and defeat of the February
revolution in Paris and in the provinces. June: Destruction of
the Czech movement and dispersion of the Slav Congress of
Prague; crushing of the Paris insurrection. July: end of the
Italian national revolution. October: Failure of the Viennese
revolution. December: Prussian *coup d'état* and dissolution of
the National Assembly. 1849—March: Austrian *coup d'état* and
dissolution of the *Reichstag* of the "Hereditary States". Restoration of the *ancien régime* at Parma, Modena and Florence. June:
Inglorious defeat of the extreme Left in Paris, and at Stuttgart
the lamentable end of the Frankfurt parliament. July: the
French Republic overthrows the Roman Republic and the
King of Prussia overturns unitary democracy. August: Capitulation of independent Hungary and of the republic of Venice.

The balance? Napoleon III breaks down the pretence of
being a conservative president and, after a brief republican
period, eighteen years of the Second Empire succeed eighteen
years of the July Monarchy. For the Italian patriots maintenance of the Constitutional Statute is a meagre recompense for
the presence once again of a foreign power in the peninsula.
In Austria the heedless authoritarianism and the somewhat

330 ]

disdainful tolerance towards the "awakening of the peoples" comes to an end; a Germanic and absolutist centralism prepares pitilessly to suppress the liberal and national aspirations of all the subjects of the Empire. In Germany the triumph of the counter-revolution results in a sort of division of labour, not however co-ordinated, between Frederick William and Schwarzenberg: the arms of the former eliminate the young representatives of the republican ideal, the audacity of the latter restores life to the dishonoured corpse of the Diet. A terrible disaster for all those who have lived in the glare of the foot-lights: Parisian workers, Viennese proletarians, the common people of southern Germany, democratic leaders and club members everywhere, the deputies of the Prussian National Assembly, of the Austrian *Reichstag*, and of the German parliament!

But also a great social victory for millions of peasants in the Empire and the many German States! Fear lest the jacqueries of March be repeated, the desire of winning over a compact electoral mass had made of pariahs, usually ignored or despised and for the most part impervious to subversive doctrines, the spoilt children of the revolution to whom democrats, constitu-tional monarchists, conservative ministers and reactionary rulers each in their turn multiplied promises and formal engagements. The abolition of serfdom and of seigniorial dues was a silent revolution[1] which has eluded the soft-hearted historians of the streets of old Paris.

Certainly the actors of 1830 knew their roles well. The proletarians set up their barricades and overthrew the régime in three days. The King, burdened by the history of 1792, did not dream of calling upon the provinces in the manner of Henry IV. Revolution, without inverted commas, was firstly, as always, political, but also social. The "communism" of the secret societies, of the system-makers and of a working-class élite seemed, in the February mists, able to prevent a return of the

---

[1] The abolition by the provisional Government of slavery in the colonies (4 March) was a spectacular measure already sketched out by the July Monarchy. The emancipation of the Jews decided by the Frankfurt parliament was only realized later and progressively within the framework of the individual States.

sufferings born of a long economic crisis; the "red" republic succeeded the monarchy without transition. Too rapid an advance for the provinces? What did it matter! Who held Paris held centralized France, on condition that the majority of Frenchmen were not asked to approve the antics of a minority. Between the notables and the champions of democracy and socialism backed up by a few tens of thousands of Parisian artisans the peasants did not hesitate. Their manner of asserting their independence was to vote for the myth of Bonaparte. The most able of the committed writers who discussed endlessly the second thoughts of this or that member of the Provisional Government underestimated an essential fact: universal suffrage in itself meant the condemnation of social democracy which preached the brotherhood of peoples under the leadership of France.

The advanced republicans believed naïvely that Europe was the image of France. But everywhere the weight of the countryside was heavier; almost everywhere the artisans were, with the exception of a few oases formed under Parisian influence, a more backward proletariat. Everywhere the intellectuals scattered throughout the particularist States burned to unite the fragments of the fatherland which they had forged. Social and political aspirations were merged with a passion for unity little inclined to place itself under the French banner of European democracy.

This aspect was not apparent to the children of an old nation until the end of the spring. In a Europe where the ideological currents of the forties had, in an atmosphere of economic difficulties, led the Swiss and Baden radicals and the Italian liberals to stir in 1847 without awaiting a signal from Paris, the scenario of 1830 was repeated with a tenfold force. Governments considered weak by historians but which had at their disposal, thanks to their police and their armies, a crushing superiority over puny adversaries, surrendered almost spontaneously. Panic overcame those who had resisted the fears of 1830.

From Vienna can be noted the extraordinary effect of the February barricades in Italy and in Germany and also the transformations undergone by an imported revolution. Nowhere did anyone think of proclaiming the republic. If the King of Bavaria disappeared, it was in favour of his son. Italian and German "revolutions" were, taken as a whole, pacific. The former succeeded in the spring of 1848 in introducing the "1830 revolution" into the peninsula, the latter led to the real democratization of States already "liberalized".

The national revolution in Italy was, despite the "crusaders", a Sardinian enterprise. Nonetheless, it had sufficient drive to end in consequences which the liberal claims had never fore-seen: the flight of the Princes of Modena and Parma, and then, after Custozza, the creation of democratic régimes, without future it is true in a fragmented country with a weak middle class, but symbols of a dishevelled romanticism, of which the *farà da se* and the refusal to accept French military aid were astonishing features. Italy was one of the countries where the centenary of the 1848 revolution was celebrated with the greatest display, despite the "Cavour complex". The judgement of Crispi undoubtedly stems from this complex: to Cavour, who knew how to make use of French and Prussian arms, the statesman was to prefer Mazzini and Garibaldi, who fought without hope like Charles Albert at Novara.

In Germany the great national revolution which peaceful notables began on 5 March in Heidelberg and which came to an end either before the Prussian firing squads, in the Baden prisons or in emigration to the United States (many political leaders were thus lost to Germany), has been discredited and classified off-handedly under the heading of "the mad year". To decide on the convocation of a parliament, to elect it and make it work, despite the princes, the Emperor and the King of Prussia, was to give proof of an unparalleled audacity. The "faults" of that parliament, so often denounced, were imputable not to an upper middle class, few in number and in any case poorly represented in Frankfurt, but to the nation as a whole. The "pan-Germanist" claims, for example to Schleswig, which so disquieted autocratic Russia, liberal Great Britain and republican France, were inspired by an ideology already widespread in the eighteen-forties. The "time lost" in beginning discussions on the constitution is explicable, though everyone keeps a conspiracy of silence about it, by a desperate desire not to deceive a people in no way prepared for a separation from their "German brothers" in Austria. As for the reproach of having talked without acting, it is based on a misconception of realities; stunned by the February barricades, the rulers let events take their course but retained their material powers. To say that it would have been possible to take over the administration of the States is to believe that all the proletarians of Berlin, of the Rhineland, of Bavaria and of Saxony had the revolutionary spirit of the petty bourgeois, of the artisans and of a section of the peasantry of the south-west educated politically before 1848. Would not universal suffrage have in the end condemned such forceful takeovers? Think of the results of the parliamentary elections before the "treason" of the *Akademiker*, terrified by the democratic movements of September 1848 and May 1849! Certainly the end of the parliament, inevitable after 28 April, lacked panache. It remains nonetheless that unity in the form of an imperial and democratic monarchy would have clashed with the insurmountable resistance of Austria, with the fear which that inspired, and with the particularism of the King of Prussia and his people. Unlike most of his contemporaries Bismarck, who was no romantic, was to remember the lessons of a setback which he, as a good Junker, had desired. Convinced that Hapsburg power was a myth, he would drive it out of Germany and thus realize the dream of the "little Germans". His success was to win over the repentant forty-eighters; and reputable historians were to finish his work by erasing from German history a single page in the honourable whole. Thus in Germany the democratic idea was to be dissociated from the national idea.

This dissociation appeared even during the revolutions of central Europe. Hatred of Germanic unity and Magyar domination threw Czechs, Croats and Rumanians into the arms of reactionary Austria, which the Vienna democrats and the Magyar aristocrats alike were fighting. Blinded by party spirit, the German democrats and certain French democrats paid no heed to the imperatives of the *Volkstum* but loudly proclaimed the right of all peoples to rule themselves as they wished and reserved for the Magyar oppressors a place of honour in the international democratic pantheon and treated the Czech intellectuals and the Slav peasants as tools of obscurantism.

In these attempts at application the principle of nationalities exacerbated the conflicts between Germans on the one hand and Danes and Poles on the other and created lasting hatred between Czechs and the Germans of Bohemia. This was aroused on linguistic grounds, whose violence does not seem exhausted. Nationalist passion was, except in France, the essential element of the revolutions. Its moderation in States already unified and yet so different perhaps explains the calm of the United Kingdom, of Belgium, of the Netherlands, of Spain and of Portugal. 1848 revealed the explosive power of nationalism and its capacity for drawing into similar aberrations men whom political and religious passions (the case of Pius IX as temporal sovereign excepted, as the Papal States were swept away in the spring) and class interests normally separated (in the socialist countries "bourgeois nationalism" was from time to time denounced). National traits were accentuated in the course of pitiless struggles: Germanic pettifoggery, Czech inertia, Magyar brutality, Croat resolution and Polish mysticism.

The era of brotherhood not only failed to respond to noble utopias (Ruge and Cattaneo had vainly launched the idea of a congress or federation of free peoples) but above all taught the lessson that blood speaks louder than words. After Sadowa when the imperial Government was to reconstitute a deeply shaken State and come to terms with the harshest of its adversaries the Magyars were to imitate it. The compromise of 1867 was to institutionalize, under the patronage of a former forty-eighter, Deak, the dualism of the spring of 1848. From 1868 the Hungarian Government, by a compromise of Austro-Hungarian type, was to exempt from a more and more vigorous Magyarization only the compatriots of Jelačić. The Poles, finally, by the immoderate but very emotional activity of the "pilgrims", bore witness to the desire to live of a people deprived of its territory. In the service of Charles Albert, of the Viennese insurrection, of the Magyar revolt, of the Dresden riots, of the Baden revolution, they had all, everywhere, been waging the same war: for the resurrection of Poland!

The memory of the France of February persisted for the Poles, the Moldo-Valachians, the Serbs, soon for the Italians and later for the Czechs. London would, well after Louis Philippe, Metternich or Prince William, welcome the *internationale* of the vanquished, and the European Democratic Committee of Mazzini, Ledru-Rollin, Ruge and Kossuth launched grandiloquent appeals for insurrection, but Paris remained, under the Second Empire as under the Third Republic, the "capital of the revolution in Europe". With French participation the Rumanian principalities and Italy before 1871, Poland, Czechoslovakia and Yugoslavia after 1918 were to realize the dreams of 1848.

Neither France nor Europe were to know another 1848. Taught by experience, their real force increased tenfold by technical advance, the Governments would no longer surrender to internal threats, whereas in the ranks of the opposition the mystique of the barricades was to decline. Revolutions of another type and of another significance were to mark the twentieth century. They were to have neither the spontaneity nor the ingenuousness of 1848. The result of military disasters or the support of friendly arms (what would have been the consequences for Austria of a Russian abstention in Hungary, or those of a French intervention in Italy?) they took care no longer to play with the diabolic invention of the unforeseeing Romantics—universal suffrage!

# Chronological References

| | |
|---|---|
| 1801 | Annexation of Ireland |
| 1812 | Spanish constitution; Sicilian constitution |
| 1814 | Fundamental Law in the Netherlands; Norwegian Democratic Constitution |
| 1815 | Creation of the *Bund*; Swiss Federal Pact; Corn Laws voted |
| 1816–1819 | Radical agitation and repression in the United Kingdom |
| 1816–1820 | Constitutions of Nassau, Bavaria, Baden, Wurtemberg, Hesse-Darmstadt |
| 1817 October 18 | Unitary demonstration at the Wartburg |
| 1819 | Beginning of agricultural protectionism in France |
| 1819–1820 | Federal reactionary measures in Germany |
| 1820 | Spain: military *coup d'état* and restoration of the 1812 constitution |
| 1820–1821 | Revolutions in Naples, Sicily and Piedmont |
| 1821 April 8 | Austrian victory over the Piedmontese revolutionaries at Novara |
| 1822 | Portugal: constitution similar to the Spanish constitution of 1812 |

| | |
|---|---|
| 1823 | Beginnings of the Irish agitation (O'Connell); creation of provincial Estates in Prussia |
| 1824–1825 | United Kingdom: right of association |
| 1825 | Hungary: foundation of the Academy and resurrection of the Diet |
| 1826 | Neusatz (Novi Sad) (Hungary): foundation of *Matica Srpska* |
| 1827 November 19 | First barricades of the nineteenth century in Paris |
| 1828 | Buonarotti: *History of Conspiracy for Equality, So-called of Babeuf* |
| 1829 | Emancipation of Catholics in the United Kingdom |
| 1829–1835 | Portuguese civil war |
| 1830 July 27–9 | The Three Glorious Days |
| August 25 | Revolution at Brussels |
| October 4 | Declaration of Belgian independence |
| 1830–1831 | Polish insurrection against the Russians; Swiss cantonal revolutions; constitutions of Hanover, Saxony, Brunswick, Hesse-Cassel |
| 1831 | Mazzini founds Young Italy at Marseilles; foundation of the Czech *Matica*; advent of Charles Albert in Sardinia; troubles at Modena, Parma and in the Papal States, and Austrian repression |
| 1831 November | Lyons: first purely workers' insurrection; Belgium: Treaty of the 24 Articles |
| 1831–1832 | The Russians give Moldavia and Valachia identical constitutions |
| 1832 | Hambach (Palatinate): unitary demonstration; new federal reactionary measures in Germany; electoral reform in the United Kingdom |
| 1832 June 5–6 | Parisian workers' insurrection (red flag) for the republic and for Poland |

| | |
|---|---|
| 1833 | Frankfurt: attempted putsch against the Diet; *Ode to the Fatherland* by the Catalan Carlos Aribaud |
| 1833–1834 | United Kingdom: social laws |
| 1833–1845 | Mazzinian conspiracies |
| 1834 | Mazzini founds Young Europe at Basle; Denmark: provincial Estates in the kingdom and the duchies |
| | United Kingdom: Poor Law |
| | Paris: creation of the Federation of the Exiles |
| April 9–12 | Lyons: republican insurrection |
| April 14 | Paris: massacre of the rue Transnonain |
| 1834–1839 | Spain: Carlist war |
| 1835 | Agram (Zagreb): foundation of the *Croat Gazette* |
| 1836 | Ghent: foundation of the Flemish Society; Paris: foundation of the Federation of the Just; Palacky begins publication of *The History of Bohemia* |
| 1837 | Suspension of the Hanoverian constitution: the "Seven" of Göttingen |
| 1838 | United Kingdom: foundation of the Anti-Corn Law League |
| 1839 | Prussia: law on children at work; Louis Blanc: *Organization of Labour*; first Chartist setback |
| May 12 | Paris: insurrection of the Seasons |
| 1840 | Rhineland crisis; accession of Frederick William IV |
| 1841 | France: law on children at work |
| 1842 | United Kingdom: second Chartist setback; foundation of *The Nation* at Dublin |
| 1843 | Ireland: Clontarf, setback of O'Connell; rise of Young Ireland; Brussels: Gioberti, *Of the Primacy . . .* |
| 1844 | Paris: *Franco-German Annals* of Ruge-Marx; Balbo: *Speranze d'Italia* |
| 1845 | Croat becomes the language of the Agram (Zagreb) Diet; the Bohemian Diet tries to |

|  | become a legislative assembly; foundation of the *Prague Gazette*; foundation of the *Slovak Gazette*; Engels: *Condition of the Working Class in England* |
|---|---|
| December | Foundation of the *Sonderbund* |
| 1846 | Foodstuffs crisis; subsistence troubles; Ruthene jacqueries in Galicia; Irish agrarian crimes; abolition of the Corn Laws; the "revolution of 1846"; Franco-Spanish marriages |
| February | Setback of Mieroslawski in Poznan; occupation of Cracow by the Austro-Prusso-Russians |
| May | D'Azeglio: *Degli ultimi casi di Romagna* |
| June | Election of Pius IX |
| July | *Open letter* of Christian VIII on the duchies; Pius IX declares political amnesty |
| November | Annexation by Austria of the republic of Cracow |
| 1847 | Economic crisis; Michelet: *History of the Revolution*; Louis Blanc: *History of the Revolution*; Lamartine: *History of the Girondins*; Belgium: victory of the Liberals and Rogier's cabinet; Factory Act (ten hours' act); the Hungarian Diet dominated by the opposition |
| January | Foundation of the Irish Confederation |
| April/June | Prussian *United Landtag* |
| July | Pius IX creates a civic guard |
| July 9–Dec. 25 | Campaign of the banquets (for electoral and parliamentary reform) |
| August/Dec. | Austria occupies Ferrara in the Papal States |
| September 12 | Assembly at Offenburg (Baden), first revolutionary demonstration (democratic, social and unitary) in Germany |
| October 10 | Liberal colloquy of Heppenheim (Hesse-Darmstadt) |
| November | Revival of the Chartist campaign; Marx and Engels prepare the *Communist Manifesto*; Swiss radicalism victorious over the *Sonderbund* |

| | |
|---|---|
| December | Gottschalk founds a section of the Federation of Communists in Cologne |
| 1848 | |
| Jan./Feb. | Chartist meetings |
| January 2–4 | "Cigar riots" in Milan |
| January 12 | Palermo insurrection |
| January 28 | *Rescript* of Frederick VII (incorporating the duchies into Denmark) |
| February 10 | Constitution at Naples |
| February 11 | State of siege in Lombardy |
| February 12 | Bassermann motion in the Baden Chamber (proposal for a German parliament); John Mitchell launches an appeal for an Irish insurrection |
| February 14 | Pius IX creates a commission of reform |
| February 17 | Constitution of Florence |
| February 22–4 | Revolution in Paris; proclamation of the Republic; Provisional Government |
| February 25 | Paris: the right to work |
| February 27 | Mannheim (Baden): popular assembly (the Four Demands) |
| February 28 | Paris: the National Workshops; the Luxembourg Commission |
| March first fortnight | The "March ministers" in the German States and agrarian riots in south-west Germany (abolition of the last seigniorial dues) |
| March 1 | Revolution of Neuchâtel (Switzerland) |
| March 2 | Paris: decree for the reduction of the working day |
| March 3 | Demands of the Hungarian Diet |
| March 4 | Lamartine's manifesto to Europe |
| March 5 | Charles Albert promulgates the Constitutional Statute; Heidelberg (Baden): beginnings of the German national revolution |
| March 5–6 | Troubles in Glasgow |
| March 11 | Assembly in Prague |
| March 12 | Lowering of property qualification in Belgium |
| March 13 | Viennese revolution; flight of Metternich |

| | |
|---|---|
| March 14 | Rome: constitution |
| March 16 | Paris: demonstration of the "bearskins" |
| March 17 | Paris: popular demonstration for postponement of elections |
| March 18 | Berlin revolution |
| March 18–22 | Milan: The Five Days |
| March 19 | Abdication of Louis I of Bavaria; Offenburg: popular assembly, republican thrust |
| March 21 | Capitulation of Frederick William IV |
| March 22 | Revolution in Venice |
| March 23–4 | *Franzosenlärm* |
| March 24 | Charles Albert declares war on Austria |
| March 26 | Riots in Madrid |
| March 27 | Jassy: failure of revolutionary attempt |
| March–April 13 | *Vorparlament* at Frankfurt; war of duchies |
| April 8 | Bohemian Charter |
| April 10 | London: Chartist setback |
| April 11 | Sanction of the Hungarian constitutional laws (dualism), "abolition" of the seigniorial régime |
| April 12–20 | Baden republican insurrection |
| April 16 | Paris: failure of a fresh popular demonstration for the postponement of the elections |
| April 23 | France: check of the extreme Left in elections for the Constituent Assembly |
| April 26 | Frederick William IV annexes the German areas of the Grand duchy of Posen |
| April 27 | Dossenbach (Baden): defeat of the Paris Legion |
| April 29 | Pius IX condemns the Italian war |
| May 7 | Riot at Madrid |
| May 9 | France: institution of the Commission of Executive Power |
| May 13 | Autonomy of the Serbian Voivodina |
| May 15 | Paris: antiparliamentary riot (Poland); Naples riot and beginning of the reaction; Viennese riot; demonstration of Transylvanian Rumanians at Blaj |
| May 18 | Opening of Frankfurt parliament |
| May 22 | Opening of Prussian National Assembly |

| | |
|---|---|
| June 2 | Opening of the Congress of Prague |
| June 10 | Vienna confirms the integrity of the kingdom of Hungary and dismisses Jelačić |
| June 12 | Prague riot and end of the Czech movement |
| June 14–17 | Frankfurt: First Democratic Congress |
| June 15 | Berlin: workers' riot |
| June 23–26 | Parisian workers' insurrection |
| June 24 | Cavaignac, chief executive |
| June 28 | Dissolution of Prague Congress |
| June 29 | Frankfurt: Archduke John elected *Reichsverweser* |
| June/Sept. | Revolution of Bucharest and its setback; measures in favour of the Prussian peasants |
| July 3 | Venice adheres to Charles Albert |
| July 12 | Abolition of the Germanic Diet |
| July 15–Aug. 18 | Frankfurt: Artisans' Congress of artisans (masters) |
| July 20–Sept. 20 | Frankfurt: Congress of guild members |
| July 22 | Vienna: opening of the *Reichstag* Constituent ("Hereditary States") |
| July 24–7 | Frankfurt: parliament declares greater part of Poznania as part of the *Reich* |
| July 25 | Custozza: defeat of Charles Albert |
| July/August | Setback of the Irish insurrection; Frankfurt: Leiningen ministry, first German Government |
| August 9 | Austro-Sardinian armistice |
| August 12 | Venice: Manin again assumes power |
| August 16–9 | Berlin: the *Junkerparlament* |
| August 23 | Vienna: workers' insurrection |
| Aug. 23–Sept. 3 | Berlin: congress of workers' associations (Born) and foundation of the Brotherhood |
| August 26 | Malmö armistice |
| End of August | Austro-Hungarian rupture |
| September | Expedition of Ferdinand II against Sicily |
| September 7 | Abolition of the seigniorial régime in the "Hereditary States" of Austria |
| September 10 | Jelačić, restored as *ban*, attacks Hungary |
| September 12 | Swiss constitution |

| September 16 | Frankfurt: parliament ratifies the Malmö armistice; Schmerling prime minister |
| September 18 | Frankfurt: republican riot; state of siege |
| September 21–4 | The Baden republic of Struve |
| September 28 | Pest: assassination of Lamberg |
| Beginning of October | Magyar victory |
| October 6 | Beginning of the Vienna revolution; assassination of Latour |
| October 26–30 | Berlin: second Democrats' Congress |
| October 27 | Frankfurt: vote on first constitutional articles |
| October 31 | Berlin: demonstration in favour of the Vienna revolution; Windischgrätz victor over the Viennese revolutionaries |
| End of October | Florence: democrat minister Guerrazzi |
| November 8 | Berlin: Brandenburg-Manteuffel ministry |
| November 9 | Vienna: execution of Robert Blum |
| November 15–6 | Roman revolution |
| November 21 | Schwarzenberg Prime Minister and Minister of Foreign Affairs |
| November 22 | Austrian *Reichstag* re-opened at Kremsier |
| November 25 | Flight of Pius IX to Gaeta |
| November 27 | Austrian declaration on "the state unity of the empire"; von Gagern succeeds Schmerling; Frankfurt: foundation of the *Zentralmärzverein* |
| December 2 | Abdication of Ferdinand I; Francis Joseph, Emperor of Austria |
| December 5 | Dissolution of the Prussian National Assembly; constitution conceded |
| December 10 | Louis Napoleon, President of the French Republic |
| **1849** | |
| January 5 | Windischgrätz occupies Pest |
| January 23 | Berlin circular to the Governments: Prussia ready to play a controlling role with the agreement of the rulers |
| January 26 | Defeat of the Magyars at Kapolna |

| | |
|---|---|
| January 28 | Frankfurt: proposed constitution submitted to the Governments |
| February 8 | Proclamation of the Tuscan Republic |
| February 9 | Proclamation of the Roman Republic |
| February 15 | Frankfurt: formation of the "great German" group |
| February 17 | Frankfurt: formation of the "little German" group |
| February 26 | Denmark denounces the Malmö armistice |
| February–April | Victorious Magyar counter-offensive |
| March 7 | Dissolution of the *Reichstag* at Kremsier and concession of a centralized constitution to the Empire (dated the 4th) |
| March 9 | Austria proposes the formation of a Central European Federation |
| March 14 | Austria: confirmation of the abolition of seigniorial dues |
| March 20–3 | Charles Albert attacks Austria and is routed at Novara; Victor Emmanuel II King of Sardinia; restoration of former authorities at Parma, Modena and Florence |
| March 28 | Frederick William elected "Emperor of the Germans" |
| April 5 | The Vienna Government recalls the Austrian deputies from Frankfurt |
| April 14 | Debreczin: proclamation of Hungarian independence |
| April 25 | The King of Wurtemberg accepts the constitution of the *Reich*; the King of Hannover dismisses his Chamber |
| April 28 | Frederick William refuses the imperial crown |
| May 1 | Russo-Turkish treaty of Balta-Liman; reaction in the principalities; Palatinate: people's assembly at |
| May 1 | Neustadt and beginnings of insurrection |
| May 3–9 | Dresden: republican rising |
| May 9 | Riot at Elberfeld |
| May 10 | Frankfurt: resignation of von Gagern |

| | |
|---|---|
| May 11 | End of Sicilian revolution |
| May 12 | Baden: secession of the Rastatt garrison and beginnings of the revolution |
| May 13 | France: success of the conservatives in the legislative assembly; Offenburg: revolutionary congress of the Baden democratic associations |
| May 14 | Frederick William annuls the mandates of the Prussian deputies at Frankfurt |
| May 18 | Treaty of alliance between the Palatine insurgents and the Baden revolutionaries |
| May 19 | Last number of the *Neue Rheinische Zeitung* |
| May 30 | The parliament leaves Frankfurt; Berlin: promulgation of the edict of the three classes/estates |
| June 4 | The Government of Kossuth returns to Pest |
| June 13 | Paris: anti-parliamentary riot (Roman expedition) |
| June 18 | Stuttgart: the Wurtemberg Government drives out the parliament |
| June 26 | The Prussians at Karlsruhe |
| July 1 | Rome capitulates |
| July 23 | Capitulation of Rastatt |
| August 6 | Austro-Sardinian peace treaty |
| August 13 | The Hungarians capitulate to the Russians at Vilagos |
| August 22 | Capitulation of Venice |

# Index